IMAGINATIVE LOVE IN JOHN

BIBLICAL
INTERPRETATION
SERIES

VOLUME 2

IMAGINATIVE LOVE IN JOHN

BY

SJEF VAN TILBORG

E.J. BRILL
LEIDEN • NEW YORK • KÖLN
1993

The Biblical Interpretation Series *accommodates monographs, collections of essays and works of reference that are concerned with the discussion or application of new methods of interpreting the Bible. Works published in the series will ordinarily either give a practical demonstration of how a particular approach may be instructively applied to a Biblical text or texts, or make a productive contribution to the discussion of method. The series thus provides a vehicle for the exercise and development of a whole range of newer techniques of interpretation, which will include feminist readings, semiotic, post-structuralist, reader-response and other types of literary readings, liberation-theological readings, ecological readings, and psychological readings, among many others.*

Manuscripts are assessed for publication by an international team of leading scholars in various fields. Publication proposals should be sent to: Dr David E. Orton, Executive Editor, Biblical Interpretation Series, E.J. Brill N.V., P.O. Box 9000, 2300 PA Leiden, The Netherlands.

The paper in this book meets the guidelines for permanence and durability of the Committee on Production Guidelines for Book Longevity of the Council on Library Resources.

Library of Congress Cataloging-in-Publication Data

Tilborg, Sjef van.
    Imaginative love in John / by Sjef van Tilborg.
      p.   cm. — (Biblical interpretation series ; v. 2)
    Includes bibliographical references and index.
    ISBN 9004097163 (cloth : alk. paper)
    1. Love—Biblical teaching.   2. Bible. N.T. John—Criticism,
interpretation, etc.   I. Title.   II. Series.
    BS2615.6.L6T558   1993
    226.5'06—dc20
                                                92-44594
                                                 CIP

ISSN 0928-0731
ISBN 90 04 09716 3

CONTENTS

PREFACE

In New Testament studies love is a recurring topic. It is a reality which also assumes a central place in the texts of the New Testament, particularly so in the Johannine Gospel. This study examines love in John's Gospel. Consequently, this publication situates itself within this exegetical and biblical tradition. To assume such a task is a precarious enterprise, as the multitude of studies in this particular area seems to indicate that no point of view has been left unexplored.

This, however, is true only to a certain extent. The connection with narratology in this study is like charting a new road in a virtually unknown terrain. The study attempts to answer the question in what way love in the Johannine Gospel receives its narratively-imaginative stature. The study does not treat the content of the word 'love', but is concerned with the way in which the various characters within John's Gospel realise their various relationships. Because of the particular characteristic of the Johannine Gospel, the study concentrates on the protagonist of the story, Jesus, in his relationships to the other characters. Consequently, the different narratives play an important role, as well as the mutual connections between these narratives and the option to interpret the discursive texts in a narratively-imaginative way. Love becomes a reality only in a concrete, historical and social context. Like any other narrative also John's Gospel concretises a number of circumstances of its characters. Thus it develops a love story which is different from any other narrative.

In order to obtain a better view of this particular imaginative reality, the study presents a reconstruction of the contemporary social reality from the Hellenistic and rabbinic literature. Due to its special treatment of the material this contextual background initially remains relatively discursive, but at a later stage of the study it progressively participates in the narrative development of the book. Love as a complex of love relationships and as a concrete human activity has always set in motion people's imagination, literarily, ethically, as well as juridically, socially, politically and religiously.

As a human reality love is situated within the context of a particular culture. At the same time, however, it continually transcends the confines of a particular culture. Without imagination there is no love. That is true also in ancient times. The study examines aspects which are important for the Johannine Gospel. In particular it emphasises its relevant choices, options and selections.

For the structure of this study I have used the biographical code, i.e. family, discipleship and mastership, the disciples and one beloved disciple among them, the preferential relationship with other persons: women and men. This creates a narrative sequence which does not run parallel to the narrative as told. However, this appeared to be extremely fruitful for the interpretation of separate narratives within the Gospel of John.

Moreover, it has functioned as a model in order to obtain an overview of the narrative in its totality. From the many imaginative possibilities presenting themselves, the Johannine Gospel has told this particular love story. In this Jesus' relationship with his beloved disciple plays a central role. The study concludes that all other (love) relationships —the relationship of Jesus with his father, mother, brothers and sisters, with his disciples in general and with particular women and men—, derive their colour and content from the specific relationship between Jesus and his beloved disciple. It means, it is a relationship which determines the social role of Jesus as his sense of identity as well. The study pays explicit attention to the cultural contextualisation of this love relationship and shows that, according to its main features, it can not be adequately understood unless one perceives the juridical, ethical, social and religious links to the Hellenistic practice of the preferential love of a male teacher for his younger male disciple. In contrast with modern discourse regarding homosexuality such behaviour strengthens the masculine code in ancient discourse on love.

CHAPTER ONE

FAMILY LOVE

Developing the argument several trajectories are possible. Narratively the most likely is for me to start with the Johannine presentation of the family relationships of the book's main character: in what imaginary way does the narrator present the relation of Jesus to his father, his mother and other relatives. John's Gospel has made choices which can be described specifically. They are part of the possible imaginary options of a narrator. Contemporary-culturally ἀγάπη belongs here.

Anticipating the results of this chapter I can say that Jesus is presented as someone who has a unique relationship to his mother; a non-relation with his father; a conflicting relationship to his ἀδελφοί, and a very close and extensively described relationship to 'his father who sent him'; a father who, narratively, exists only in Jesus' 'imagination', in the way Jesus presents matters. It is, so to say, an imaginary relationship in the second degree. In the description of this last mentioned relationship —which is communicated to the listeners only indirectly, i.e., in sentences which Jesus uses about his father and about his own sonship and in authorial sentences in which the author gives his (positive) evaluation of this relationship—, the narrator uses also contemporary codes. It is really proper to the fourth Gospel that only in this context the culturally correct words like ἀγάπη, φιλέω and τιμάω are used.

1. JESUS' RELATION TO HIS MOTHER

1.a. the story of Cana (Jn 2,1-12)
It will be clear that my reading of John will be only in a very specific way in line with today's scientific discourse. I want to clarify how Jesus, as the protagonist of the story, is related to his own family. It is a kind of biographical research into the relations

between Jesus and his own *oikos* and/or the *oikos* which he accepts as his own. These relations are historical, psycho-biographical data for the narrator and for the point of view of the story itself. For me as a reader in the context of today's scientific discourse they are narratively-imaginary possibilities. That means that the interpretative process of the narrator and that of the reader go in opposite directions. The narrator of the narrative (the narrator of the fourth Gospel in this case) creates a narrative reality from the imaginary possibility. He relates his story as something that actually happened. The reader (I myself as the person who interprets the story in this 20th century) looks at this narrative reality as something which could be imaginarily possible; as a familial constellation of which I place the psycho-biological possibilities in various contexts.

I will start with the most famous scene, the Cana story in which —obviously together with a mass of other meanings—, we learn about the relationship between Jesus and his mother, (and his ἀδελφοί. The closing sentence 'then he came down to Capharnaum, he and his mother and his brothers and sisters and his disciples' (2,12) seems to indicate that the ἀδελφοί were present at the celebration, even though practically no exegete speaks of this. Biographically there is no reason why they should not have been there and the closing sentence places them between his mother and his disciples who are both explicitly mentioned as being present. In any case, they do not play any role in the events but their alliance with Jesus is, narratively, not without significance, as we shall see. Introducing the reader in the relation between mother and son is, obviously, more important for the Cana story.

It is well-known how this relation is expressed in an ambiguous way and how this linguistic construction has caused a multiplicity of interpretations. It is part of the larger Cana narrative which itself is open to more than one interpretation. After all, the most miraculous trait of the Cana narrative is the fact that the miracle itself is not explicitly narrated. The story consists of a number of short dialogues which are not brought into relation with each other except by the fact that they are part of one narrative: the dialogue between Jesus and his mother (2,3-4); the mother's command to the servants (2,5); Jesus' command to the servants (2,7-8); the dialogue between the master of ceremonies and the bridegroom (2,10). None of the people knows what the others do or say and yet there is a chain of events which is linked together. It means that the reader must do most of the work in re-constructing the narrative.

Although I do not think that the implied author of John's Gospel, continuously, misleads the implied reader, in this way of reading I am following the commentary of Staley on the Cana narrative (Staley 1988, 83). I will limit myself to the opening scene: the way Jesus' mother acts in relation to the way Jesus acts (2,3-5). The way in which the individual reader judges this scene determines the process of signification of the rest of the narrative. What is the purpose of the sentence 'they have no wine'? Is it 'just a preparation for the following miracle' (Schnelle 1987, 89; Bultmann 1941, 80), or is the intention also to say something about the position and the meaning of the person who puts the question? These questions are not mutually exclusive. The opening sentence of Jesus' mother serves as an introduction to the miracle story in order to make clear that there is a situation of need; at the same time it is 'coloured' by the fact that the mother of the main character of the story is introduced as an active participant. The mother of a main character is seldom irrelevant if she is mentioned. That is true here in a special way, since she is already mentioned in the opening sentence, in vs 2,1, where the characters, the time and place of the narrative are introduced. Her action is already prepared for the reader. Vs 2,3 develops this.

Jesus' answer shows that the mother-son relation is also for him in question: 'Woman, why turn to me. My hour has not yet come.' (2,4). This answer has caused an extensive exegetical discussion. Staley makes clear that this has not erased the ambiguity of the text. If we combine this 'why turn to me, woman' with the preceding sentence, we could accept an 'earthly' meaning: 'what is this (i.e. the lack of wine) to you and me?' But when we read on and come to 'my hour has not yet come', the question 'what is this to you and me' takes on a 'heavenly' meaning: 'what has this concern of yours to do with me?' (Staley 1988, 88). In his answer Jesus redefines the mother-son relation. It is not the mother who determines what is to be done. In a way it is not even Jesus himself who determines this. The hour to which also the son is subject must determine the time and place of Jesus' *doxa*-filled action. The distancing from his mother's initiative —that is what it is, notwithstanding all ambiguity —, is forcefully expressed in the word γύναι which, in a relation between a son and his mother, is unique in the classical Greek and

Jewish literature, no matter how respectful one wants to understand it.

It is a good thing that the Cana story goes against all the 'logical' rules of a narrative. If the reader takes Jesus' answer seriously and believes him on his word, the story should take a different turn. His mother sticks to her plan and Jesus does what he —at least seemingly—, said he would not do.

Jesus' mother tells the servants that they should do what Jesus tells them to do (2,5). Some exegetes think that she understood what Jesus was saying: be ready for the commands of the miracle-worker (Bultmann 1941, 81; Schnackenburg 1967, 336). Obviously, I can not contradict this. In fact, I think that such an interpretation expresses the exegete's need to read a simple, coherent meaning into the text. Jesus' answer to his mother in 2,4 does not imply narratively and communicatively her specific action in 2,5. One can, as reader, construct such a meaning. In that way one fills the gap in the text in a way which guarantees best the narrative unity of the text. But it is also possible to leave the break in the text and that too has narrative and communicative consequences for its interpretation.

It means, narratively, that Jesus' mother takes a new initiative: Jesus' mother as the initiator in the story. In this case it is even more so than in the first part of the story, because her command determines the whole set of events which follow. When the servants do what Jesus tells them to do, they act, from now on in the story, 'on the command of his mother'. Through this second initiative, the mother has taken a narrative position which no one can take away from her.

It means, communicatively, that the mother is presented as someone who does not listen to what Jesus says. That may sound less friendly than what the narrator is trying to communicate. It is a literary device which the author uses quite often for characters in his stories. It plays an important role in the farewell discourses: see e.g. Thomas who tells Jesus that he does not know ('we do not know') where Jesus is going, while Jesus has just told them that in the preceding sentences (14,4 in relation to 14,2-3); the same with Philip about the visibility of the father (14,8 in relation to 14,7 and 14,9); also where the disciples speak about the origin of Jesus (16,29 in relation to the whole preceding part and Jesus' answer in

16,31). In the narrative policy of the story's narrator, the fact that the disciples do not listen is no reason for Jesus to keep quiet.

It is the same in the Cana story. In what follows Jesus does exactly what his mother has prepared. He assigns tasks to the servants in preparation of the water-wine change; an act which, in a way, is even more difficult to reconcile with what has been said in 2,4 than his mother's reaction in 2,5. Exegesis has proposed as solution to see the closing sentence of 2,4 'my hour has not yet come' as an affirmative interrogative: 'has my hour now not come?' (a.o. Kurfess 1952/53, 257; Michl 1955, 505; Ceroke 1959, 325; Vanhoye 1974, 157-167): Jesus, not his mother, determines whether his hour has come. It is an elegant solution for the narrative problems of the text. But there are problems too. It aggravates the abruptness of his mother's action in 2,5. This figure of speech does not appear anywhere else in John. It is not in line with the negative meaning of the parallel sentences in 7,30 and 8,30. The constative-negative translation of 2,4 —'my hour has not yet come'—, remains, therefore, more in line with the author's option. Notwithstanding the narrative text-problems, this interpretation carries a real advantage. It causes the reader to have a keen interest in the meaning of 'the hour of Jesus'. The narrative breaks in the text force the reader, as it were, to ask whether the hour of Jesus has come or not. The narrator will exploit this reader's question in the sequence.

Summing up we can say that, from the perspective of the narrator, the mother and her son evaluate their relationship from a different point of view. The mother believes that she has the right to point out the situation of need to her son. Furthermore, she positions herself as the dominant character in the story and thus also as the dominant of her son's behaviour. Her command to the servants forces Jesus into a double bind. Jesus can not escape any more his mother's command. The son distances himself from her in unmistakable words, but does not succeed in eluding her influence. In his actions he follows the path which his mother outlined without taking a critical distance.

1.b. the closing scene at the cross (Jn 19,25-27)
The parallel scene at the end of the book where Jesus and his mother appear again, presents new interpretative problems. So many meanings have been read into the text that it is difficult to

remain unbiased. The face value of the text, in which I am more interested, is snowed under by the many 'symbolic' meanings which are proposed.

The scene opens with an opposition: οἱ μὲν ... δὲ: four women are mentioned together with the four anonymous soldiers. The soldiers have received their reward which, according to Roman law, is due to them when they execute someone. They threw dice for the *chitoon*. The author sees this as a fulfilment of Psalm 22, an intertextual reference which, maybe, wants to call forth in the reader's mind verses 10-11 (LXX):

"for you have brought me forth from the womb;
my hope from my mother's breasts.
I have been placed on your lap from my birth;
from my mother's womb you have been my God."

Anyway, we have the four women and the four soldiers. Such a contrast, obviously, carries meaning, but the reader is given much freedom to fill in the blanks, because the functions of the characters are nor clearly identified: men who, because of their function, bring death against women who silently witness Jesus' death; soldiers who demand their share in the spoils against female relatives and friends who are present (mourning /or not allowed to mourn) (Schottroff 1982); unbelievers against believers (Barrett 1967; Gnilka 1983) etc.

For our reading it is important that Jesus' mother is present. In the next sentence, which can not be qualified as well formulated, Jesus sees (in literal translation) 'the mother and the disciple standing whom he loved'. Apart from the four women it is now clear that also a man is present: the disciple whom Jesus loved, someone who will later on return in our attention. Jesus speaks the now famous words to them 'woman, this is your son'; 'this is your mother', the basic sentences of the scene which is closed with the narrative remark that 'from that hour he took her into his house' (19,27).

In the construction of the meaning of this passage it seems important to relate this scene to the writer's remark in 19,28: 'Then, knowing that everything has been completed Jesus said...'. The words which Jesus said to his mother and to the disciple have brought his actions to their τέλος. There is a connection with 13,1 and 19,30 and, probably, also with τελειόω: the fulfilment of the task which the father had given to Jesus (4,34; 5,36; 17,4). But as is clear from the inclusion of πάντα τετέλεσται —— τελειωθῇ (19,28) —— τετέλεσται (19,30), there is also a connection with the 'fulfilment' of the Scripture. With his remark in 19,28, the writer thus places the scene against the background of the mission which Jesus received from his father —to be an obedient son—, of which mission the fulfilment of the Scripture is an important part (cf. 12,38; 13,18; 15,25; 17,12, but also 2,22; 5,39; 7,38; 10,35 and 20,9). With the words he speaks to his mother and his beloved disciple, Jesus fulfils the mission he received from his father faithful to the end in faithfulness to the Scripture.

If this is a correct interpretation, it has important consequences for the understanding of the scene. It becomes possible, then, to read the scene against the background of the Scripture, as the fulfilment of a biblical command. What is happening? Leaving out the possibility that an adoption text is used —a possibility to which I will return later when I speak about the beloved disciple—, Jesus provides a place for his mother to live. He shows that he cares for her. Some exegetes think that this is below the theological expressiveness of John (Schnackenburg 1975, 325; de la Potterie 1974, 216). Others do not have much difficulty with it (Schürmann 1969, 108; Dauer 1972, 322), but they bend the meaning in a more spiritual direction: Jesus entrusts his mother to the beloved disciple. In fact, nobody seems to ask the question how this concrete story was imaginarily possible for the narrator.

The point of departure seems to be that the narrator wants to communicate in his narrative that Jesus follows the Scripture 'till the end', i.e., that he keeps the Law. In this case that means the torah about the *kibbud ab we'em*: the honouring of father and mother. I must now not speak about the honour Jesus gives his father by his death on the cross. John prepares this theme extensively (cf. esp. 17,1-5 and its references) and it must be seen in connection with 19,28 as we said already. Important in my option is the honour which Jesus gives his mother by his gesture.

The torah about honouring father and mother is based specifically on Ex 20,12 (=Dt 5,16) and Lv 19,3: the 'honouring of father and mother' in Ex 20,12, and the 'reverence for mother and father' in Lv 19,3. Based on these two texts, Jewish interpreters developed important halachot. (In what follows I base myself entirely on the extraordinarily instructive study of Blidstein

1975). The change in order, in which the father and mother are mentioned in the Exodus and the Leviticus text, shows that both are to be equally important for the child. The two different verbs used —'to honour' and 'to revere'—, have been interpreted as a double commandment in the tannaitic time:

> "Our rabbis taught: What is reverence and what is honour? Reverence means that he (the son) must neither stand nor sit in his (father's) place, nor contradict his words, nor tip the scale against him.
> Honour means that he must give him food and drink, clothe and cover him, and lead him in and out." (Kidd 31b, transl. Blidstein 1975, 38).

That means that from the beginning a distinction has been made between the obligation to give filial support (the *moreh*) and to provide a financial contribution (the *kibbud*). This tannaitic doctrine is the point of departure for the teaching of the Amoreans in the Palestinian as well as the Babylonian Talmud. New is the question as to which person should pay.

In the palTalmud we read: "What is reverence ?...and what is honour?.. At whose expense? Hunna b. Hiyya said,'At the expense of the older man (the parent).' Others wished to say, 'At his own expense.'...R. Yannai and R. Jonathan were sitting. A man came up and kissed the feet of R. Jonathan. R. Yannai asked, 'What did you do for this man that he repays you so?' R. Jonathan answered, 'Once this man came to me and complained about his son, that he does not support him. I told him, 'Go, gather the congregation in the synagogue and publicly shame him.' R. Yannai asked ,'And why did you not compel the son to support his father?' R. Jonathan responded, 'Can one compel that?' Rabbi Yannai answered, 'You don't know that?'. R. Jonathan then began to teach as a fixed rule, 'One may compel a son to support his father'...R. Jose said, 'Would that I were as certain of all my traditions as I am of that one that 'one may compel a son to support his father'." (pKidd 1:7; 61b, transl. Blidstein 1975, 64).

However, in the babTalmud we read: "What is reverence and what is honour?... At whose expense? R. Judah said, 'At the son's expense'. R. Nathan b. Oshaya said, 'At the father's expense'. The sages taught R. Jeremiah...that the decision was as he who said, 'At the father's expense'." (bKidd 32a).

Blidstein concludes therefore: "It would seem, then, that the Talmuds differ on the obligation of filial support and financial contribution. The Palestinian (TP) obligates the son, and holds that both personal service and economic care fuse in the organic category of concern and centrality called *kibbud av*. The Babylonian (TB), on the contrary, discriminates between the two; personal service is a valid demand, but financial responsibility lies outside *kibbud av*. TP, moreover, concludes that the son can be compelled to provide for his parents; TB does not consider this issue, inasmuch as it frees the son from such responsibility altogether". (Blidstein 1975, 66).

Returning to John's text it is now clear that Jesus, in his sentences, performs an act of *kibbud em*. By fulfilling his filial obligations for the support of his mother beyond his own death, he honours his mother 'till the very end'. In so far as this carries financial consequences —and that seems to be the case, because he transfers his mother from his own *oikos* to the *oikos* of his beloved disciple—, Jesus acts according to the Palestinian tradition which, in the Palestinian Talmud, has been expressed textually in the discussion between R. Yannai and R. Jonathan. In a way Jesus acts beyond that, because it goes beyond his own death.

Juridical positions now come into play. Of course, from the perspective of the narrative that has been presented, Jesus' right is perfectly clear —he has been shown to be the pre-existent Logos, the one to whom the Father has given all things, the one who decides ultimate issues of life and death. From this point of view, Jesus' right to entrust his mother to the beloved disciple is self-evident. It does not *need* a special juridical background. But at the same time there is also a more down-to-earth explanation of Jesus' behaviour. If Jesus is the *kyrios* of his own mother —if his father has died and he, as the first born, stepped into the position of the husband of his mother—, he has to do something. Such a juridical fact would lead to a behaviour of this kind in the whole of the Eastern Mediterranean area. In other words, all readers in this area 'would' read the text (also) from this supposition and/or would 'spontaneously' fill in this textual blank in this way.

In Judaism the regulations which are written down in the Mishnah treatise Ketubot apply. A woman may stay and live in the house of her deceased husband: "The people of Jerusalem used to write (—in the *ketubah* = marriage settlement—), 'Thou shalt dwell in my house and thou shalt be supported from my goods as long as thou stayest a widow in my house'. The people of Galilee used to

write as did the people of Jerusalem; but the people of Judea used
to write,...'until the heirs are willing to give her her marriage
settlement', therefore if the heirs were so minded, they would give
her her marriage settlement and send her away." (Ket 4,12). The
difference between Galilee and Judea is connected with the fact that
the possession of the woman is not always transferred as inheritance
to the *oikos* of the deceased husband (For another explanation, see
Falk 1978, 340). If the woman did not bear children, the
inheritance returns to the *oikos* of her father. Relevant for us here is
Ket 12,3: "If a widow said, 'I do not want to depart from my
husband's house', the heirs can not say to her, 'Go to thy father's
house and we will maintain thee', but they must maintain her in her
husband's house and give her a home in accordance with her status
(מדור לפי כבודה)." A widow has the right to remain in the
house of her deceased husband; that is, she has the right to join
permanently the actual οἰκοδεσπότης. If this *kyrios* is her own (first-
born) son, he is also her heir and he is financially responsible for
her maintenance as long as she lives. Jesus does precisely what this
mishnah prescribes, when he provides a home for his mother in
accordance with her *kabod*. He goes beyond this where he stretches
his responsibility beyond his own death. He is not obliged to do this
and it shows the extreme limits of his acts. This way he prevents
that his mother must go to (one of) his ἀδελφοί (in so far as this is
about men) or to the *oikos* of her father.

This procedure may seem rather complicated, but it is a juridical
structure which we find from of old and everywhere within the
Hellenistic system in exactly the same way. In Attic law we find:
"Women who had lost their husbands were generally classified
under two headings -those who had children and those who were
childless... Widows with children had the choice of remaining in
their dead husband's house or of returning to their lord's house. If
a widow chose to remain in her husband's house, she had to be
supported by her sons or, if these were under age, by guardians."
(den Boer 1979, 34/35; for the legal texts, Lacey 1968/1983,
204/205; about the typical use of the word ἐκδίδοσθαι, Wolff 1961,
162/163). Roman law is in the process of abolishing the *tutela
mulieris* (Kaser 1955, I, 311; II, 158), but the legal text which
mentions this (Gai Institutiones I, 193) shows that in Bithynia there
is a different situation: "Apud peregrinos non similiter, ut apud
nos, in tutela sunt feminae; sed tamen plerumque quasi in tutela

sunt; ut ecce lex Bithynorum, si quid mulier contrahat, maritum auctorem esse iubet aut filium eius puberum." Hellenistic Egypt is in complete accordance with this. It is not surprising that the Jewish papyri presuppose this legal structure. In legal matters the woman is always represented by a man, by her own husband (CPJ II,145.146. 430), by her mother's brother (CPJ II,143.144), and, interesting enough, by her own son (CPJ I,26). The same is true for the Greek papyri (Taubenschlag 1955/2, 171). It is then not strange that this is also true for Philo (Heinemann 1929-32/1962, 310; cf. also the patristic interpretation of this text, see Neirynck 1979b and 1981, as for example in Epiphanius, PG 42,716: "if she had a husband, if she had an *oikos*, if she had children, she could have retired to her own house", Neirynck 1979b, 358; 1981, 84f).

Narratively-imaginatively it is clear that there is a continuing line between the Cana story and the farewell narrative as far as the relation between Jesus and his mother is concerned: he is the obedient son of his mother. Where in the Cana narrative he is presented as a son who is not disobedient, in the farewell scene he transcends even the legal requirements. It is too much to think that Jesus protects his mother against his brothers and the *oikos* of her own father. In fact, he liberates her from it and lets her live in the protection of his own *oikos* by making sure she is accepted in the *oikos* of his beloved disciple. Obviously, this has religious consequences but, in the first place, it says something about the author's imaginary representation of the relationship between Jesus and his mother: as the mother does not abandon her son, the son does not abandon his mother.

2. THE RELATION BETWEEN JESUS AND HIS BROTHERS AND SISTERS

In a reconstruction one does not respect the narrative data in the order in which they are given. The farewell scene between Jesus and his mother will not be well understood —notwithstanding the silence of the exegetes—, if one does not bring in somehow the relations between Jesus and his ἀδελφοί. In John's story the ἀδελφοί play an important role, although it is textually a limited one. The relation between the main character and his ἀδελφοί is, obviously, very important in a psycho-biographical research project.

First we must pay attention to two reader-concretizations which remain impossible to fill in. There is no indication whether the narrator uses the word ἀδελφοί inclusively for men and women or exclusively for men. An inclusive use seems more reasonable because the plural is used, because of statistical possibilities and because of the Synoptic tradition (see lately Seim, 1987, 58). In Lazarus' *oikos* with his two sisters Mary and Martha this possibility is narratively exploited also in John's text. Anyway, the self-evident male determination which, generally, is supposed in exegetical texts, is not correct. To maintain the ambiguity of the text I will alternately speak about ἀδελφοί and about Jesus' brothers and sisters.

Also the question about the kind of family relationship between Jesus and his brothers and sisters is insoluble. They could be ἀδελφοί of the same father and mother, but also of the same father and a different mother, or the same mother and a different father, and, as is well known, they could also be nieces and nephews from father's or mother's side. The answer to this question is narratively unimportant.

The story in John 7 makes clear that Jesus comes in a conflict with his ἀδελφοί. To clarify how this happened, narratively, I need to explain a technique of story-telling which is typical for John's Gospel. The narrator of this Gospel is a superb master in 'double connections', in narratively ambiguous connections. A typical example is the opening of chapter 7. On the one hand, the story finds life in its narrative connection with the preceding chapter: should Jesus stay in Galilee or go to Judea? But, on the other hand, it is intimately connected with the narrative which follows: the celebration of the Feast of Tabernacles in Jerusalem. Shortly, John 7,1-9 is the dramatic conclusion of the Galilee story which is filled with conflict *and* it is the dramatic introduction of Jesus' contentious way of acting in Jerusalem during the Feast of Tabernacles. The story about Jesus and his brothers and sisters has, thus, narratively a linking function.

To perceive the meaning of this conflict we must, therefore, stay in touch with this two-sided narrative connection. The connection with the preceding narrative line always disappears in scientific exegesis as far as I can see. Its reason seems to be that one does not emphasise much to the narrative meaning of John 6. G.A. Philips' study (1983) made that clear to me. I even think that we can go further. John 6 narrates a dramatic event around Jesus himself:

He comes into conflict with 'the Jews' of Galilee: narratively expressed in the lexemes /grumble/ (6,41) and /fight/ (6,52)—,

a conflict which is pursued in the discussion with his own disciples, narratively expressed in the lexeme /grumble/ (6,61)—,

a conflict which comes to a halt in the (small) group of the twelve disciples (6,67)—,

one of whom is called 'devil' (6,70).

However, the conflict does not stop with chapter 6. It goes on in chapter 7 with the contention between Jesus and his ἀδελφοί: Jesus comes into conflict also with his own *oikos*. Against this background 2,12 takes on a greater narrative significance —the more so when one may presuppose that the brothers and sisters were also present in Cana. Having told the story of the gradual establishment of Jesus' contact with his environment in the first chapters of his book:

- the winning of the first disciples in 1,19-2,11;

- the good contact with his own *oikos* in the person of his mother and his ἀδελφοί (2,11-12);

- the expansion of the Jesus group in Samaria and Galilee (4,1-54),

the narrator relates the breakdown from chapter 6 on:

- Galilee is no longer the hospitable country it promised to be (4,43-45 over against chapter 6);

- the group of disciples is drastically reduced and even contains in its inner core the seed for Jesus' death;

- even his own *oikos* no longer provides him with a home.

Jesus does not go to Jerusalem together with his ἀδελφοί (7,10). For Jesus the Feast of Tabernacles is no (longer a) family occasion. Jesus goes by himself and in secret to the Feast: the group around him which was expanding, now diminishes to a very small group.

The connection between 7,1-9 and the following text has always attracted more attention among the exegetes: John 7,1-9 as the start of the story about the Feast of the Tabernacles, a contentious discussion in which each of the partners speak three sentences which result in a complete break. Two author's remarks determine how the sentences about the ἀδελφοί must be understood.

The first one, at the beginning of the text (7,1), indicates what moves Jesus: he does not want to go to Judea because the people there want to kill him. That refers to 5,18, the last time he was in Jerusalem. Judea is for him the land of death. His brothers and

sisters are presented as people who are unaware of this, who have
no idea of what moves their own brother. For them Judea is
publicity. If Jesus is consistent, he should go there and show
himself. The works he does demand publicity and he will not find
that in Galilee. Their objective reasoning bypasses the danger of
death threatening Jesus. That is not an expression of *philadelphia*,
to say the least.

The second author's remark —staying after the sentences of the
ἀδελφοί (in 7,5)—, comments their sayings. It reveals what moves
the brothers and sisters: they do not believe in Jesus. First of all
this refers to their advice that Jesus must show his works to the
cosmos. This is bad advice. Different from the ἀδελφοί the readers
know already that Jesus' works are not a revelation to the cosmos,
but rather a revelation of his heavenly origin. The narrator makes
us surmise with this remark that the break between Jesus and his
brothers and sisters has everything to do with the break between
him and the cosmos.

Although Jesus' answer to his ἀδελφοί seems superficially to be
quite simple, it appears far more mysterious when we look a little
more closely at the text.

The opening and closing sentence deal with the *kairos* (7,6 and
7,8): the right and decisive moment that things happen. Jesus
distinguishes between his own *kairos* and that of his brothers and
sisters. He knows one single time which is determined from outside
himself and to which he is subject. The ἀδελφοί do not have such a
kairos: all time is their time.

As becomes clear from the sequence of the sentences, this has to
do with their relationship to the cosmos. The difference between
Jesus and his brothers and sisters lies, therefore, in this relation to
the cosmos. Jesus is hated by the cosmos because he indicts the
cosmos and its works. The ἀδελφοί and the cosmos are on the same
side. The sentences which Jesus speaks make the reader look anew
what the ἀδελφοί have said, i.e. the reader is once again influenced
in his interpretation of the scene: the brothers and sisters who want
Jesus to show himself in publicity and to the cosmos want this
because their interests are in line with the interests of the cosmos.
This is, somehow, connected with τιμή, an honour which one can
receive from people in the cosmos.

The problem with Jesus' answer lies in the closing sentences:
'you can go up to the Feast; I am not going' (7,8). Why, then, does

Jesus go immediately afterwards? Can't we take Jesus and the narrator on their word? These are readers' questions which run parallel to the readers' questions in the Cana narrative. Has Jesus' *kairos* (ch. 7; Jesus' hour ch. 2) now come or not? Exegesis has tried to find an answer in various ways (see esp. Schnackenburg 1971, 198; Staley 1988, 103 thinks, obviously, again that the implied reader has been had). The difference with the Cana story is that here we do not have a mother who takes the initiative. The ἀδελφοί let the break continue: whether Jesus comes with them or not, they are going to Jerusalem.

Summing up we can say that, narratively, the ἀδελφοί do not get a good evaluation from the narrator. Jesus is in the right. The ἀδελφοί can not understand their brother's significance for the world. They even refuse to understand. Selfishly they do not pay attention to the danger to which their brother is exposed. On condition that Jesus accepts their understanding of him as a person, they want to promote their own *oikos*. When Jesus refuses to go along with this, i.e. when he makes it clear that he has a mission which is more important than he is and which creates the conflict with the world, the ἀδελφοί stand together as a group and exclude him. Jesus' reaction is in line with this. He breaks with his relatives and goes his own way. In the story this will bring us to the scene at the cross where Jesus also excludes his ἀδελφοί. They are presented as a group and that makes the break more total. This is even more so where the ἀδελφοί are brothers *and* sisters. The exclusion is, then, more total and Jesus' isolation even more pronounced. Jesus is a stranger who is not accepted by his own. He does not belong in this family and this he knows.

3. THE RELATION BETWEEN JESUS AND HIS FATHER

3.a. the absent father

Jesus has a very special relationship with each of his relatives. His relation to his father is different from that to his mother or the one to his brothers and sisters. First of all, Jesus' father —in the familiar-biological sense—, is in a way the great absent one. We encountered this reality already in discussing the farewell scene of Jesus and his mother. As her son he can decide for her as *kyrios*, as he in fact does, only when the father/husband is absent through death or divorce. In the then existing juridical situation this is the only way. The text indicates that because none of the characters involved —not even the author—, raises any objection. It is a silence in the text which, according to me, is meaningful.

This supposition is supported by the almost total absence of the father in the story as told. He is not mentioned in the Cana story, nor in the story about the conflict with the ἀδελφοί, nor in the narration of one of the trips to Jerusalem which, normally speaking, would be considered *oikos* events.

His name is mentioned twice only:
- in 1,45 by Philip in the dialogue with Nathanael whom he persuades to go to Jesus. He describes Jesus, then, as 'son of Joseph from Nazareth'. This is intended as a positive identification (Sproston 1985, 77) which ties Jesus for the readers to an *oikos*. That the importance of the *oikos* is at stake follows from the sequence of the dialogue where Nathanael asks for the significance of Nazareth: the place as a closer identification of an *oikos*: 'can anything good come from Nazareth?'
- the second time Jesus' father is mentioned is in 6,42, in the contentious discussion between Jesus and 'the Jews' in Galilee in connection with the discussion about the bread from heaven: 'is this not Jesus, the son of Joseph, whose father and mother we know?' This is no longer positive. The question is part of the 'grumbling', the lexeme which refers to the Exodus tradition of the manna in the desert. Jesus can not be the manna from God because they know where he is from (cf. 7,27).

Where exegetes express themselves about the meaning of the phrase: 'the son of Joseph whose father and mother we know', the apposition 'whose father and mother we know' is seen as applying to Jesus. Brown translates: 'Isn't this Jesus, the son of Joseph? Don't we know his father and mother?' (Brown 1966, 269; see also Schnackenburg 1971, 76). That is possible syntactically but semantically it seems improbable. Having mentioned the father, that father would be mentioned again. Such a redundancy is not usual in John. It seems more probable that it is said of Jesus that he is the son of Joseph and that Joseph's father and mother are known: Jesus, the son of Joseph, the son of father x and mother y; and they know this father x and this mother y. The fact that it is mentioned that they 'know' this father and mother and thus, implicitly, that they do not 'know' Joseph, underscores again the narrative supposition that Joseph has been dead for some time (cf. the older commentaries Westcott 1881/1975, 104; Bernard 1928/1976, 202).

In whatever supposition, it is clear that Joseph as the father of Jesus is of no importance in either place. In 1,46 Joseph is not mentioned in the dialogue which follows. In 6,42 Jesus speaks immediately afterwards about 'the father who sent him' and Joseph has nothing to do with this.

There is one more text where Jesus' biological origin plays some kind of role. The story of the Feast of the Tabernacles (ch. 7-8) centres the discussion between Jesus and the Judeans on the question who can claim Abraham as true father. At a certain point in the discussion the Judeans say, 'we are not born ἐκ πορνείας' (8,41). The implication could be that Jesus is born ἐκ πορνείας. Discursively this refers to a Jewish-Christian controversy with deep roots in early Christianity (cf. Dozeman 1980). Narratively it is a inner Jewish controversy where 'we-Judeans' stands over against 'I-Jesus'.

What kind of πορνεία is meant in 8,41? The fact that the narrative context is about Abraham and that the Judeans are mentioned in the plural, does not indicate a text-understanding from the problem of direct origin of the Judeans and/or of Jesus, i.e. the text does not exploit possible 'Jewish' rumours that Jesus would be illegitimate; that Jesus would be born ἐκ πορνείας from Joseph or from his mother. In other words, because the text can not deal with a possible πορνεία of the fathers (and mothers) of the Judeans present, —as a group such a general expression can not be used, or at least can not be proven—, neither can it deal with a possible πορνεία of Joseph as Jesus' father or of his mother. The topic of the text deals with a possible πορνεία of Abraham and the consequences this would have for the Judeans (contra Schaberg 1987, 157).

Such a discussion about an unlawful act by a remote ancestor evokes a lot of emotions. In classical literature we have the famous example of the family of the Alcmaeonidae who carried until Pericles' time the ἄγος that their ancestor, unlawfully, murdered people who asked for asylum in the temple of Athena (Herod 5,71; Thuc 1,126; Plut Solon, 12; cf. den Boer 1979, 20.131.197). John's text speaks about a πορνεία which affects a whole nation and that is, obviously, quite a different thing. But, structurally, it is the same question: the unlawful behaviour of the ancestor has

consequences for the position of all his offspring. The affection
involved is demonstrated by a number of biblical etiological stories
such as the stories about the origin of Edom, Moab, Assyria,
Egypt, etc.

That these questions on the origin of a nation are still a sensitive
problem in first century AD is clear from the way they are treated
by Josephus. Limiting myself to the way he tells the story of
Abraham —his own origin is involved—, it is striking how Josephus
puts emphasis on the γνήσιος-character of Isaac (Ant 1,154: about
the adoption of Lot by Abraham, 'since Abraham did not have a
legitimate son'; 1,186f; 215 about Hagar as a female slave; 1,214
about Ishmael as the son of a concubine: and in 1,253 about Isaac
who presents himself to Laban, 'it is this Abraham who sends me
to you to ask this damsel in wedlock for his son -his lawful son,
who has been brought up as sole heir to his whole estate'). Even
more clear and more to the point is TJ I Gen which says about
Isaac that he is a son 'who resembles his father' and that Sarah can,
thus, not be guilty of πορνεία (TJ I Gen 21,2 and 25,19); and
which makes God. say to Abraham: 'they will name your
(=Abraham's) children through Isaac, but the son of the female
slave will not be part of your genealogy' (TJ I Gen 21,12); cf. also
TJ I Gen 5,3, a text about Cain which is antithetically parallel (see
Jn 8,44!) and which says: 'Eve bore Cain who was not his
(=Adam's) and who did not resemble him. Abel was killed by
Cain. Cain was then driven away and his offspring was not
mentioned in the book of Adam's genealogy'(TJ I Gen 5,3).

If we can interpret the phrases of Jn 8 against this background,
the underlying reasoning of the text becomes much clearer. Jesus'
words in 8,40: 'you seek to kill me, a man who spoke the truth as I
received it from God. Abraham did not do that', can be connected
with the story in Genesis 18-19 about the visit of the three men
—angels in human form cf. Jos Ant 1,197; Philo Abr 113; TJ I
Gen 18,2.8.16—, at the oak in Mamre. Abraham listened to what
the man had to say about the birth of his son. He was not hostile as
the inhabitants of Sodom were, —and as the Judeans who now
threaten Jesus' life (cf. Bouwman 1990 on the story of Sodom;
different from Neyrey 1987, 528; 1988, 37 who identifies Jesus
with Isaac. I do not think that in this text Jesus is presented as a son
of Abraham).

In 8,41 the Judeans answer that they are not born from πορνεία, that is, that they are not offspring of the unlawful contact of Abraham with some woman; or maybe a little more precise, that they are not offspring of Abraham and his female slave. Therefore, they are in the *oikos* of Abraham not (illegitimate) slave-children, but free children (cf. the discussion in 8,33-37). God is their father, i.e. they are offspring of Abraham's son who is a son of God —cf. the theologoumenon which is developed in Philo about Isaac's birth (see Leg All 3,219; Mut 130f; 137; Somn 1,173).

Jesus tells them in 8,42 that they should, then, love him because he is from God. He is the man who, in God's name, spoke to Abraham about Isaac's sonship (cf. Jn 12,41 about the vision of Jesajah and Jn 8,46 about the vision of Abraham; see especially Ashton 1991, 141ff who has shown that this identification of Jesus with some angelic being plays a yet more important role at the end of the discussion in ch. 8). But the Judeans do not understand the language Jesus uses, because they are not capable of listening. They are 'from the devil', i.e. they are offspring of Cain and not children of God via Isaac; respectively they are not children of God via Adam.

What is in question is Jesus' mission by God and from God. It has nothing to do with a possible accusation of πορνεία in relation to his birth.

3.b. the imaginary father

It is clear that these considerations can not be the last word. From a different perspective the father of Jesus is all over the book, from the first page till practically the end. We can summarise that in two sentences: 'God is the father of Jesus' and 'the father of Jesus is God'. With Jesus' sonship God is subject and predicate of fatherhood. It is mentioned in phrases which have a defining character, as an essential description, and with a sense of reality from which the narrator derives his pretence to speak the truth: 'these things are written so that you may believe that Jesus is the Christ, the son of God' (20,30).

This 'ontological claim to truth' does not mean that there is not something else going on narratively. The divine fatherhood is expressed only in discursive phrases in which Jesus (partly dependent on John the Baptist as will be shown in the next chapter), presents himself in words (connected with works) as son of the father-God. The narrator unites himself textually with these phrases, but he is totally dependent on what Jesus himself has to say about it. The great debate with the Judeans about the divine sonship of Jesus makes this clear. Not every hearer in (and of) the story agrees with what Jesus says about himself.

There has to be made a distinction between the discourse and the narration of the text. Discursively God is the father of Jesus and the father of Jesus is God. Narratively the main character in the story makes, in his words, God into his father and his father into God. That means: embedded in the imaginary reality of the story as told, the main character of the narrative creates an imaginary world in which he and God appear in a father-son relationship which is accessible only from the imagination of the main character, from the fantasy, the imagery and desires of Jesus. Sometimes this happens in phrases which are in the I-form: I and the father, and, my father and I. More typically in Jn, however, it happens in phrases in the third person singular: Jesus who speaks to his audience about 'the son' in his relation to 'the father'; in sayings which, reflexively, are, as it were, half-way, in phrases which in the third person singular speak about the self as if it were someone else and which, yet, are not about someone else. The narrative implications of this textual phenomenon have not yet been explored as far as I can see.

A discussion of this father-son relationship is, obviously, necessary in a research about the psycho-biological data of the main character of the Johannine Gospel. The problem is that the multitude of data necessitates a reader-reconstruction. Connecting with scientific exegesis I emphasise some data from the text. In its own way this gives an insight in the origin of the use of metaphors in the Johannine Gospel.

3.b.1. Jesus and his oikos

One of the opening scenes of the book, the first Jerusalem-story, relates how Jesus goes —also here alone—, to Jerusalem because of the Jewish Feast of Passover, and how he finds men selling cattle, sheep and pigeons and the money-changers (2,13-22). Yet keeping close to the narrativity of the story, the reader is introduced here in the typical Johannine father-son relationship. The narrator lets Jesus say to the men selling pigeons: 'Take it away. Do not make the house of my father into a marketplace'. In his rather dull commentary on Boismard, Neirynck (1979, 89) sees in this saying a reference to what Jesus says in the Synoptic Temple story. It is one opinion. The rather distant reference to God in the Synoptic text ('Is it not written: my house is a house of prayer?' Mc 11,17 a.p.) becomes in John, in fact, a personal reference: the house of my father. Jesus identifies with the interests of his father-God. The Temple in Jerusalem is the material *oikos* of his father for which the son commits himself. There are rights of usage in question here. Therefore, Jesus fights the sellers and the money-changers and acts as someone who has the right to determine what is acceptable in the house of his father. Later, the disciples will remember the text from the psalm which foretells this happening: 'The zeal for your house will devour me' (Jn 2,17 and Ps 69,9), a psalm-text which, just before this phrase, reads: 'I became a stranger to my ἀδελφοί, an alien to my mother's other sons' (cf. 2,12). In the first Jerusalem story Jesus presents himself as the only son of the father-God who stands for his father's *oikos*.

It is intriguing to see that readers have various possibilities to connect the Temple story about Jesus' father with the preceding Cana story about his mother. One can point to the typical use of μου in the lexeme /my father/ (2,16) which points to ἡ ὥρα μου in the Cana story (2,4) (cf. Staley 1988, 91).

But one can also point to much wider parallel structures in 2,1-12 and 2,13-25:   (Koester 1989, 331)

setting Cana 2,1-2	setting Jerusalem 2,13
	main action 2,14-17
verbal exchange 2,3-5	verbal exchange 2,18-20
main action 2,6-10	
narrator's comment 2,11	narrator's comment 2,21-22
transitional scene 2,12	transitional scene 2,23-25

It is even possible to see the structures wider still: Jn 2,13-3,26 as a whole referring to Jn 1,19-2,12:

- Jn 3,22-36 which points literally to Jn 1,19-34 (3,26 to 1,28; 3,28 to 1,20; 3,30 to 1,30; 3,33 to 1,32; 3,34 to 1,32);

- Jn 3,1-21, the dialogue with Nicodemus which reinstates in its own way the dialogue with the first disciples (1,35-51);

- the Temple story (2,13-25) where Jesus shows his strength in the house of his father which rhymes with the Cana story where Jesus shows his glory at the intercession of his mother:

story about John and the relation Jesus-John	1,19-34	3,22-36	story about John and the relation Jesus-John
dialogue between Jesus and disciples	1,35-51	3,1-21	dialogue between Jesus and Nicodemus
Cana story	2,1-12	2,13-25	Temple story

The imaginary relation between Jesus and his father-God is embedded in the narratively 'real' relation between Jesus and his mother and his ἀδελφοί. The discussion of Jn 6,41ff about Jesus' origin, seemingly, comes back in several other places (cf. also the explanation of Jn 19,26-27).

For the Temple story we must add something. Jn 14,2-3 says: 'in the οἰκία of my father there are many rooms'. It speaks about a building (cf. Neirynck 1979, 89), but again as the material part of the *oikos*: the *oikos* of God-father in heaven to which Jesus is returning because that is where he came from; the house of his father as locality and as home where Jesus goes to prepare a place for his disciples-friends, for they have a right to a place there because of the son. From the viewpoint of Jesus' sonship one must connect the text with 8,34-38 as applied to Jesus. In the house of the father Jesus is not a slave who is part of the *oikos* only for a limited time. He is the son who is there for always. He is the son who can prepare a place for his friends in the *oikia* and who can receive them so that 'they can be where he is'.

In John's vision the Temple as *oikos* of God and the heaven as his *oikia* are realities which are intimately connected. In this Temple story the narrator has brought these two realities together by the authorial remarks of 2,19-22. The tearing down and building up of the *naos* of Jesus' body is identified with the tearing down and building up of the *naos* of the Temple. Jesus' journey to heaven via his death and resurrection has taken the place of the broken down and not re-built Temple for the faithful. It is a kind of symbolic language which is not easy to follow but which wants to express the oneness of the interests of God and his son. Via Jesus' body the access to God has become possible. Jesus is part of the *oikos* of his father even in his corporeal being. In the narrator's vision Jesus' body has become itself the *oikos* of God.

3.b.2. the father-who-sends and the son-who-is-sent

A serious subject for discussion in the Johannine Gospel is the question whether Jesus is correct in saying of himself that he is sent by God, his father. Seen from the words of Jesus which are the basis for the faith of the narrator, it is true. Seen from the side of the Judeans who form the opposition, it is a pretentious claim. In Johannine research it is seen as a metaphor which is central for the world of thought operative in the Gospel. Jesus is the father's envoy in the cosmos as his only son (3,16.18 in his own words; 1,14.18 in the words of the poet who wrote the prologue). The father 'sent' Jesus into the world out of love (the technical terms are $\pi\acute{e}\mu\pi\omega$ and $\acute{\alpha}\pi o\sigma\tau\acute{e}\lambda\lambda\omega$) to be his envoy in this world. It is a mission which Jesus fulfils out of respect for his father (cf. the lexeme /$\tau\iota\mu\acute{\alpha}\omega$/ in 5,23; 8,49 and /$\delta\acute{o}\xi\alpha$/ in 5,41-44; 7,18; 8,54; 17,4.5.23.24). The fulfilment of this mission coincides with 'saying the words which Jesus heard from his father' (3,34; 5,30; 6,45.63; 8,26.40.47; 14,10; 15,15; 17,8) and with 'doing the work which the father gave him to do' (4,34; 5,36; 9,3.4; 10,25.32.37.38; 14,10; 15,24; 17,4). Once the mission is fulfilled the son will return to the house of his father.

No other author linked himself so closely to this theologoumenon as J.-A. Bühner (1977). He believes that it is the basis for the whole of the Johannine Gospel. This is a myopic vision but it takes nothing away from the truth that Bühner helped to further Johannine research. The legation of Jesus is a metaphor taken from the secular world: the son-envoy who speaks or acts outside the confines of his own family in the name of the clan.

To prove his point Bühner posits a series of basic phrases, which he calls legal clauses, and which he concretises with texts from the Johannine Gospel:

- the mission is given orally to the envoy and he needs to listen to it
(ἀκούω). Witnesses (μαρτυρία) are not always present, but full
powers are always conferred upon him (ἐξουσία: 10,18; 17,2).
- if the mission is entrusted to one of the sons of the family, this
son is the envoy of the *oikos*. He is the appointed בֵּן בַּיִת of whom
it is said in bSheb 46b: "He is not just someone who (in the house)
goes in and out, but he is someone who takes on labourers for the
house and dismisses them; who buys and sells fruit for the house".
In the Johannine Gospel Jesus is, at one and the same time, the
envoy of his father and the son of the house '
'in whose hands all is given' by law (3,35; 13,3).
- the envoy is 'under obedience'. If he acts beyond his powers the
legation ceases. John uses this clause in an inverted way: Jesus'
obedience proves that he is the envoy of his father-God: 4,34; 5,30.
- the envoy represents the one who sends him. This is even more
stringent when it is the father and son, as in John's text: 10,30.38;
12,44; 14,10.20; 17,11.21.23.
- the envoy's first concern must be the interest of the one who
sends him. If this does not in fact happen, the one who sends him
can retract his mandate; not he but the envoy is then responsible:
see esp. 7,18 and 8,29.
- the one who sends can not be represented in matters beyond his
control: see 13,16
- the envoy must announce himself as such. Otherwise he acts in his
own name and he is then a ψεύστης (8,55). Whoever hides his
mission, acts in his own interest (7,18). John again uses this in an
inverted way: Jesus proves that he is an envoy, because he fulfils
all the prerequisites.
- the envoy can appoint a substitute. This third person will, then,
have the same powers as the second and the first (13,20; 20,21).
Jesus, however, does not lose his own special position in this case,
different from the normal social procedure.
- the envoy must return to the one who sent him to give an account
of his words and deeds and to return the powers that were given
(for the return of the son, see 13,1ff; for the return of the ἐξουσία,
see ch. 17). (Bühner 1977, 181-267).

This list looks quite impressive. But not every 'similarity' has
the same force. Furthermore, it is a reader's construction: as well
in relation to the institute of the 'son-of-the-house-envoy' as well as

in relation to the Johannine Gospel. There is no immediate influence of juridical institutions on a narrative text, but that does not mean that Bühner did not make a point.

For our own context, the remark —which Bühner sometimes adds about the Johannine reversal—, is quite important. According to Bühner, John argues sometimes in an inverted way: because Jesus proves that he fulfils the presupposition, he proves that he is the son-envoy of the father. That is, however, not incidental. At every point proof needs to be given that Jesus is the son-envoy. The narrator does that by relating what Jesus does and even more by relating what Jesus says. He lets Jesus call witnesses, lets him argue, discuss, make objections and reject them, he lets him pray to the father, all the time needing to prove that the father in heaven is the source and origin of his mission into the cosmos. The legation of Jesus as son-envoy, respectively the sending of Jesus by his father, are imaginary language constructions of the main character of the book in which the narrator believes and of which he tries to convince his readers. John's Gospel has a proper rhetoric structure which, in exegesis, quite often is forgotten.

If we want to understand the impact of the Johannine presentation something else is also important. The Gospel deals with a very special kind of son-envoy legation. The presentation implies more than just a son who acts for his father or for the *oikos* of his father. That happens quite frequently in business transactions (see e.g. Taubenschlag 1955/2, 145.149.309). John's text, however, presupposes much more. It has combined this legal institution with some other social situations. John's text is about a son who is being sent to a far country as representative of the *oikos*; he is sent to an unfriendly place, a place where the position of his father is not without enemies. This combination, however, is less frequent than Bühner suggests. As far as I can see, there are in the literature only two social situations which, then, can be considered: the king/monarch who sends his own son as envoy (as e.g. Agrippa who carries the responsibility for the East as the son-in-law of Augustus, or Germanicus who is Tiberius' envoy as son); and second, the rich οἰκοδεσπότης who considers it necessary to send his own son as a trade-envoy to foreign and/or inimical territory (as e.g. in the Synoptic parable of the vineyard where the father sends his son to hostile tenants). It is clear that in the Johannine Gospel only the first of these can be considered: Jesus as the royal son-envoy who, in the name of his father-king, defends the interests of the *oikos* of his father with word and deed in a strange country.

3.b.3. the father-teacher and the son-disciple

The Feast of the Tabernacles was the occasion for the conflict between Jesus and his ἀδελφοί. In the middle of the week of that feast Jesus goes to the Temple to 'teach'. The Judeans who are present are surprised and wonder: how does he understand γράμματα without being taught? Jesus answers that his teaching is not his own, but that it is given to him by the one who sent him (7,14-16).

It is a special kind of dialogue. Jesus' legation is seen in the context of his education. The expression εἰδεῖν γράμματα means literally 'know the alphabet', as its parallel μαθεῖν γράμματα means 'to have learnt to read'. The Judeans are surprised that Jesus appears to teach publicly, when he has not even had the most elementary education. Jesus rejects this argument basing himself on the education he received in the house of his father.

He told the Judeans this already in a preceding scene, in the long discourse in relation to their accusation that he cured a cripple on the sabbath (5,17-30). The discussion begins with Jesus' statement that he will not stop work because the father did not do that either (5,17). This, probably, refers to Ex 31,17: 'in six days God made heaven and earth but on the seventh day he rested and took a breather'. God stops his work of creating but does he also stop administering justice?, the rabbis ask themselves. And they answer: no, because, then, the text would not have read, 'and he took a breather'. That means that God continues to be occupied with breath, with the life of people. Exodus 31,17 wants to teach us that administering justice never stops in God in opposition to Gen 2,2 where this 'breathing' of God is not mentioned. The fact that God works even on this day, means that the sabbath rest does not exist for him as far as administering justice is concerned, i.e. maintaining life and taking it away (cf. Mek R.Ishmael Shabb 1, on Ex 31,17, see esp. Odeberg 1929/68, 202). And in the same way as his father-God did not stop administering justice on the seventh day Jesus also does not stop (see also Neyrey 1988, 25 who connects the strain of thought with Philo's distinction between δύναμις ποιητική and δύναμις βασιλική —which distinction is remarkably parallel to the Mekilta-text (not-quoted by Neyrey). I do not understand why Neyrey changes Philo's δύναμις βασιλική into 'eschatological power'. 'Royal power', 'kingly power' would fit very well with John's presentation of the power of Jesus as 'king under his father's authority').

The Judeans protest against this statement of Jesus and they conclude correctly that Jesus makes himself equal to God. Therefore, Jesus begins a discourse in which he speaks —in third person singular—, about the father and the son as about a father who introduces his son as a king-judge:
- the son can not do anything except what he has seen the father do;
- whatever the father does, the son does;
- the father shows the son everything he does because he loves him;
- as the father resurrects the dead and gives them life, so also the son (5,19-21).

The basic metaphor is taken from the earthly reality of a father who teaches his son a trade (cf. Gaechter 1963 and Dodd 1968b, 30-40). The son sees what his father does and the father shows him what he does. What the father does, the son does too and what the son hears his father say, the son repeats (see also 3,34; 8,28.38.47; 12,50; 14,10; 17,8; the λαλέω of the father over against the ἀκούω of the son in 5,30; 8,26.40.47; 15,15; 16,13). A son is introduced lovingly in the trade of his father and he does exactly what he sees his father do (3,11; 6,44; 8,38). That means: Jesus says about himself that he has been trained in the house of his father by his own father. From him he learned how he should be king-judge and he now acts in the name of his father.

This is a special way to present reality. The school plays an important role in the existing learning system, in the Jewish as well as the Hellenistic educational system (cf. Gerhardsson 1961; and Marrou 1965). Various texts indicate what should be taught according to an age differentiation. The pseudo-platonic treatise Axiochus says: "The child will be given pedagogues, teachers and gymnastic trainers from his seventh year on; later on the teachers for literature, geometry and warfare will be added; when the child has become *ephebe* there will be a teacher of morals and then follows the lyceum and academy" (366D-367A; see also Plut., De liberum educ. 4A(7)ff. Abot 5,21 says about the Jewish system: "The age of five is good to begin the study of the Scriptures; the age of ten for the Mishnah, thirteen for the commandments and fifteen for the Talmud, eighteen for marriage etc." (For the special ordering in Qumran, see 1QSa 1,6-20; 1QM 6,14-7,3; CD 10,6f; 14,6-9).

Such a system does not take away the responsibility of the father. He keeps certain tasks which the school system does not take away. He must set a good example: "be a παράδειγμα so that his children, by looking at the fathers' lives as at a mirror, may be deterred from disgraceful deeds and words" (Plut., De liberum educ. 14A(20)). Within the Jewish system it is especially emphasised that the father must teach his son Torah (but not Mishnah). He must also teach him a trade (Tos Qidd 1,11). The theorists from this time repeat time and again that the father has final responsibility for the education of his children (cf. Callicratides, in Stob. IV.28.18.p.687; Ps-Arist., Oeconomica I.3.4; III.2 (father *and* mother are responsible); Xenophon Oeconomica III.11; within Judaism see Falk 1978,325).

The unique element in the Johannine story is that Jesus is 'educated' by his father alone: he received his schooling 'at home' as it were. That is normally only possible for the rich and even then the father would make sure that there are pedagogues and teachers by paying a free man or by buying competent slaves (see Plut., De liberum educ. 7C (10); 8E (11); 12 B(16); Paulus Emilius 6; how wide-spread this custom became in the Jewish community is clear from the fact that the Greek loan word *pidagoog* is being used so often, cf. SDeut & 19; SNum & 87 —parables in which the king provides a pedagogue for his son—; TJ I Num 11,12). There is a story about Marcus Cato which relates this as an exception. He taught his own son to read and write. He taught him law and even gave him physical training (Plut., Marcus Cato 20(42); see also Suetonius, Aug 64,3 on the education of his grand-children; Plinius, Epistulae VIII.14.6 about the 'olden times'). It is presented as very old but also as truly authentic. The Johannine story fits in this picture. Jesus' father gave him all the time and care. He is a father who completely fits the image which the Wisdom of Sirach proposes for a father: he loved his son; he educated and taught him; he made his son like unto himself (Sir 30,1-5). The narrator makes Jesus repeat time and again that he had an extraordinary father, but also that he himself is an extraordinary son.

3.b.4. the father-kyrios and the obedient son

The Johannine Gospel uses, as it were a magnifying glass. The relation father-son and son-father has taken on enormous proportions. Between Jesus and his imaginary father everything is grandiose. His father is the greatest (10,29), the strongest(10,29), the most loving (17,24.26); the son is the chosen one (1,18), he is unique (3,16.18). The oneness between father and son can not be broken even by the ruler of this world (10,30; 17,11.22). The father will not abandon the son nor the son the father (8,16.29: 16,32). The oneness exists in possessions (16,15; 17,10), in knowledge (10,15; 17,25) and in love (3,35; 10,17; 14,31; 15,9; 17,24.26) which is completely incomparable. Therefore, the son has access to the father and nothing will be denied him. He can ask anything (11,42). He can also intervene for others who want to ask something (15,16; 16,23; c. 17). All this is still re-enforced because it exists on 'the highest levels', on the level of a king-judge who has the power of life and death (5,21; 19,11); of God himself who guarantees life for eternity (6,38-40) from before the foundation of the cosmos (17,24).

Finally it is important to see how the words from the contemporary ideology about the father-son relationship are brought together.

On the father's side we find the lexemes /command/ and /want to/: the command which Jesus received to speak the father's words (12,49); to lay down his life and take it back again (10,18); to make known to the cosmos how he loves his father (14,31). The father wants him to bring the work to fulfilment (4,34), the work which, essentially, is the return of Jesus to the father, a return which opens for mankind the possibility to live forever (6,38-40). The commands and wishes of the father are, therefore, directed to give people life. The patriarchal point of departure —the commanding— appears to intend to give life. To say so, the authoritarian structure erases itself from within.

The repeated use of the words /to love/ and /love/ from the father towards the son underlines this ($\dot{\alpha}\gamma\alpha\pi\dot{\alpha}\omega$ in 3,35; 10,17; 14,31; 15,9; 17,23.24.26; $\phi\iota\lambda\dot{\epsilon}\omega$ in 5,20). This is emphasised even more by the sayings that the father 'gives honour' to the son, in the double meaning which this word has in the Johannine Gospel: $\delta o\xi\dot{\alpha}\zeta\omega$ in 8,54; 12,28; 13,32; 16,14; 17,1.5, and $\tau\iota\mu\dot{\alpha}\omega$ in 12,26.

Jesus' father is not a jealous God. He brings to reality what, culturally, is available as the best: to be the perfect father.

The son from his side is the mirror-image of the father. It is his life to do the will of the father. He does what his father asked him in words and in deeds. He fulfils the work for which his father sent him to the cosmos. As we said already, that work is to show that he comes from God via his return to him through the cross, in order to open the way for the return to God for the scattered children of God.

We have sufficiently elaborated on the fact that the son's giving of δόξα and τιμή to the father is the fulfilment of the double Torah command: Ex 20,12 about the honour to be given to father and mother and Lv 19,3 about revering one's mother and father (cf. the exegesis of Jn 19,26.27 and Blidstein 1975). The honour which Jesus gives his father has everything to do with the work which he must fulfil: make visible that he is united with the father in a union which nothing can destroy and which will bear abundant fruit in the disciples (see for δοξάζω 12,28; 13,32; 14,13; 15,8; 17,1.4; and for τιμάω 8,49). As with the father so also with the son we see that this fundamental attitude is coloured by and embedded in 'love': 'the cosmos must know that I love the father and that I act according to his will' (14,31). The fulfilment of the father's will is for the son not the obedience to an external, authoritarian commandment. There is an inner, steadfast acceptance because the work of the father is in favour of the cosmos. The son is perfect too and he too brings to reality the best that the culture has available. 'Until the end' is the expression the narrator uses at a crucial moment in the narrative (13,1).

Evoking the relation between Jesus and his father, between God and his son, the narrator immeasurably enlarges the cultural codes of his time.

Summing up we can say that Jesus' relation to his father is very complex. The absence of a biological father is opposed to the presence of an imaginary father which is broadly painted. From the opening sentences till practically the end (except for chapter 21) the imaginary father is textually omnipresent. Such a disproportion, obviously, carries meaning, notwithstanding the silence of the exegetes. The absence of one creates the space for the presence of the other. Because there is no 'real' father, the fantasy is not hindered and can grow to 'divine' proportions. Yet, the writer uses contemporary-cultural codes from the *oikos* ideology: the only son who acts, as envoy, in the interests of the house of his father, in obedience to his will, in mutual love in favour of the life of God's children. It may be clear that, through this 'fantastic' elaboration the male code has become enormously expanded, qualitatively as well as quantitatively.

4. BEING BORN FROM GOD

John's Gospel knows a few other sentences in which family relationships are implied. They are Jn 1,13 and 3,5-6. In both these pronouncements, being born is seen in contradistinction to being born from God, from on high, from water and spirit. As the positive use of the metaphor in Jn 16,21 makes clear —the woman wailing in birth pain and rejoicing after the birth of her child—, there is nothing 'wrong' about human birth. Nevertheless, John puts it to its readers that the events surrounding birth are unimportant in comparison with what happens to people in their originating from God.

The results of this 'message' is that the physiology —and connected with it the anthropology—, which sounds in the background, are undervalued in exegesis. An exegesis which, from the point of view of gender orientation, wants to investigate the different positions of men and women in their mutual benevolent relationships can not leave out this reality. Although the treatment of these texts interrupts, in a certain sense, the development of the main argument, I want, nevertheless, to elaborate these backgrounds more explicitly. As we will see, it puts the family relationships of Jesus in a more general context and it makes clear that John's Gospel knows to criticise the culturally determined male dominance.

4.a. John 1,13

To those who believe in the name of the light-man who came into the cosmos, the power was given to become children of God. At the point where the prologue reaches a new height, just before it states that the logos appeared as flesh in this world, John speaks about the birth of man from men in a negative commentary: 'those who are born not out of multiple blood, nor out of the will of flesh or the will of a man, but of God'. After the dative 'to them who believe in his name', a nominative sentence follows, 'those who are not born', as if to fill in an empty space in the thought process: how is it with people who believe in the name of the light-man?

4.a.1. 'not born out of multiple blood' (1,13a)

First of all, starting with the birth theories of ancient classical theory, I want to describe the positive implications of the threefold negatively formulated Johannine sentences. As said, there is far more physiology -and, thus, anthropology-, hidden in the words used than most authors think. I will start with the expression οἱ [οὐκ] ἐξ αἱμάτων.

4.a.1.1. the origin of the seed

Most important in our own context is the theory which, ultimately, found the most adherents in antiquity: that the seed originates directly from the blood (cf. John 1,13: 'born from multiple blood'). Diogenes of Apollonia, a pre-Socratic, is the first to teach this so called 'haematogene' origin of the seed: "As to the blood, the thickest part is taken up by the fleshy parts; when it reaches the testicles of the womb, it becomes more fluid (λεπτόν), warm (θερμόν) and foaming (ἀφρῶδες)." (Diels 51 B6 cf. Lesky 1951 13; von Schumann 1975).

Aristotle accepts this physiology in principle. The seed is the περίττωμα τῆς αἱματικῆς τροφῆς: 'the residue from that nourishment which is in the form of blood' (De gen. anim. I.726b.10f). He proposes three proofs for his theory: semen emitted under strain due to excessively frequent intercourse, has been known in some cases to have a blood-like appearance when discharged; the loss of semen is just as exhausting as the loss of pure healthy blood; and it is the reason why we should expect children to resemble their parents (De gen. anim. I. 726b.9f). This presentation is clearly connected with the actual anatomical understanding: 'the liquid contained in the passage which lies alongside the testicle is still blood-like..., whereas in the passages which bend back towards the canal of the penis the liquid is white in colour' (De gen. anim. III.510a.20f). This kind of anatomical knowledge has prevented the recognition of the working of the testicles in the forming of seed for centuries (Lesky 1951, 132).

Galen nuances somewhat the traditional theory that the blood is the single origin of the seed. Since he knew from his own anatomical observations that the blood contains some whitish fluid before it reaches the testicles, he still maintains that the blood is the real origin of the seed (de semine, ed. Kuhn IV,582). The seedy fluid in the arteries before the testicles changes into real seed by 'the force of the boiling channels': ἰσχύς τῶν πεπτόντων ἀγγείων (de usu partium, ed. Kuhn IV, 184). The blood is the origin of the seed and the boiling is the cause.

4.a.1.2. the seed as the foam of the blood

In this last quote from Galen it is clear that blood and seed are not considered the same. Summing up shortly, we can say that the seed is conceived as 'the foam (ὁ ἀφρός) of the blood'. This idea can be found already by Diogenes of Apollonia. Some blood channels are called 'seed-arteries (σπερματίδες) where the blood, eventually, comes out 'foaming' (ἀφρῶδες) (Diels 51 B6). In a passage from this Diogenes which is handed down by Clemens of Alexandria (!) it is said: "the foam of the blood. The man's blood, already warm, is whipped up in the embrace and expelled; it foams and is passed on in the seed-arteries. Because of this foam (ἀφρός), Diogenes of Apollonia believes that the pleasure of love has received its name 'aphrodisia'" (ἀφροδίσια from ἀφρός) (Diels 51 A24).

Aristotle has taken up this theory in his own way. He connects it to the difference between man and woman. The man can boil the food in his blood till the last degree of ripeness because of his warmer blood. So he can expel seed. The blood is united to *pneuma* and the heat of the *pneuma* creates a kind of boiling process which separates the foam (=seed). Woman does not possess this potential because she is cooler. The pneumatic union with her blood leads to a pre-phase, the blood of menstruation which serves as food for the boiling blood of the man. The heat of this seed is transferred to the menstrual blood in the woman and brings it to ripeness. The seed thickens and begins to grow into new life (De gen. anim. I, 728; II, 736b; IV, 772a).

In a more general form, i.e. without the specific application to menstruation, this blood-foam-seed theory is widely present in Hellenistic, Greek-Roman and Jewish texts. I have already quoted a text from Galen about the 'force of the boiling channels'. But we find the same kind of thinking also in Philo: "Now seed is the original starting-point of living creatures. That this is a substance of a very low order, resembling foam, is evident to the eye. But when it has been deposited in the womb and become solid, it acquires movement, and at once enters upon natural growth." (De Opif. Mundi 67).

That this has become widely accepted in Jewish thinking appears from a number of Talmudic texts. The various texts about 'the boiling' (בשל) make this clear (Preuss 1969, 125), as e.g. in Jeb 76a: "It happened once in Pumbeditha that someone's seed canal was obstructed and that the seed came out via the ureter. Rabbi Bebaj ben Abajje wanted to declare this kosher. Rabbi Papi, then, said: Because you are weak people, you speak weak words. It is boiled in its own place, it is not boiled in a place not its own".

It is so widespread, that it has got a place in proverbs. In the instruction which Rabbi Akiba during his imprisonment passes on to his disciple Rabbi Simon ben Jochai it is said: 'Do not boil in the pot which your neighbour used for boiling', (Pes 112a), which is meant as a warning not to marry a divorced woman. In jSanh 8,26a we find a mashal on the evil and disobedient son: 'If the seed boils within, the pot will become black outside', i.e., when a boy begins to grow pubic hair, he is capable of producing fertile seed. The boiling of the blood ripens the seed.

This 'boiling of blood' is even linked to the verb זיד, which is interpreted from the double meaning: 'act in an uncouth manner' and 'boil': "In Hizqija's school it is taught: 'if a man boils' (יזיד) (=Ex 21,14): a man can boil and impregnate; a child can not boil and impregnate. Rabbi Mordekai said to Rabbi Ashi: How can it be proved that *mazid* means 'boil' (לבשלי)? It is written: 'and Jacob boiled a dish' (ויזד נזיד) (Gen 25,29)" (Sanh 69a).

4.a.1.3. the female seed

There is another factor which for us is rather strange. Many ancient authors believe that the woman also provides seed (see esp. Gerlach 1938 and recently Rouselle 1983/88, 27ff). Alcmaion mentions it (Diels 14 A14), but Hippon does not. He believes that the woman does not possess creative power but only provides food (τροφή) (Diels 26 A14). Aristotle very strongly resisted the idea of female seed. Based on specific genetic observations, as for instance how to explain that a son resembles his mother or a daughter her father, the Hippocratic writings had accepted that male as well as female seed had male and female characteristics. In their opinion, heredity was a question of ἐπικρατεία: what is the more powerful force in certain circumstances; what power does win in the always continuing contest? This antagonistic/agonistic principle which has a central place in Greek culture, appears already in the first written texts on the doctrine of heredity. The Hippocratic writings continue this tradition. In *De Generatione Animalium* Aristotle argues against it. As mentioned already, menstrual blood is for him, biogenetically, of a lower order than the male seed. Woman provides through a residue of the menstrual blood the matter (the ὑλή), and the food (the τροφή), while man through his seed provides the form (the εἶδος), and the movement (the κίνησις). Combined they make the embryo and development can take place. He writes on the female seed: "There are some who think that the female contributes semen during coition because women sometimes derive pleasure from it comparable to that of the male and also produce a fluid secretion. This fluid, however, is not seminal...; there is a discharge from the uterus, which though it happens in some women does not in others" (De gen. anim. I.727b.728).

With this Aristotle pinpointed the problem. For what could one imagine this female seed to be? In the Post-Aristotelian period (end 4th century BC), Herophilos of Chalcedon had discovered the ovaries anatomically. That provided the best chance, yet, to understand woman's own contribution in the origin of the embryo, but it did not work out that way. That he calls the ovaries 'female testicles', can still be understood against the background of existing theories. But he believes that the 'seed channels' open up in the urine-bladder. Soranus, a medico in Ephesus living in the beginning of the 2nd century AD, concluded from this that the female seed could not contribute anything in the embryo formation (Lesky 1951, 162). It was Galen who discovered (middle 2nd century AD) that Herophilos was mistaken in his anatomy and that the female 'seed-channels' opened up in the uterus (de sem ed. Kuhn IV,598; de utero ed. Kuhn II,900). With that he had to reject Aristotle's theory of the non-existence of female seed and to return to the theories of the Hippocratic writings, the atomici and Alcmaion who postulated the existence of female seed. Galen's theory found adherents till late in the Middle Ages.

What these ancient theorists could imagine this female seed to be, remains a difficult question. According to Lesky and Rouselle, it is for Galen probably the mucus from the ovarian ducts (Lesky 1951, 179; Rouselle 1983/88, 30). From certain texts in the Talmud I have come to the conclusion that the rabbis thought of the orgasm moisture. That women do produce seed, followed from certain texts of the Old Testament such as Gen 3,15 and especially Lev 12,2 which, talmudically, should be translated as 'if the woman provides the seed, she bears a boy'. The rabbis saw proof in this text of how a boy or a girl originates and how one could manipulate the birth of one or the other. "Rabbi Isaac said that Rabbi Ami said, 'if the woman sows first, a boy will be born; if the man sows first, a girl will be born, because it is written: if the woman provides the seed, she bears a boy (=Lev 12,2)'" (Nidda 31a, see also Nidda 25b; 28a; Ber 60a). From practical experience the rabbis knew that this was not foolproof and so we also find other advices for conception. As far as my question is concerned, however, it is probably clear that 'the sowing of the woman', parallel to that of the man, is connected with the orgasm and that the female seed, thus, is seen as orgasm fluid.

4.a.1.4. not out of multiple blood

The plural αἵματα in this sentence provides surprises till the end. For me it is clear that via the idea of the boiling of the blood to become sperm, the male element in conception is provided for. It would be strange, if next to the expression οὐδὲ ἐκ θελήματος ἀνδρὸς the male contribution would be completely absent. But the plural form αἵματα makes it very probable to think that also the female element in conception is not forgotten.

The Euripides-quote (Ion 693) ἄλλων τραφείς ἐξ αἱμάτων = 'nourished by alien's blood', which in exegetical literature appears time and again (see Theobald 1988, 243; Hofrichter 1986, 48; Barrett 1967, 137; Bultmann 1941, 38; Bernard 1928, 18) and which often is seen as a perfect parallel and which would prove that the Johannine sentence only wants to pay attention to the female contribution in the conception is, most probably, not really a parallel at all. The text suggests -the hearers of the drama are already much better informed-, that the young man Ion of this text, is fed by the blood of a woman who is not the wife of the protagonist: i.e. the participle τραφείς has to be understood from the substantive τροφή : the woman's blood as τροφή (cf. the theory of Hippon and Aristotle, but see also Aesch., Eumenides 665 'fed in the darkness of the womb'; Soph., Ajax 1229 'fed by a noble-born mother' and 4Macc 13,20). That is quite a different interpretation than the supposed meaning that the blood of woman is the cause of birth. But this is not all that has to be said. The verb τρέφω is used with the tragici also of the father (Soph., Philoctetes 3; Ajax 557) and takes, then, the meaning of 'to sire'. It is not to exclude that this signification could also be applied in the Euripides-text. In that case one should translate the text as 'sired by the multiple blood of aliens'. /ἄλλων/ relates, then, to the supposed mother as well as to the supposed father. No matter how, in the drama the 'father' Xunthus plays, in any case, the role of an alien who has forced his way into the royal household of Athens (see in the antistrophe vs 998.701.705. 721; and about his fatherhood: 553; in any case, Ion is the 'real' son of Apollo and Creusa).

Rather than to stand still by this Euripides-quote which is quite difficult to interpret, I would think of the interpretation by Augustine: 'mixtis sanguinibus, masculi et feminae, commixtione carnis masculi et feminae' (Serm CXXI.4, quoted by Bernard). Together with the blood of the man the woman's blood contributes to the origin of new life, cf. Hipp Coll 12,1: 'if the seed which comes from both parents remains in the womb of the woman, it is first of all thoroughly mixed together —for the woman of course does not remain still' (cf. Rouselle 1983/88, 27/28; Brown 1988, 12/14). The 'mixing' is a more or less technical terminology: the μείγνυμι and its derivations μίξις and ἐπίμιξις in Aristotle and the בלל from the Talmud (see bChullin 69a).

It is possible that parallel to the way of looking at the male sperm, they saw the female sperm as a blood-residue. But, more probably, they thought of uterus-blood in relation to the female contribution either in connection with menstrual blood or not. How all this is seen, can appear from the following texts:

Wisdom 7,2: "In the womb of my mother I have been formed into a body, in ten months, after I had been set in blood (sg.), out of the seed of man and the lust which comes with sleep."

Nidda 31b: "Rabbi Isaac said, It is said in the school of Rabbi Ami: a woman will not become pregnant unless close to her menstrual period, because it is said: See, I was born in your guilt (Ps 51,7). Rabbi Jochanan said: close to the bath of purification, because it is written: And in my sin my mother conceived me (Ps 51,7)." (This means that the chance for conception is greatest just before or just after the menstrual period).

Nidda 31b: "The rabbanan taught: Three cooperators are active (in the coming into existence) of men: the Holy one, blessed be He, his father and his mother. The father sows the white from which bones, muscle, nails, the brains in his head and the white of the eye are formed. The mother sows the red from which the skin, flesh, hairs and the black of the eye are formed. And the Holy one, blessed be He, gives him spirit and breath, the form of his face, the sight in the eyes and the hearing in the ears, the speaking of the mouth and the walking of the feet; knowledge and insight and intellect. When his time comes to leave this world, the Holy one, blessed be He, takes his part and leaves the part of father and mother before their eyes."

LevR 14,9: "A woman's womb is full of blood, some of which goes out by way of the menstrual flow, and by the favour of the Holy One, blessed be He, a drop of white matter goes and falls into it and immediately the foetus begins to form. It may be compared to milk in a basin; if one puts rennet into it, it congeals and becomes consistent, if not, it continues to be loose." (For the comparison of milk and rennet, see Job 10,10!, and more elaborate Aristotle De gen. anim. I.729a.13f; II.739b.23f; a text as Tertullianus, de carne Christi, 19,3-5 should be understood from this context. Hofrichter 1978, 72 is puzzled by this text, because 1/ he refuses to think of the role of the male's blood; 2/ he seems not to be aware of the Aristotelian theory about the equalization *calor sanguinis = despumatio*).

The theoretically adapted Parmenides-fragment (see Lesky 1951, 48) comes closest to the expression which is used in Jn 1,13. It is handed down by Soranus (beginning of the 2nd century AD, Ephesus!), in the Latin version of Caelius Aurelianus:

"femina virque simul Veneris cum germina miscent
venis informans diverso ex sanguine virtus
temperiem servans bene condita corpora fingit"

"When woman and man mix the seed of love, the force which originates in the arteries forms well-built bodies from the different blood, if equality is maintained."

(Diels 18 B18)

The act of begetting of man and woman creates a force *diverso ex sanguine*. If the mix is equal, a well-formed person is born out of the multiple blood. 'To be born ἐξ αἱμάτων' calls forth 'to be born ἐκ θελήματος σαρκός'.

4.a.2. 'not out of the will of flesh' (1,13b)

Via the blood man and woman are together responsible for the birth of a child. What does the rest of Jn 1,13 add to this? It seems most probable that the text runs backwards chronologically: the will of the flesh precedes the mixing of the blood -and this is preceded by the will of the man. It is a literary form which we find more often in John: see e.g. 1,29; 3,13; 8,28; 21,18 and which gives direction to the interpretation also in Jn 1,13: the will of the flesh as introduction to the mixing of the blood.

It is a very particular expression which as such is rather unique, not only in biblical writings but, in a certain sense, in the whole of classical literature. This has to do with the fact that this reality - i.e., the willing of the flesh-, is described no longer by physiologists but by moralists. The description is surrounded by normative statements and reflections about the *sarx* in which 'the seemly', 'that which should be' (τό καθῆκον) predominates. This colours the underlying physiological reality.

The more or less classical studies on the *sarx* (as for instance, Käsemann 1933; W.D. Davies 1948; Lindijer 1952; Schweizer-Meyer 1964; Lazure 1969; Jewett 1971) do not add much that is relevant for understanding Jn 1,13. Because they reach as a rule for Pauline texts, they are more interested in appositions like ἡδονή (pleasure), ἐπιθυμία (desire, yearning), πάθος (emotion, passion), and φρόνημα (thought, purpose) than in the almost neutral θελήμα from the Johannine text. Jn 1,13 does not say much more than that the flesh knows a willing which leads to conception.

Obviously, the subject of the phrase is the sexual desire. That seems so self-evident that, as far as I can see, no one puts this in a literary context of signification. Dateless magic papyri which Bultmann mentions (1964, 38 and of which Brown 1966, 12 says, "*Thelèma*, 'will, desire' appears for 'lust' in some of the Greek papyri of this period"), do not add anything to the meaning of the text. And the reference to the Hebrew standard expression 'flesh and blood' as equivalent for 'man' (as a.o. Schweizer 1964, 139) deconstructs the text too conceitedly to be of any use: 1/ the word

sequence in the Hebrew expression is different from Jn 1,13; 2/ the
blood is not multiple; and 3/ the really specific mention in Jn 1,13
of 'the will of the flesh' is not respected any more (cf. Brown
1966, 12).

The expression 'from the will of flesh' is the description of a
single moment in a complex event, the coming into existence of a
human being from human beings. It leaves its readers with the
question whether -as in the expression 'from multiple blood'-, the
activities of man and woman are described or whether one should
think only of the male. But, then, why is it followed by 'and (not)
from the will of man'? To find an answer to this readers' question
we must search the (contemporary) *oikos*-treatises in which a.o. the
intercourse between man and woman is described in a mixture of
descriptive and obligatory sentences. In fact we must, then, look at
Musonius, Ps-Ocellus and Plutarch. These names represent
differing positions because, as I have said above, the descriptions
are placed in the context of prescriptions: of what is 'seemly for
man and woman'.

Nevertheless, there is some kind of a common point of
departure: the mutual desire which is common to man and woman.
I quote the relevant passages:

Musonius: "With what purpose did the creator divide us in two
genders; why did he, then, give us two sexes, one to be for the
man and the other for the woman; why did he put into both of them
a strong desire (ἐπιθυμία) to come to union; and why did he give
each a strong longing (ποθός) for each other, man for woman and
woman for man ?" (Stob. IVa 22,20 p. 498 l.14-21; cf. Jagu 1979,
67/68; Geytenbeek 1962, 68).

Ps-Ocellus: "The potential and the organs and the desire
(ὄρεξεις) to the intermingling which are given to men (ἀνθρώποις)
by God, are not given for pleasure (ἡδονή), but for the perpetual
preservation of mankind" (De univ.nat. 4,2).

It is clear that these authors do not use the word 'will'. I found
that only in Plutarch, in the introduction on his *Praecepta
Coniugalia*, where he pleads for the combination of pleasure and
grace in marriage 'so that married people should succeed in
attaining their mutual desires (διαπράττωνται παρ' ἀλλήλων ἃ
βούλονται) by persuasion and not by fighting and quarrelling.'
(Praec. Coniug. 138 C/D). It is a will which includes -among other
things- sexual relations as is clear from the immediately following

opening sentences where the bride is advised to take a quince before retiring so that her lips and her speech will be pleasing (to the groom, I suppose).

The will of the flesh of the woman is the most under pressure. The one acceptance of mutual desire is constantly limited normatively by prescriptions which demand from the woman as wife a σωφροσύνη (a moderation in sensual desires), quite different from the moderation demanded from the man as husband. The different authors take their own positions here. Hierocles and Musonius write that the same norms should apply to man and woman. Antipatros, the other Neo-Pythagoreans (Bruson, Callicratides, Perictyone, Phintys, Hierocles) and Plutarch accept a difference in norms. Considering that Jn 1,13 continues with 'and (not) out of the will of man', it seems likely that this text, ideologically, is connected with these last authors: the will of man is explicitly mentioned next to the mutual will. This needs to be elaborated.

4.a.3. 'and not out of the will of a man' (1,13c)

If I am right to read Jn 1,13 in this way, the expression 'out of the will of a man' does not intend to say 'that the man is the principal agent in generation'(Brown 1966, 12; Bultmann 1964, 38) but, rather, that the will of the man precedes the mutual will of the flesh and (must) give direction to that.

Among the various ancient authors, it is in Plutarch that we find the most explicit statements (see Ziegler 1951; Goessler 1962; Babut 1969; Wicker 1975). The man leads: "whenever two notes are sounded in accord the tune is carried on by the bass; and in like manner every activity in a virtuous household is carried on by both parties in agreement, but discloses the hushand's leadership and preferences" (Praec. Coniug. 139 D). It depends on the man how a woman will comport herself. He can make her "all paint and powder, meretricious and licentious, but also discreet and well-behaved" (140 C). Plutarch uses the example of the Spartan woman who is asked whether she had already made advances to her husband and who answers: 'No, but he has made them to me'. That behaviour is worthy of an οἰκοδεσποίνη: "on the one hand not to avoid or to feel annoyed at such actions on the part of her husband if he begins them, and on the other not to take the initiative herself;

for the one course is meretricious and froward, the other disdainful and unamiable" (140 D, see also Moralia 242 B; Amat. 751 D).

The unilateral masculinity of Plutarch's opinion is evident from the incongruity of the relationships. Man's hegemony is, according to him, an art as well as a duty. That the woman is to be led, is only a duty. The man must take care that he keeps dominance over his wife, "and control ought to be exercised by the man over the woman, not as the owner has control of a piece of property, but, as the soul controls the body, by entering into her feelings and being knit to her through goodwill. As, therefore, it is possible to exercise care over the body without being slave to its pleasures and desires, so it is possible to govern a wife, and at the same time to delight and gratify her" (142 E; in essence we find the same in Antipatros, Stob. IVa. 22,25 p. 510 l. 9-10). But if the woman wants something or, rather, when she does not want something, her position is quite different. To clarify that, Plutarch mentions an anecdote about Philip: "A woman once said to Philip, who was trying to force her to come to him against her will,'Let me go. All women are the same when the lights are out'. This is well said as an answer to adulterous and licentious men, but the wedded wife ought especially when the light is out not to be the same as ordinary women, but, when her body is invisible, her virtue, her exclusive devotion to her husband, her constancy, and her affection, ought to be most in evidence" (144 F).

That the willing of the man and the woman do not coincide at the same time, seems to be an old marriage problem. The strongest wins or is treated better. In this respect there is no great difference between Hellenistic and Jewish writings. In the Mishnah it is stated as a Torah:"If a woman is refractory against her husband, he may reduce her marriage settlement by seven dinars every week. R. Judah says, seven half-dinars. How long is the reduction to be continued? Until it reaches the full amount of her marriage settlement. R. Jose says, He may continue to diminish it, in case an inheritance may fall to her from some source and he can, then, claim from her. And likewise also if the husband is refractory against his wife, they may add to her marriage settlement three dinars a week; R. Judah says, Three half-dinars" (Ket 5,7). Notwithstanding a certain equality, there is still a big difference: the woman who does not want, is under pressure of a double diminution of money; furthermore, the woman has no say, if the man does not want. She must rely on other people (father, uncle(s), brother(s), judge(s)) to obtain her right: 'he may reduce, they may add'.

So we arrive at the last possible meaning which is implied in John's text. The unequal division of power between the married man and the wife leads (sometimes) to different possibilities in behaviour: the man is allowed more than the woman and the woman must approve of his behaviour. It is surprising how matter-of-factly this is reported.

We find in Plutarch: "The lawful wives of the Persian kings sit beside them at dinner, and eat with them. But when the kings wish to be merry and get drunk, they send their wives away, and send for their music-girls and concubines. In so far they are right in what they do, because they do not concede any share in their licentiousness and debauchery to their wedded wives. If therefore a man in private life, who is incontinent and dissolute in regard to his pleasures, commit some peccadillo with a paramour or a maid-servant, his wedded wife ought not to be indignant or angry, but she should reason that it is respect for her which leads him to share his debauchery, licentiousness, and wantonness with another woman" (Praec. Coniug. 140 B; see also Perictyone, Stob. IV, 28,19, p. 692 l. 1-2; for further parallels, see Wilhelm 1915, 199).

Specific male practices are glossed over, and at the same time the texts impose a double tolerance on the woman. One could argue that such a male oriented moral attitude would be unimaginable for Jn 1,13. In the group of people where the text of John has been conceived and received, other and stricter rules prevail, because one could presuppose a greater influence of biblical marriage values. That is indeed probable. Yet, if 'the will of man' is to be translated in Hebrew as רצון הבעל —and, therefore, will be understood by Jewish readers via this lexeme—, the 'freedom' of the man does remain quite a bit greater than the woman's. The man determines the conditions of the marriage contract. He has in principle the possibility to marry more women. As long as he is willing to marry her, a man may have sexual relations with any woman who is not engaged or married to another man.

In Philo one can see how this works out in the strictest way (see especially, De Spec. Leg. III, 7-82), but, staying within the Jewish tradition we can also point to the practices of Rabbi Rab and Rabbi Nachman (quoted by Urbach 1975, 478). The Talmud writes that they were accustomed, when they arrived in certain places, to have it announced, 'what woman wants to belong to me for one day?' (Joma 18b; Jeb 37b). These practices, obviously, called forth a great deal of resistance, at least theoretically, and the Talmud rejects them according to the traditional halachah on marriage, and /or interprets them 'in a spiritual manner' ('The rabbis only used to withdraw themselves with these women, because it is not the same whether one has bread in one's basket or not', i.e. they only discussed the Torah with them -and they did not sleep with them). But the Talmudic objections and corrections are not intended to diminish the male רצון.

Only in cases of adultery the equality of man and woman appears. Progeny is, then, in question. Plutarch writes about this: "Man and wife...should keep themselves pure from all unholy and unlawful intercourse with others, and they should not sow seed from which they are unwilling to have any offspring, and from which if any issue does result, they are ashamed of it, and try to conceal it" (Praec. Coniug. 144 B). Probably he considers only the children of free people, and this might be the reason why he considers them equal. Philo certainly does so (see De Spec. Leg. III, 69.80), and that proves again that 'the will of the man' is more respected.

The will of the man is the starting point of sexual intercourse. The man is supposed to take the initiative. He has the right and the duty to give form and substance to the 'will of the flesh'. He determines the space and the manner where the woman can play an active role. The mixing of the multiple blood, the origin of new life originates from this mutual will.

The most important feature in John 1,13 is its negation: 'born not out of multiple blood, nor out of the will of flesh or the will of man'. Jn 1,13 negates its own moralised heterosexual physiology. Compared to the birth from God, everything that happens in the birth of man in sexual relations is without value.

Jn 1,13 is not treated very extensively in exegesis, and is usually negatively evaluated. It can not stand up, poetically, to the opening sentences of the prologue. Only those exegetes who see the prologue as a chiastic textual structure, consider Jn 1,12.13 sometimes as the most important turning point within the text (see e.g. Boismard 1953; Culpepper 1981; Staley 1988): the birth from

God based on the trust in the name of God's word is unique in the prologue, more so than all other sentences which, in whatever way, refer to each other. Jn 1,12.13 is a case apart.

And Jn 1,13 is still apart in that: the relativisation of the sexual relationship between man and woman which results in the birth of a human person, brings a particular, polemical note to the logical line of thought in the prologue. The text presupposes a certain surplus value of the man in the sexual relationship between man and woman, but the surplus value of God in the relationship between God and every person born from God, is much more important.

There is most probable a connection with 1 Jn 2,16-17: 'everything that exists in the world -the desire of the flesh, the desire of the eyes and the pride of wealth-, does not come from the father, but comes from the world. And the world and its desire passes away, but whoever does the will of God, lives forever', i.e. timeliness connected with human birth and sexuality can not be compared (or only negatively) with the permanence which comes from a birth from God.

Jn 3,5-6 is the only other text in John which elaborates on this problem.

4.b. 'born from water and spirit' (Jn 3,5)

Jn 3,5f is part of a longer conversation: the dialogue between Jesus and Nicodemus during the night: 3,1-21. It is the turning point in the discussion so far and as we will see, it is intimately connected with the pronouncement in Jn 1,13. It caused a lot of confusion in exegesis, because the logic of the dialogue seems to be broken. The reader expects that Jesus will explain the ἄνωθεν of 3,3. The expression 'to be born from water and spirit' frustrates this expectation. Via 1,26 and 1,33 it is supposed that the expression ' 'water and spirit' is connected to Jesus' baptising activity 'in water and spirit'. But this is not completely satisfactory. In 1,26.33 the 'baptism in water' and the 'baptism in the (holy) spirit' are set in opposition. The baptism in water is the baptism of John and the baptism in spirit is the baptism of Jesus and that is presented as an opposition of preparation and fulfilment. Furthermore, the expression 'baptism *in* water' and 'baptism *in* spirit' is not the same as 'being born *from* water and spirit'. Why did vs 3,5 not say 'born *in* water and spirit'?

It is inexplicable also that the text in 3,6 continues only on the
opposition between a birth from the *sarx* and a birth from the
pneuma, and especially that 'the water' disappears completely in
this sentence. A reader's reaction like Bultmann's who attributes the
ἐξ ὕδατος to his supposed ecclesiastical redaction, is symptomatic
for the experienced lack of logic in 3,5. The bone of contention
-the textual presence of 'the water'- is then removed, but the
question is at what price.

In 3,6 these readers' problems are solved. Jesus distinguishes
two kinds of birth from two different principles. On the one hand,
there is the birth from the mother's womb and from the *sarx*: a
birth which happens only once and which can not be undone: man
as a transient, perishable and mortal being; born from the mother's
womb, man becomes old. Flesh produces flesh. On the other hand,
the birth from the *pneuma*, a birth which, in some way, parallels to
the birth from 'on high', and the birth 'from water and spirit': a
birth from God which stands for permanence and immortality; a
birth which can take place independently from the birth from the
sarx and which is, then, more lastingly important.

The text, clearly, indicates two evaluative lines of thought which
can be distinguished as follows:

negative evaluation	positive evaluation
3,3: be born ἄνωθεν in the meaning: 'again'	3,3: be born ἄνωθεν in the meaning: 'from on high'
3,4: re-enter his mother's womb and be born again	3,5: be born from water and spirit
3,6: born from the σάρξ	3,6: born from the πνεῦμα
3,6: σάρξ	3,6: πνεῦμα

It is self-evident that contrary codes are activated here. One can
think of the oppositions:

/changeable/ - /unchangeable/
/transitory/ - /permanent/
/passing/   - /remaining/

These are connected with the lexemes /ἄνωθεν/ , /σάρξ/, and /πνεῦμα/, understood against the background of Jewish, Platonic, Middle-Platonic as well as Christian texts (cf. o.a. Kleinknecht-Bieder-Sjöberg-Schweizer 1959). But this does not solve the readers' problem of vs 3,5 as indicated above.

I believe that a solution can only be found, if one adds the codes /female/ and /male/ to this series of contrary oppositions . No one will argue with the fact that the code /female/ fits the left hand side. The lexemes /mother's womb/ and /ἡ σάρξ/ are univoque. The problem is in the right hand side: how are the lexemes 'born from water and spirit' and τὸ πνεῦμα connected to the code /male/? I believe that, via the reference to 'the male sperm', this connection can be made: the womb of the mother as opposed to the sperm of the father.

This suggestion is not totally new. There is a tradition in exegesis which has seen in vs 3,5 an allusion to the male sperm. Odeberg (1929/1968, 48, followed by Barrett 1967, 174, but not any more in 1982, 92) points out that in (a limited number of) Jewish texts 'the water' (מַיִם) stands for sperm:

-Nidda 16b:"Rabbi Chanina bar Pappa expounded: The angel that is appointed over the conception is called Laila (=Night) and he takes the טִפָּה (the drop of semen) and brings it before the Holy One, Blessed be He, and he says before him: 'Lord of the Universe, what shall arise out of this drop? A strong man or a weak man, a wise or a fool, a rich or a poor?' And if the words 'a righteous or a wicked' are not included in the question, this is in accord with R. Chanina's opinion, for R. Chanina used to say: 'Everything is in the hands of Heaven except the fear of Heaven'."

- Abot 3,1: "Akiba ben Mehalalel said: 'Know whence thou art come' -from a fetid drop (טִפָּה); 'and whither thou art going' -to a place of dust, worms and maggots; 'and before whom thou wilt in future render account and reckoning' -before the supreme King of kings, the Holy One, Blessed be He."

Based on these texts, it seems likely to Odeberg that the ὕδωρ from Jn 3,5 stands for the male sperm, as a metonymy for the *sarx* in 3,6 and, thus, opposed to the *pneuma* of 3,5 and 3,6.

It is not surprising that this suggestion did not make it in exegesis: 1/ the identification of ὕδωρ and טִפָּה is not right: טִפָּה stands for every drop, not only for a drop of 'water', but just as well for a drop of rain or poison; furthermore, even the rabbis knew that semen was not pure water; children are not born from pure water. 2/ More importantly, the suggestion aggravates the problem of 3,5. The expression 'water and spirit' must, then, be taken as a hendiadys for 'spiritual seed': man must be born not of earthly but of spiritual semen. Barrett (1982, 92) writes as conclusion of his discussion of Odeberg's suggestion: "If we could allow that water, ὕδωρ, would quite naturally suggest seminal fluid, this would be a very attractive suggestion indeed, and would remove baptism from the context completely."

I believe that exegetes stopped their search too quickly. In my research in classical sexology, it has become clear to me that the combination /water and spirit/ appears in this physiology precisely as indicating the male sperm.

Aristotle's text from De gen. anim. II, 735a-b can be taken as the origin of this doctrine:

"A puzzle which may now be propounded is, what is the nature (φύσις) of semen? Semen when it leaves the animal is thick and white, but when it cools it becomes fluid like water and is of the colour of water. This may seem strange, because water is not thickened by heat, yet semen is thick when it leaves the inside of the animal, which is hot, and becomes fluid when it cools. Moreover, watery substances freeze, but semen does not freeze when exposed to frost in the open air; it becomes fluid, which suggests that is was heat that thickened it.

...This then is the puzzle. Suppose that semen is water..., or suppose it consists of earth or is a mixture of earth and water... (This does not solve the puzzle. One must start from the idea that it is a mixture ἐξ ὕδατος καὶ πνεύματος). The semen is coherent and white, when it comes forth from within, because it contains a good deal of hot *pneuma* owing to the internal heat of the animal. Later, when it has lost its heat by evaporation and the air has cooled, it becomes fluid and dark, because the water and whatever tiny quality of earthy matter it may contain stay behind in the semen as it solidifies. Semen, then, is a compound of *pneuma* and water (κοινὸν πνεύματος καὶ ὕδατος) (*pneuma* being hot air), and that is why it is fluid in its nature; it is made of water (ὑγρὸν ... ὅτι ἐξ ὕδατος)."

From the texts of the following authors, it appears that this 'water and spirit' theory continued to exist also after Aristotle. It is to be supposed that the school system played a role in its tradition. During a rather long period this specific theory on the male sperm is handed down in the (medical) schools. It seems to be proved that the pneumatic-medical direction —which flourishes in the Claudius-Trajan era—, had immediate access to Aristotle's texts. Therefore, this school is directly linked to Aristotle's theory (cf. Verbeke 1945, 206ff; Festugière 1954, III, XCIII).

I give a list of quotations from authors from the 4th century BC till 2nd century AD:

Zeno (Arnim fr. 128): "Zeno says that the sperm which man ejaculates is πνεῦμα μεθ' ὑγροῦ, a part of the soul and a particle of the seed of the ancestors". (In Arnim II, 741 this same idea is attributed to Chrysippus; in II, 742; 743 to the 'Stoics').

The πνεῦμα in the early Stoics is seen materially as a spark of the fire from the stars. (cf. Pohlenz 1948, I, 86; 1949 II, 50). It touches all senses: the five senses of perception, and the senses of speech, intellect and the organs for generation (Arnim fr. 143, cf. Verbeke 1945, 32): a theory which can be found in Zeno as well as in Chrysippus (Verbeke 1945, 79).

Diocles of Carystos (4th century BC): "Diocles says about the sperm that it is γεῶδές τι καὶ ὕδωρ καὶ πνεῦμα. When the warmth is blown out, the watery remains; it thickens because it has something earthy; it is white because it is foam (ἀφρός)" (cf. Festugière 1954, LXXXIX, in the translation back to the Greek by Jaeger).

Ps-Galen, De Def.Med., ed. Kuhn XIX,370, (according to Mewaldt, Pauly-Wissowa s.v. Galenus, written by someone from the pneumatic-medical school): "Sperm is bundled force in moist matter (δύναμις ἐν ὑγρῷ)....; or according to another definition: sperm is moist matter from warm *pneuma* (ὑγρὸν ἐκ θερμοῦ πνεύματος) which is in the testicles and from which, normally, man originates; or, sperm is πνεῦμα ἔνθερμον ἐν ὑγρῷ which moves from itself and has the potential to generate, thus, the matter from which it comes".

Philo, De Opif. Mundi 67: "Now seed is the original starting-point of living creatures...Nature...forms living creatures, by distributing the moist substance (τὴν μὲν ὑγρὰν οὐσίαν) to the limbs and different parts of the body; the substance of life-breath (τὴν δὲ πνευματικὴν) to the faculties of the soul, affording them nourishment and endowing them with perception."

Clemens of Alexandria, Paedagogus I.6.49.1: "All these considerations prove that the blood is the substance of the human body. What descends into the mother's womb, has originally a

moist (ὑγρός) structure as milk (cf. the ἄφρος-theory!); after blood
has been withdrawn from it, the structure changes in flesh; after
this has thickened, the embryo is formed in the womb under the
influence of the natural and warm πνεῦμα and the living creature
originates" (cf. Verbeke 1945, 431).

The great differences in theoretical background and suppositions
do not take away the continuity of the sperm ideas. Male sperm is a
mixture of water and spirit. The word ὑγρός, sometimes,
substitutes for the word ὕδωρ. Against the background of the
four-elements-theory where 'the moist' is characteristic of 'water',
this seems an acceptable variant. The common element is that the
pneuma is seen as the most important principle, even though the
different authors see the *pneuma* quite differently: for Aristotle it is
the principle of movement; for the Stoics it participates in the
heavenly fire; Philo sees it as a participation in the divine breath;
while the pneumatic medical school considers it the active principle
which transforms and gives form.

These various ways of looking at this reality are not unimportant
to see the proper possibility of meaning in John's text. He connects
it with his own signification of the word *pneuma*. 'Born from water
and spirit' is 'born from the sperm of God'. The secret key is the
meaning of *pneuma*. In vs 3,3 Jesus speaks about 'to be born
ἄνωθεν'. Nicodemus says that it is impossible for man to return to
the womb, i.e. to start life again as sperm. Jesus alludes to that
sperm. He does not use the word but the wording 'from water and
spirit'. In the follow-up sentence (in vs 3,6) he discloses the secret
language: there is an essential difference between 'born out of *sarx*'
and 'born out of *pneuma*'. *Pneuma* is a divine principle. It can not,
then, be hidden from any listener/reader that in vs 3,5 he has
spoken about the birth from God.

If this interpretation is correct, it demonstrates once again how
subtle John manipulates his readers. It would bare a
misunderstanding of not a few readers/exegetes! There is even little
reason to deny allusions to baptismal practices and doctrines. Such
a refined use of language leaves all doors open. Anyway, two other
Johannine texts show that the proposed interpretation is at least a
possible one. First, Jn 6,63 where it is said of the *pneuma* that it is
τὸ ζῳοποιοῦν, a word which describes the *pneuma* as an active
life-principle and which refers in Jn 5,21 (cf. the Pauline literature)

to calling from death to life. Opposed to the *pneuma* as the origin of life is the *sarx* of no importance. Secondly, and even more direct, I may point to 1 Jn 3,9 where 'the sperm of God' is mentioned explicitly as the principle of origin of being born from God: for those who are born from God, God's seed is a remaining strength which protects even against sin.

As Jn 1,13, Jn 3,1-10 is connected with 1 Jn 2,16-17. It, clearly, accentuates the opposition /permanent/ vs /transitory/, combined with the codes /unchanging/ vs /changing/ and /remaining/ vs /passing/. New in Jn 3,1-10 is the explicit evaluative connection with the codes /male-positive/ opposed to /female-negative/. In Jn 1,13 this was an implicit suggestion. It is now expressed much more clearly. It makes the main message of the text —that compared to what happens in the birth from God, the surplus value of the man in the fertile sexuality between man and woman is of no great importance—, much more incisive.

5. THE FAMILY CONSTELLATION

Returning to the main argument of this chapter —the family constellation of Jesus—, we can see now how from the point of view of the narrator and of Jesus, the absence of an 'earthly' father is related to the presence of a 'heavenly' father. Jesus realises the birth from God in an extreme sense. God is his only Father. But, as explained, not only the absence-presence of his father but also the conspicuous presence of his mother and the conflict with his brothers and sisters belong to this specific family constellation. It is this special, dynamic constellation which determines how the familial love is narratively expressed.

In accordance with the focus of this study, I see this familial constellation as an 'imaginary reality', i.e. as a narrative realisation of an imaginary possibility. For its evaluation it would be important to compare John's story with the Synoptic parallels which vary the family constellation in different ways: an opposing and absent mother, opposing brothers and sisters and an absent father in Mark; a contested fathership, a more favourable mother, opposing brothers and sisters in Matthew and Luke. The variations make clear that a rather large field of imaginary possibilities existed.

Anyhow, a research in contemporary first century literature has made clear to me that, at least, the narrator of the Johannine Gospel created a very special reality with his story. I re-read a number of the more important biographical collections from this point of view —Cornelius Nepos, Plutarch, Suetonius. This made me conclude that the Johannine Gospel is rather unique. All aspects of this special familial constellation appear individually. An absent father —unknown, disappeared or dead—, is for different reasons a fairly common phenomenon (cf. the biographies of Scipio, Fabius Maximus, Philopoemon, Pyrrhus, Damon, Simon, Sertorius, Cato jr, Demosthenes, Demetrius, Antonius, Marcus Brutus and Aratus). The absent father is (usually) replaced by a guardian who, then, often plays a very important role in the lives of the adopted sons (see Scipio, Fabius Maximus, Marcus Brutus, Augustus; Epaminondas is the great father figure in the life of Philopoemon). A mother who is evidently present is not an exception, at least in the stories of Plutarch (see Coriolanus, the Gracchi; Agis, Cleomenes and Artaxerxes). It can also be found in some biographies of Cornelius Nepos (in Datames and Timoleon). Conflicts with brothers (and sisters) sometimes play a role (in the biographies of Artaxerxes, Flaminius and Timoleon). But these separate familial realities seldom or never come all together in one story.

A kind of exception is the biography of Persius (cf. Leo 1965/1901, 18 this *vita* is not by Suetonius but by Valerius Probus). It is a very short biography. Persius' father dies as his son is six years old. His mother marries again but this man dies quickly too. Persius himself reveres (*coluit*) a certain Nonianus as his father. His mother plays an important role in his life as also his sister and an aunt. Persius dies very young. As he dies he bequeaths all his possessions to his mother and his sisters (in the plural now). His mother takes it upon herself to publish the poems of her son. She is advised in this by Cornutus, the long-time friend of Persius himself (*Persius nusquam ab eo discederet*). Apparently there are no brothers. There is no conflict with the sister(s). Apart from this, the biography resembles structurally the story which the narrator of the Johannine Gospel tells us about the life of Jesus, at least from the point of view of family setting.

The result of this research is quite remarkable. It so happens that the quasi-total absence of structurally similar narratives in antiquity stays in complete opposition to the multitude of stories which speak of similar familial constellations in modern discourse. At least since

Freud's 'Three Essay on the Theory of Sexuality' (1905, English Standard Edition VII, 130ff), the very special familial constellation —as constructed in the foregoing text—, has been extensively discussed in modern discourses on familial relationships. The discussion concerns the etiology of what Freud (in the beginning) calls inversion and what later on in the century is described as the family background of (male) homosexuality. The domineering mother, the detached father, and the peers —sometimes including brothers and/or sisters—, who behave differently, are the ever returning characters in the narrative about the origin of male homosexuals as told in our age.

The narrative develops continually. The joy of discovery in Freud which has started the discussion, fades away little by little. It 'hardens' into a point of departure which receives a 'scientific' base. That is not Freud's fault. He did not keep himself to one model. He even says that he never saw his analysis of the origin of homosexuality as complete (Standard Edition, XVIII, 231), a statement which can be demonstrated by pointing out some relevant and rather conflicting differences in his own writings: in the 'Three Essays' he speaks about a hostile father, the father as deterrent; in his study 'Leonardo da Vinci and a Memory of his Childhood' (1910, Standard Edition XI, 165ff) the absence of the father is important; in his study 'Some Neurotic Mechanisms in Jealousy, Paranoia and Homosexuality' (1922, Standard Edition XVIII, 223ff), he develops the meaning of the sometimes exceedingly hostile and aggressive attitude towards the own brothers and the absence of *horror feminae*.

Bieber's study (Bieber et al. 1962) can stay model for the changing point of view. This was a research project from a co-operation within the American Society of Medical Psychoanalysts. A large group of analysts (77 persons) produced material from their own practice about 106 male homosexuals who were compared etiologically with 100 heterosexuals. The researchers came to the conclusion that it would be too simple to limit oneself to a one-parent interaction in an etiology of male homosexuality: an overprotective mother or a detached father. In their view, a 'triangular' family system led to homosexuality:

"The 'classical' homosexual triangular pattern is one where the mother is Close Binding Intimate and is dominant and minimizing toward a husband who is a detached father, particularly a hostile-detached one. From our statistical analysis, the chances appear to be high that any son exposed to this parental combination will become homosexual or develop homosexual problems" (p.172).

On the basis of this Bieber and colleagues formulated a developmental model to explain how the interaction between the growing child and his parents could lead to homosexuality. The marriage is unsatisfactory and the father retreats from intimacy with both his wife and the prehomosexual youngster. The mother devalues her husband, idealises her son, and forms an excessively close bound with him:

"By the time the H-son has reached the preadolescent period, he had suffered a diffuse personality disorder... Pathologically dependent upon his mother and beset by feelings of inadequacy, impotence and self-contempt, he is reluctant to participate in boyhood activities thought to be physically injurious -usually grossly overestimated. His peer group responds with humiliating name-calling and often with physical attacks which timidity tends to invite among children" (p. 316; see also Bieber 1965/4).

The 'conclusion' of the Bieber-study has been accepted as definitive for a long time. It even became a 'classic', cf. Socarides in the 'American Handbook of Psychiatry', and the text in the 'Diagnostic and Statistical Manual III' of the American Psychiatric Association. From time to time this conclusion found support in similar research studies with a slightly different setting and/or from a diverse *status quaestionis* (cf. the research-report in Friedman 1988, 58ff).

But the limitations of the Bieber research became slowly evident. The familial background which supposedly enhanced male homosexuality was evidently not the only cause. The same familial background existed in a fairly large part of the control-group who were heterosexuals (for numbers and percentages, see Friedman 1988, 58ff). Marmor could write in conclusion:

"The common denominator in a host of clinical studies (i.e. on the etiology of male homosexuals) appears to be a poor relationship with a father figure which results in a failure to form a satisfactory masculine identification, and a close but ambivalent relationship with a mother figure which presumably results in strong, unconscious fears or hatred of women. The difficulty with this as a specific cause of homosexuality, however, is that dominating and seductive mothers and weak, hostile, or detached fathers, as well as variations of this constellation, abound in the histories of countless heterosexual individuals also. I do not mean to imply that such family constellations are irrelevant to the etiology of homosexuality. There does seem to be a reasonable amount of evidence that boys exposed to this kind of family background have a greater than average likelihood of becoming homosexual. But since cases of homosexuality can and do occur with quite varied family histories, the family background described by the Bieber group -although an important and relevant factor- is not specifically etiological in the sense that the tubercle bacillus is specific for tuberculosis." (Marmor 1980, 10; cf. Green 1980, 255-266; Dannecker 1981/ 1978; Friedman 1988 57-78; Isay 1989).

It will be clear where this modern discourse about familial relationships leads us. The special familial constellation which, narratively, is elaborated in the Johannine Gospel as an imaginary possibility, is largely parallel to innumerable case-studies of familial situations in modern discussions. Therefore, the text of the Johannine Gospel can rightly be read from this context; or conversely one can also say that the silence of scientific exegesis is, thus, unjustified. Via a detour in Freudian-oriented thinking it has become clear once again that a son in such a family does not necessarily have to be predetermined to be a homosexual. However, it is neither excluded. The question how this developed in Jesus —how the author imaginarily wrote this into his life—, is still open, but it becomes more important to find an answer.

That will have to be done in subsequent research.

CHAPTER TWO

THE TEACHER'S LOVE FOR HIS FAVOURITE

There is a narrative reality in the Johannine Gospel which comes closest to what moderns would call male homosexual behaviour: the love of an (older) man for a younger one. From chapter 13 on we find the anonymous character: —'the disciple whom Jesus loved'—, who from that moment on will play a very important role in the narrative. The beloved disciple is a character who is unique for the Johannine Gospel among the gospel stories. Obviously, this evoked a mountain of literature but the characteristic of 'to love' and 'to be loved' is conspicuously absent. In the scientific exegetical discourse it is not mentioned at all —which is very peculiar, indeed. I can not evade the question in my research.

The study starts from the a priori assumption that, via the lexeme of the /beloved disciple/, a reality is imaginarily evoked which has its own structure in classical and Hellenistic antiquity: the teacher who has a special, affectively loaded relationship with one of his pupils and who gives him a special role in the future succession of teacher and pupil. In antiquity, this relationship is more or less an institutional reality as I intend to show. Therefore, I can not restrict this study to the relationship between Jesus and the beloved disciple. I need to look at the relation between John (the Baptist) and Jesus as well. Narratively we see a repetition in the Johannine Gospel: as Jesus is being placed in a special position by John, so Jesus also places the beloved disciple in a special position. It is interesting from a biographical narrative point of view to delve into this teacher's love after having studied the family constellation.

1. THE RELATION OF JOHN (THE BAPTIST) TO JESUS

Research into a more precise definition of the narrative relationship between John (the Baptist) and Jesus in the Johannine Gospel is aggravated by the (almost) exclusive focus on the historical reconstruction of the baptiser-movement(s). The studies which explicitly treat John the Baptist (cf. a.o. Schütz 1967; Wink 1968; Hollenbach 1979; Lichtenberger 1987; Ernst 1989; Murphy-O'Connor 1990) are all historically oriented. The texts of the Johannine Gospel are, therefore, exclusively or mainly seen in so far as they can have possible informative value for such an historical reconstruction. The Johannine Gospel is interesting, because it gives a view of John the Baptist totally different from the Synoptics or Josephus. The polemic plays an important role and demands that it be precisely described and defined. I would not do these people justice, if I said that they leave out a synchronic approach to the text. Schnackenburg (1967, 393ff), for example, treated Jn 3,31-36, yet, as an 'Beilage', placed it before 3,13-21 and supposed that the one who speaks the text, could without further ado be identified with the author of the book (he called this self-constructed pericope 'Das Johanneische Kerygma'). In opposition with this form of textual manipulation, the afore mentioned other authors see 3,22-36 as a narratively coherent scene. This is not to say that they show to have any understanding of the difference between a narrative and a discursive analysis of the text. It is possible to read the texts discursively as an intervention within the conflicting situation between the followers of the Baptist and the followers of Jesus. Narratively, however, the texts treat the relationship between John (the Baptist) and Jesus. It is very difficult to forget one's own scientific past in this regard as is clear in an author like Culpepper (1983, 54) who gives a clarifying analysis of Jn 1,19-34 but, then, finds the position of John (the Baptist) of no further interest. John (the Baptist) does not play any significant role in his plot description (p.89-97). In the chapter on the characters we find John as one of the minor figures (p.132). I hope to show that this kind of treatment does not do justice to the texts themselves.

Some presuppositions are important here:

a/ The language of John (the Baptist)
Every reader has noticed that, in the few sentences which are attributed to John (the Baptist), he uses a language which, in a way, is not different from the language Jesus uses, —and this is not really different from the language of the narrator of the story. This evokes serious questions in a reading of the text which is

historically oriented. One tries to distinguish between what is historically possible and what is not, and one uses for this —as was mentioned already—, the baptizer movements from the second half of the first century. In a narrative analysis one must forego such an escape. But this does not solve the specific problems. One needs to ask whether John (the Baptist) uses the language of Jesus or whether it is the other way around: Jesus who speaks in and with the words of John. I believe that, *narratively*, we must opt for the second possibility. The narrator of the story indicates this narratively as well as chronologically. John is, narratively, the first person who is allowed to speak: in 1,15 (and following); in 1,19-28; in 1,29-34 and in 1,35-37. The first sentence of Jesus comes in 1,38. John is introduced as 'the first' also chronologically. That is the content of the first sentences about him (in 1,6-8) and of the first sentence which is attributed to him (in 1,15). This content is, furthermore, a continuous line till the last sentences he speaks (3,27ff) and till the last sentences spoken about him (in 5,32-35).

Jesus adopts the language of John (the Baptist). This way of looking at things is totally different from what has always been presupposed. Yet I want to use this as my point of departure in my analysis. Where the reverse is true (as I think it is in a certain interpretation of 3,22ff), I can show the difference.

b/ The 'teaching' of John (the Baptist) and its influence on Jesus
Use of a particular language is never without significance. If Jesus is narratively dependent on John for his use of language, there are important consequences. One can not adopt language without also adopting the content of the language. This seems a reasonable presupposition in the relation between John (the Baptist) and Jesus which can be used as a point of departure for further investigation. Because this has never been treated as a specific topic in exegesis, I can only make the first steps here. I would like to try it.

Does this mean that John is also Jesus' teacher and/or that Jesus is his disciple? That is not true in the direct meaning of those words. It seems as if the narrator of the story evades these words rather subtly. We read that Jesus 'goes to John' (1,29); that Jesus has been 'with John' (3,26), but we do not read anywhere that Jesus was John's disciple or that John is his teacher. Yet John has success with two of his own disciples in manifesting Jesus to Israel. They follow Jesus and ask where he 'is staying' (1,35-41), i.e.

Jesus, among all the people, is for John the preferred one and he introduces him to his own disciples as such. Indirectly, he points to Jesus within the circle of his own disciples as the eminent one and as such Jesus is drawn into the circle of his own disciples. We must analyse this more precisely in relation to both.

c/ The testimony of John (the Baptist)
The central word to describe John's function is $\mu\alpha\rho\tau\upsilon\rho\iota\alpha$ (/witness/,/testimony/). The word appears in every passage in one form or another: witness, give witness, speak out, shout, confess, do not deny, to have seen. There is no need to prove this further. However, one question remains and that regards the content of the testimony of John as expressed in the prologue. It is clear that his testimony relates to 1,15: 'who comes after me is before me, because he existed before me'. The question is whether the following verses (1,16-18) are intended as a reflection of John's witness.

Few readers give a positive answer, apparently, for a variety of reasons:
- in 1,30 John (the Baptist) reflects only on 1,15. The other verses (1,16.17) are not taken into consideration, at least not in the literal sense.
- the content of 1,16-18 can not be brought in line with any historical teaching of John (the Baptist).
- the function of 1,18 is ambiguous. It is a poetical ending of the whole prologue providing a dramatic closing sentence but also pointing back to 1,1 and thus forming an inclusion. The verse would/could, then, not be linked to 1,15a.

Yet, there are arguments on the other side too (see esp. de la Potterie 1984, 372 and 384, note 63 where he gives the history of this interpretation from Heracleon and Origines to Trocmé and Barrett):
- 1,16 and 1,17 both begin with $\delta\tau\iota$, a particle of causality which starts a subordinate sentence. Vss 1,16 and 1,17 are, thus, not independent sentences. After 1,15, John (the Baptist) continues his speech in 1,16.
- the ambiguous poetical function of 1,18 is not a real argument. All it means is that different readings are possible, dependent on the way the reader approaches the text. It can be read, stylistically, as the closing sentence of the prologue, as climax and inclusion. But,

communicatively, it can (also) be understood as a continuation of what John (the Baptist) has to say to the Johannine community, including himself.

- 1,19 opens with a new reference to the μαρτυρία of John (the Baptist). It closes the prologue, but, at the same time, it is a new reference to 1,15a, a reference which makes the prologue less isolated from the main text.

- Finally, when we attribute 1,16-18 to John (the Baptist), we are not impugning the historical reliability of John the evangelist —whether the statements are historically reliable—, but we do question his —to use that word—, historical poetry —whether it is historically reliable that John the evangelist puts such words in the mouth of John (the Baptist). This seems at least possible. A writer who speaks about Jesus in the way he in fact does, has (at least) the freedom to introduce Jesus' antagonists imaginarily as is done in 1,15-18.

I want to use this freedom and I presuppose, therefore, that 1,15-18 can be seen as the opening-μαρτυρία of John (the Baptist).

1.a. The first John (the Baptist) pericope (1,15-36)

This way of reading has important consequences. In this way we have a John (the Baptist) pericope uninterrupted from 1,15 to 1,36. The reference in 1,19 to the μαρτυρία of John is retrospective as well as prospective. After John has spoken about the importance of Jesus, he says about himself that *he* is not the Christ. It becomes thus clear once again that one can read the Johannine text in different ways and that each reading generates new meaning.

1.a.1. the chronology

The passage has a special narrative structure. There is no chronological order but the story proceeds with analepses and prolepses in a way which is unique for the Johannine Gospel. Most often the Johannine text is chronologically straightforward. Culpepper (1983, 54ff) showed that this is not the case here. The reconstruction of the chronological order is, therefore, quite important. This strategy of reading the text gives a better insight in the story which lies at the base of the narrative, a story which deals precisely with the imaginary relation between John (the Baptist) and Jesus.

Since the proposed manner of reading and the resulting starting point is quite different from those of Culpepper, I come to a different reconstruction.

Culpepper writes:

"The story time is no more than two days, but the narrative of those two days gives the reader an overview of much of the story to be presented in the rest of the narrative. Jesus actually preceded (i.e. was before) John (1). Isaiah prophesied prior to John also (2). John himself was sent with a specific commission (3) and came baptizing (4). At first he did not know Jesus (5), but identified him when he saw the Spirit descend upon him (6). Some time later, the Jews sent priests and Levites to question John (7). John's testimony is contained in his answers to their questions (8), and in these he refers both to Jesus' anonymity (9) and to his imminent coming or public appearance (10). When Jesus does come, John announces him (11), and in some sequence relative to these events the priests and Levites will report to those who sent him (12). Still further into the future, Jesus will take away the sin of the world (13) and baptize his followers with the Holy Spirit (14)."

I will pass the 'events' beyond the narrative, i.e. those in nr.1-2 and 12-14, not because they are not important but because they are not relevant to our research now. Even if the testimony of John (the Baptist) in 1,15-18 (evidently) does not play a part in Culpepper, it is strange that so many aspects of the text remain unmentioned. It seems easiest to show this by providing a double list which describes the events more exhaustively.

Culpepper	Addition Culpepper
1/ John himself was sent with a specific commission,	1/ John is sent to baptise in water (1,33).
2/ and came baptising.	
3/ At first he did not know Jesus	2/ At first he does not know 'him' (1,31.33)
	3/ He hears the voice of his sender,

4/ but identified him when he saw the spirit descend upon him.	4/ saying: on whom you will see the spirit descend and remain, he is the one who baptises in the holy spirit (1,33)
	5/ He says: one is coming after me who was before me, because he existed before me (1,15.30).
	6/ He sees the spirit descend as a dove from heaven and rest upon him (1,32)
	7/ He gives testimony about Jesus and about his relation to Jesus: 1,30; 1,34; 1,15-18.
5/ Some time later, the Jews sent priests and Levites to question John	8/ As a result the Jews send priests and Levites to question John judicially (1,19ff)
6/ John's testimony is contained in his answers to their questions,	9/ John makes a fourfold deposition: I am not the Christ, neither am I Elijah or the prophet; I am the voice calling in the wilderness.
7/ and in these he refers both to Jesus' anonymity,	10/ Jesus is anonymously present but he will appear publicly (1,19-28).
8/ and to his imminent coming of public appearance.	
	11/ He sees Jesus coming towards him (1,29).

	12/ He points out Jesus as the lamb of God which carries the sins of the cosmos (1,29) and as the person about whom he spoke as the one who came after but is before (1,30).
	13/ With his revelation to Israel he fulfilled his mission (1,31)
	14/ Next day he sees Jesus again and repeats that Jesus is the lamb of God (1,35-36)
	15/ Two of his own disciples follow Jesus (1,37).

The precise chronological explication of the events clarifies a number of things. Everything is more active and comes more from John than appears in the resume which Culpepper gives. John has gone through a process. A voice gave him a mandate to baptise in water. When he hears a voice again, he knows it is the same voice which sent him. It is that same voice which tells him that someone will come to baptise in the holy spirit. The voice makes him speak about the 'one who comes after but is before'. The voice helps him understand the sign: on whom the spirit will descend and remain. When he sees the dove descend on Jesus and remain, he knows that this dove signifies the spirit and that, therefore, Jesus is the one announced.

This brings John (the Baptist) to great testimonies. Vss 1,15-18, 1,30, and 1,34 enunciate these. It is impossible to reconstruct the relative chronology of these testimonies. Originally John speaks about an anonymous person whom he himself did not know. When the dove appears he 'sees'. This brings him to an identification: this is the son of God. It also brings him the insight that Jesus is God's benevolence for Israel personified.

However, even if the relative chronology can not be completely reconstructed, there is —more than usually is seen—, an intrinsic connection between the individual events. Vs 1,30 self evidently refers to 1,15. It is not too difficult to combine 1,34 and 1,18: Jesus is the son of God who is at the father's side. If 1,17 states that God through Moses, by the law, wanted to let the people *hear* what he wanted from them (νομός as covenant-word), but that through Jesus he wanted let them *see* that he himself will be steadfast in his fidelity to the covenant (χάρις καὶ ἀλήθεια as covenant words which express the ongoing interest of God himself, *pace* de la Potterie 1977, 115ff, but see also Hanson 1967/77, 90-101 and recently 1991, 21-32 with a host of references), then the relation between 1,17 and 1,32 and 1,33 is also quite acceptable; cf. the permanent character of the spirit on Jesus and Jesus' baptising in the holy spirit (the πνεῦμα, again, as a covenant word).

In this presentation of the facts the event of the dove coming down from heaven is the catalysing factor. That opened heaven for John (the Baptist). *Hearing* the voice made him *see*. Hearing and seeing are judicial terms which lead to 'witnessing', to speak words as a result of what is seen and heard under divine inspiration.

There is a double reality:

Jesus' divine origin: Jesus as the first, as the son of God, at the side of the father, as the revelation of the grace and truth of God himself, making visible that God is faithful to his covenant with Israel;

ánd, the manner how John (the Baptist) relates to this, he being the first who knows he is the lesser and he himself as spokesman of a we-group who knows to be the receiver of grace: one benevolence for another; the spokesman of a we-experience who realises that God himself is above the law of revenge (the *lex talionis*). Instead of the χάρις of the gift of the law, instead of the benevolence which God showed for Israel by giving it the Torah, *we* now have the fullness of χάρις καὶ ἀλήθεια, —the logos which has become flesh. *Through* Jesus Christ, χάρις καὶ ἀλήθεια have become 'for us', i.e. have become present in the cosmos, cf. the γίγνομαι as creative act in 1,3ff. John (the Baptist) is the receiving witness who has been sent to reveal this to Israel (1,31).

In the proposed way of reading the testimony of 1,15-18 precedes the arrival of the priests and Levites. This does not entirely fit 1,29.30 which suggests that the identification of Jesus with the sentence about 'the later one who is before' happens only after this judicial inquiry. But it fits 1,34 where the identification happens in relation with or together with the appearance of the dove. A margin of unclarity remains as we already said. In the concrete text the Judeans react to the testimony of John (the Baptist) as formulated in 1,15-18. The succession of these testimonies place a heavy burden on the judicial process. The Judeans send a highly qualified legation. This brings John (the Baptist) in fact to a testimony about himself which fits with what he said before about himself and about Jesus: he is not the Christ, Elijah or the prophet; he is the voice of one who shouts in the wilderness. The voices he has heard lead him to this self identification. Jesus is invisibly present among them, but this one-who-comes-after-him is infinitely superior to him. It is a testimony which brings Jesus ever closer for the listeners to this text.

The decisive identification comes in the next scene (1,29ff). John points to Jesus as the lamb of God and as the person about whom he spoke that enigmatic sentence. This identification is not a revelation for the readers, because they have already heard 1,15-18 and 1,27. But the concrete words are still new: Jesus as the lamb of God who carries the sins of the cosmos. This is a choice of words which plays an important role in the concreteness of the story as told: Jesus who is going to be slaughtered as the lamb of God on the evening of the pesach and not a bone shall be broken.

The narratively decisive transition is found in the closing scene (1,35ff). Two of the disciples of John (the Baptist) follow Jesus on the word of their teacher. The group around Jesus begins. John places himself completely at the service of Jesus' interests.

1.a.2. The effect of John (the Baptist)'s appearance

It is remarkable that there are no affective evaluations. We find the story told in a very matter of fact manner. However, this has a strongly literary effect. The behaviour of John becomes natural, because there is no mention of any affective reaction, i.e. the model character of John is strongly emphasised. If John —who can claim the rights of the first arrived—, places himself so simply in the service of the one who came after him, then this should apply even more to the others who came later.

It is possible to explicate this in a few points:
John (the Baptist) is introduced as someone who is completely at the disposition of the voices he hears. This is true in relation to the task which the voice gives him: to baptise in water; but it is true also in relation to the voice which speaks about the coming Jesus.

He draws important consequences: especially that he who is the elder, the first, accepts that he is subject to the younger one, the one who came after him. This presentation is to be connected with the important biblical theme that the younger one is elected over the elder one: Jacob over Esau, Joseph over his elder brothers; David over his brothers and over Saul. The difference with the classical biblical stories is the fact that, in the Johannine Gospel, a story is told without the mentioning of any conflict. John (the Baptist) does not resist. More, he identifies himself with his role. Using a text from Isaiah he presents himself as the voice which proclaims that 'the path of the Lord must be cleared' (1,23).

His obedience to the voice is clear also in the answers he gives to the authorities who come to question him. The voice of God makes him answer from a *parrhesia* which serves as a pattern for the behaviour of all those who follow: Jesus first of all but also Nicodemus, the lame man, the man who is born blind, the beloved disciple. (The voice of) God is to be obeyed first of all. Human authority can not take God's place.

Most amazing is his attitude to his own disciples. He does not react, when two of them follow Jesus. His reaction will only be given in the following scene which deals with John (the Baptist). For the time-being nothing more or less is said than that he points to Jesus as the lamb of God, apparently in the presence of his disciples and that two of them (Andrew and an anonymous 'other disciple') draw the compelling conclusion to walk with Jesus. Jesus is for John (the Baptist) the eminent one who is to be preferred in all matters.

Jesus, the one about whom so much is said, is himself the one who does not speak. No reaction is mentioned until the two disciples of John (the Baptist) follow him. This does not mean that the words of John (the Baptist) about Jesus are not heard by Jesus. Two not unimportant scenes show that the testimonies of John (the Baptist) did have an effect.

First, we have 5,31-47 linked in various ways with 1,15-18. One can give a description as to content (see Theobald 1988, 360.362): the description of John as a lamp (in 1,8.15 and 5,35) and the effect of the appearance of John on the Jewish leaders (in 1,19ff and 5,31-35); the determination of the position of Moses in relation to Jesus (in 1,17 and 5,39.45-47); the statement about the access to God, direct or indirect, and Jesus' function therein (in 1,18 and

5,37-38). If one describes the similarity only semantically, the narrative effect is not brought out. I do not think that is right. Because Jesus speaks the same or similar sentences as John (the Baptist), we have narratively a plagiarism. Jesus makes his own the words which John (the Baptist) shouted to the people. It is a factual citation which can be described as a realised learning effect.

The closing scene in 10,31-39.40-42 is almost the same. The narrator makes Jesus say that 'he has said: I am the son of God' (10,38). Literally speaking that is not true. Not that Jesus did not speak continuously from such an identification, but the first one who explicitly spoke this sentence is John (the Baptist): in 1,18 for a not identified public and in 1,34 for a public where Jesus is present. That means that Jesus heard this statement about him first from John (the Baptist). In 10,38 he commits himself to it. The end of the scene shows that I, with good reasons, combine this self identification of Jesus with the testimony of John (the Baptist): Jesus retires to the spot 'where John used to baptise'. Many come to Jesus and say: 'John did not perform any sign but everything which John said about him is true' (10,40-41): a late recognition of the truth of the testimony of John (the Baptist).

The testimony of John which, narratively, has the most far reaching effect is, obviously, his saying that Jesus is the lamb of God. Jesus has no choice here. His life story realises in the most extreme way the truth of this testimony. In his death he is made lamb of God by the Judeans. This testimony of John is, therefore, an anticipation of the scene under the cross where the beloved disciple attests the truth of what he has seen (19,35): only Jesus' bones are not broken. The lamb of God brings John (the Baptist) and the beloved disciple together as in a mirror: beginning and end, origin and continuity of Jesus' appearance.

1.b. the second John (the Baptist) pericope (3,22-36)

This second pericope has also suffered from the historically oriented interest of the exegetes, be it in a different way from the first. Where in the first pericope the reader question was whether and how to combine the opening sentences (1,14-18) with the scene of the μαρτυρία of John (the Baptist), here the closing sentences (3,31-36) are made the problem. Who is speaking? John (the Baptist) or Jesus or the evangelist? (cf. e.g. recently still Schnelle 1987, 197).

1.b.1. speaking in the same words

Historical considerations again play an important role in the argument against John (the Baptist) as the possible speaker, reinforced by the fact that 3,31-36 shows semantically clear similarities as to content with 3,11-21: the previous words of Jesus which in 3,31-36 are taken up in a specific way by John (the Baptist). Narratively, however, the situation is much clearer here than in the attribution of the prologue sentences to a coherent Johannine pericope. John (the Baptist) begins to speak in 3,27 and stops in 3,36.

The occasion of this longer discourse of John is a discussion between the disciples of John and a Judean about purity (3,25). Jesus has come from Jerusalem to the land of Judea to baptise. In a short time he has, thus, become a competitor of John's group. That at least is the way the disciples of John tell their teacher: 'they all go to him' (3,26). John does not agree with this interpretation of his disciples. One final time, —matters are presented in such a way that John (the Baptist) disappears in prison soon after this—, he makes clear how *he* sees the relation between himself and Jesus.

The narrative situation is quite different from that of his first appearance. Jesus has shown himself publicly: in Cana, in Jerusalem, in the long discourse with Nicodemus. John (the Baptist) reacts to this: he is no longer the initiator but Jesus himself has become active. John (the Baptist) pronounces himself influenced by what Jesus has said and done. In itself this presents no problem. The narrator of the story indicates it already in his description of the reason for the discourse: the disciples of John (the Baptist) turn to him, because Jesus baptises and everybody turns to him.

The real question is how far one may extend the 'knowledge' of John (the Baptist). The events in Cana and Jerusalem were public facts, but can this be said also about the nightly discussion with Nicodemus? The answer to this question determines to a very large extent the way in which one should/might see the relation between John and Jesus. If one sees this discussion narratively as a public event —of which John knows the content and which places John, therefore, in the same position as the reader of the story—, then John can be said to be reacting to the words of Jesus: he makes them his own; he changes them; he interprets them etc. But if one sees the discussion narratively as a secret happening —of which John does not know the content—, then we have a parallel with regard to content which the persons involved do not know but which the reader is aware of afterwards. So we have two ways to read the text and probably one can not/should not choose between them.

A semantic analysis of similarities and differences between 3,31-36 and 3,11-21 gives the following (cf. a.o. Theobald 1988, 354ff; Brown 1966, 159ff):

3,27:
No one can take anything unless it is given to him.

If this sentence speaks about Jesus —it has been given to *him* to baptise in the holy spirit (cf. 1,33)—, it refers to 3,11 and 3,13: the divine origin of Jesus which he brings into the cosmos. It is a theme to which Jesus returns several times: see esp. 19,11.

The sentence can be understood also negatively towards John (the Baptist): it has not been given to me. In this case it would be a statement by John about himself which is in line with the descriptions of himself before: there is no comparison between Jesus and me.

3,28:
I am not the Christ, but I am the one who is sent to go before him.

In this last interpretation, 3,28 follows with a certain logic. It refers literally to the scene of the interrogation of the Judeans (1,19ff).

3,29-30:
There are no direct references here.

3,31:
coming from above; being from the earth.

Here again we have a possibility for more than one interpretation. If one sees the sentence as a statement from the perspective of Jesus, it refers to 3,13. The idea is taken up by Jesus in different ways later on in the story: in 8,23 from the viewpoint of an antithesis with the Judeans; in 12,31.32 from the perspective of the crisis; in 19,11 as a self description of Jesus.

It is sometimes said that the meaning of the sentence also contains what John (the Baptist) says about himself: next to Jesus 'who comes from above' stands John (the Baptist) who comes ἐκ τῆς γῆς (see e.g. Lichtenberger 1987, 51). This would, then, be a reinforcement of all previous self-descriptions of John (the Baptist). It bypasses the often repeated statement that John (the

Baptist) has been sent by God too (for a negative judgment of this interpretation see esp. Panackel 1988, 67).

More important for the question about possible 'plagiarism' is the observation that the ἄνωθεν has played an important role in the discussion between Jesus and Nicodemus (3,3.7): being born from above which is given to all who believe in Jesus' origin. A peculiar circle of referrals develops, because John (the Baptist) speaks precisely about this origin of Jesus.

3,32:

He gives testimony about what he has seen and heard; no one accepts it.

This is the most literal reference to the discussion with Nicodemus. In 3,11 Jesus puts this statement before Nicodemus in a 'we'-sentence which is rather difficult to interpret. John (the Baptist) makes the 'we' into 'he-Jesus' but, at the same time, he enlarges the negative character of the statement: instead of saying 'you do not accept it' (3,11) he says 'no one accepts this testimony'.

As a positive testimony about Jesus, John (the Baptist) falls in line, also as to content, with his own testimony from 1,18: Jesus as the *exegètes* of God.

3,33:

whoever accepts his testimony has certified that God is truthful.

After the negative rejection comes the positive acceptance. The acceptance of the ἀλήθεια of God refers naturally to what John (the Baptist) has said about this in 1,16 and 1,17. John is consistent in his testimony.

3,34:

The one sent by God speaks the words of God, for the gift of the spirit is superabundant.

That Jesus, as the one sent by God, speaks the words of God, has been stated also by Jesus in the Nicodemus statement: in 3,11 especially. But John (the Baptist) has also spoken about this in 1,17.18.34 and in 3,34.

The same can be said about the gift of the spirit as linked to the coming of Jesus. Jesus spoke about this with Nicodemus in 3,5-8; and John (the Baptist) got to know Jesus as such through the divine voice (1,32.33).

3,35-36:
These statements put together thematically what Jesus said in 3,16-21:
- the love of the father for the son: 3,35 and 3,16;
- the transferring of divine power into the hands of the son: 3,35 and 3,17;
- the connection between faith and eternal life: 3,36 and 3,16.18;
- the contraposition between faith and unbelief: 3,36 and 3,17.

Typical and proper to this series of statements of John (the Baptist) is the accent in closing on the ὀργή of God (3,36).

The analysis makes clear that the learning relations between John (the Baptist) and Jesus and those between Jesus and John (the Baptist) are truly nuanced. We can distinguish three topics which each go their own way:
- When speaking about himself, John does not borrow from Jesus: cf. 3,27 and 3,28 which, in so far as they point to John, refer totally to 1,15-36 (1,20-23.24-27.31). Jesus has not spoken so far about John. When he does in 5,31-36, it is in accordance with what John has said about himself and about his relation to Jesus, i.e. in his self-descriptions the initiative lies with John (the Baptist), resp. in his obedience to the heavenly voice which made him hear it.
- It is different, when John (the Baptist) speaks about Jesus. We then have a double 'origin'. John develops what he has said about Jesus in 1,17.18.34 (cf. 3,32 and 3,34 in so far as they go back to 1,17.18.34), but at the same time we see a relation with the basic sentences in 3,11 and 3,13 (cf. the references of 3,27.31.32.34). Depending on how one judges the discourse of John (the Baptist) in relation to the Nicodemus discussion, one can qualify this as an influence from Jesus on John (John 'learns' from the mouth of Jesus how he can say even more clearly who Jesus is), or one can qualify it as John's own knowledge who from his own insight, parallel to Jesus says who Jesus is, and who affirms Jesus in this way in *his* self awareness (cf. the development by Jesus esp. in 8,23; 12,31f; 19,11).
- We can make a last distinction in the sentences which deal with a possible reaction of the listeners —the way in which they react positively or negatively to Jesus—, (see 3,31.33.35.36). In 1,15-34 a possible negative reaction does not yet play a role. The

interrogation by the Pharisees probably has a negative result, but John (the Baptist) did not so far speak about it. That comes now (3,31.35.36), in sentences which connect directly with the Nicodemus discourse (3,16-18). This opens again a double narrative option. John (the Baptist) follows the negative way of speaking of Jesus, or he understood by himself that a negative reaction to Jesus' appearance is possible (cf. the reaction of his own disciples to the success of Jesus' appearance). Whatever, because John (the Baptist) says that 'no one accepts the testimony of Jesus' (3,32), Jesus' own statement in 3,11 is very much strengthened.

1.b.2. the friend of the bridegroom

The analysis makes clear how symbiotically the relation between John (the Baptist) and Jesus is imaginarily proposed. This appears most clearly in the interpretation which allows John to be narratively unaware of the discourse between Jesus and Nicodemus. Even without previous knowledge, John (the Baptist) takes over important ideas and representations from Jesus. In scientific circles in exegesis this brought readers to the insight that the text of 3,31-36 is an author's construction. Surely so, but this does not take away the narrative manipulation.

The interpretation which allows John awareness of the preceding discourse with Nicodemus, gives something similar. John is imaginarily proposed as a kind of disciple who attentively hears the words of his teacher, takes them and passes them on: the elder, the earlier one who puts himself in the position of the younger, the later one. In 3,29.30 —the only text which does not show any direct reference to what happens before—, John himself indicates how he sees his relation to Jesus. These are the most affective sentences in the whole episode: he rejoices with happiness, his joy is fulfilled.

John uses a mashal about a marriage feast: a bridegroom, a bride, a friend of the groom, happiness, grow larger, grow smaller. The mashal is told in a personified way in all its details: it is my joy, he must grow, I must become less. Therefore, it is clear for any reader what the application is: Jesus is the groom, Israel is the bride; John is the friend of the groom; Jesus speaks; John stands, listens, and is filled with joy. It is reasonable to think of a relation with the revelation about the dove from heaven who came upon Jesus to stay: the dove now as a symbol of Israel and Jesus as the legate-son of God, who, in his person, makes 'the truth and the grace' of God present. In Jesus God enters into a marriage with Israel.

Obviously, this is mythical language which refers to God's marriage with Israel (in Hos 1-2; Is 61,10; Jer 2,2), to Israel at the Sinai having God as bridegroom and Moses as best man who writes down the marriage conditions (in ExR 46 (101a); ExR 47 (101d) cf. Strack-Billerbeck 1955, I,501. If one does not see Jesus as the Messiah but as the son of God, you have complete similarity with the Jewish marriage metaphor: God (i.e. the son of God) enters into a marriage with his bride, the people of Israel. There is no need, then, to point out that, in Jewish thought, the Messiah is nowhere mentioned as a bridegroom of Israel, nor that John developed his own theologoumenon: so a.o. Panackel 1988, 58).

Jesus' marriage is celebrated imaginarily: Jesus present at his own wedding and John (the Baptist) as the one who has brought it about. John plays the most typical role. In the Jewish way of thinking he acts as the *sjosjbin* (the best man of the bride):

he introduces the groom to the bride:
> he reveals Jesus to Israel (1,31) (i.e. he has let know);
> because he saw it, he gives witness about Jesus' origin:
> this is the son of God (1,34) (i.e. he guarantees the family relation of the groom).

He directs the festivities:
> he is there and listens (3,29);
> he rejoices hearing the voice of the bridegroom (3,29).

The best man is responsible for the legalities and the celebration of the feast. He acts in the name of the groom and guarantees the family origin, the juridical procedure of the contract and the regular closing of the marriage (cf. Sanh 3,5; TKet 1,4). John (the Baptist) is the official witness that Jesus is a married man.

The Jewish institute of the *sjosjbin* is not unique, no matter what the exegetes say about this (see a.o. Schnackenburg 1967, 452; Brown 1966, 152). One finds it also in the Hellenistic and Roman culture (see Pauly-Wissowa s.v. παρανύμφιος). In a way, Jn 3,29 is closer to this because, in contradistinction to Jewish customs, where there are always two 'best men' (see TKet 1,4: one for the bride and one for the groom, cf. Archer 1990, 203-205. Most probably, there was a man for the groom and a woman for the bride), Hellenism knows only the one for the groom. The three sit in the marriage cart which goes from the house of the father of the bride to the ἑστία of the groom (see Samter 1901, 14ff): the bride in the middle and the groom and the best man on either side of her. To be a παρανύμφιος is an honour which expresses the bond of friendship between the groom and his best friend. The best man is 'the friend of the groom', Jn 3,29 says. To be chosen from among the friends shows how special the relation is.

That we must take into consideration the difference in age between John and Jesus makes this a typical text. John is the older one. He is in a certain sense 'the teacher' who brings his 'disciple' to the marriage; he is present at the feast as the most important guest. The happiness he experiences is a kind of evaluation: there is complete inner agreement. That John (the Baptist), then, uses the same words as Jesus has used before shows that, between these two friends, we have μία ψυχὴ δύο σώμασιν ἐνοικοῦσα, one soul inhabiting two bodies: the Aristotelian ideal of friendship (cf. Diogn. Laër., 5,20; Plut., De amicorum multitudine 96F). In the relation between John and Jesus, we find realised an ideal of friendship which has very old roots in classical thought and practice. Discussing the texts about the beloved disciple, I will return to this more elaborately.

2. THE RELATION BETWEEN JESUS AND THE BELOVED DISCIPLE

Jesus' beloved disciple is a special topic in the Johannine research. Whoever is involved in the Johannine Gospel, must address this reality. New studies which takes the beloved disciple as their subject, appear continuously (see a.o. Kragerud 1959; Lorenzen 1971; Thyen 1976; Minear 1977; Brown 1979; de la Potterie 1986; Ruckstuhl 1988; Kügler 1988; Neirynck 1990). It is a continuous series of which we probably have not seen the end. It is truly amazing that none of these studies pay any attention to the words 'to love' or 'to be loved', not even Kügler who, yet, wrote a large tome of some 500 pages. I find this a painful gap and what follows can certainly not fill that. Yet I want to sketch some lines which can give a direction.

By treating the texts on the beloved disciple in a chapter entitled 'the teacher's love for his favourite', I run ahead of myself. The Johannine Gospel corresponds imaginarily, through the beloved disciple, with what Marrou (1964/1948, 312) wrote in the context of the παιδεραστία as a system of education: "C'est dans les milieux philosphiques qu'a le mieux survécu la grande tradition archaïque de *l'eros éducateur*, source de vertu." The teacher who loves one of his disciples in a special way and who shows that publicly, places himself historically in a line which, in a certain sense, is the most characteristic for the Greek culture of love: the love of a mature man for a παῖς as the prototype of all love. This is a very broad subject with mythological, political, cultural-historical, philosophical as well as poetical aspects. (see Meier 1837; de Pogey-Castries 1930; Flacelière 1960; Dover 1978; Boswell 1980; Buffière 1980; Keuls 1985). However interesting this theme is, it is not relevant to develop it fully here. If we do not want to be drown in a multitude of data, we must make a selection based on an awareness of the texts from the Johannine Gospel. I will do this before I examine the texts, because the contextualising influences the reading and the construction of meaning of the texts: it is an unavoidable hermeneutic circle.

2.a. the lover and the beloved

The distinction between the one who actively loves and the one who passively accepts this love is part of the structure of this special love: it is the distinction between the ἐραστής and the ἐρώμενος, two more or less technical terms which indicate the different roles and which are culturally determined: the older man is the *erastès* and the younger one the *eromenos*. It is not necessary —although allowed—, that there is a large difference of age between the two. It is, however, improper that the *erastès* is younger than the *eromenos*. This is connected with the educative sense which is attributed to this love:

- the introduction in the adult men's world among the Doric and Spartan free men (see e.g. Strabo 10.4.21);
- the acceptance in the other *oikos* (see e.g. the story of Aristotle in Diogenes Laërtius about whom the story goes that he was either the παιδικά (i.e. the *eromenos*) of the tyrant Hermias or that Hermias gave him his daughter or niece in marriage, Diog Laër 5,3);

- the entrance to the larger ἀρετή and wisdom (in the theories of Plato in the Phaedrus and the Symposion).

The older one should, culturally, be the active one and the younger one passive. This is most clearly expressed in iconography, in the vases from the 5th - 4th century BC where the *eromenos* does not show a sexual reaction to the advances of the *erastès*, not even when he has an intercrural orgasm. The *eromenos* receives; the *erastès* gives. The poetic literature makes clear how far these theories are fictional. That does not take away the cultural point of departure. The division in active-passive is connected with the cultural code about male and female behaviour. Different from our own culture where all homosexual activity is seen as a diminishing of the male code, this specific homosexual activity is seen as a reinforcement of the male code in the Greek culture as long as the role division of age is respected, and when the *eromenos* is not older than a certain age, say 18 to 20: (the growth of the beard and the hair on the thighs determine that age limit).

The stereo-typical formula of the Johannine Gospel —'the disciple whom Jesus loved'—, in which only the word for 'to love' changes (ἀγαπάω in 13,23; 19,26; 21,7; φιλέω in 20,2) and which has evoked the term 'the beloved disciple' in the secondary literature about the Johannine Gospel finds, culturally, its most natural explanation against this background. The teacher Jesus —and as teacher he is the older one—, is the active lover. Among his disciples there is one favourite. There is no secret about it. To-be-loved-by-Jesus is the most characteristic part of the role which this anonymous disciple is given: the disciple whom Jesus loved, the passive object of Jesus' love.

2.b. the attitude towards sexuality

The reason that scientific exegesis did not connect the relation of the teacher Jesus to his beloved disciple with this typical educational background is, probably, that sexuality is present in the majority of the concerned texts, either explicitly mentioned or at least not far off. The love for the παῖς in the context of education and training has sexual connotations in Greek and Hellenistic thought and action which can not be brought in line with the a-sexual text of the Johannine Gospel, to limit myself to our subject.

I think that is right up to a point. I also believe that the narrator of the Johannine Gospel is rather laconic where homosexuality is concerned. As we have seen, he also considers procreation and the sexuality involved with it, irrelevant in confrontation with the birth from God. But this matter of fact attitude towards sexuality does not prevent him, as I will show, from associating himself closely with the Greek freedom of speech in the description of the actual behaviour of Jesus and the beloved disciple. The text of the Johannine Gospel does not suggest anywhere that this led to sexual contact, but that does not diminish the love relationship between these two men.

The combination of true love in the context of a teacher-disciple relationship without (full) sexual expression is far from unique in classical thought. It points to the Platonic ideal of love such as Plato lets Socrates speak of: the παιδεραστία as the real model of love, if it manages to arrive at the contemplation of beauty through the particular experience of the beautiful boy (Symp 211 C-E); or, even more clear in abstracting from orgasm (even though not much more than that —and if it happens on occasion, it is not considered very important, Phaedrus 256 C till D—, the παιδεραστία is the model of love, if such love manages to transmit to the beloved the experience of the beautiful, which the lover has undergone by seeing the beautiful boy, so that the beloved 'can see himself as in a mirror' (Phaedrus 255 D). The παιδεραστία is for Plato the ideal of love itself, because, as long as the requested σωφροσύνη is present, it frees for both lovers the ἀρετή which keeps one directed permanently towards the φιλοσοφία (Phaedrus 256 A).

If one can go from the Johannine text to Plato, one is in good company. There are many threads which link the two. That is not to say that there are no differences. Also in this particular reference these are considerable. Furthermore, one needs to question in what way or even whether this part of Platonic philosophy was known in the first century.

It would be nice, if one could show the history of this philosophy as an ongoing historical reality. But I doubt whether that is possible. Too many texts are lost. I am glad, however, to have a text from Plutarch which, more or less contemporarily with the Johannine Gospel, takes up this Platonic way of presentation in his own way. In his *Erotikos*, Plutarch makes the defender of the παιδεραστία say that this is the only true love, "since it is not 'flashing with desire', as Anacreon says of the love of maidens, or 'drenched with unguents, shining bright'. No, its aspect is simple and unspoiled. You will see it in the schools of philosophy, or perhaps in the gymnasia and palaestras, searching for young men whom it cheers on with a clear and noble cry to the pursuit of virtue when they are found worthy of its attention" (Moralia 751 A).

This attitude is not taken very seriously in the *Erotikos*. Furthermore, Plutarch wants to show that the love between a man and a woman is more important and the defender of love between man and man is, therefore, given less scope. Yet, in the explanation of the Phaedrus the main speaker of the story, Plutarch's father, says conciliatorily: "Yet most men, since they pursue in boys and women merely the mirrored image of Beauty, can attain by their groping nothing more solid than a pleasure mixed with pain...But the noble and self-controlled lover has a different bent. His regard is refracted to the other world, to Beauty divine and intelligible" (Moralia 765 F), so that as well Plato with his love for boys as Plutarch with his love for girls are declared right. Anyway, the text makes clear that in the first century Plato's way of looking at these things is known and that, at least in some circles of the society, the rooting of the Johannine Gospel is recognisable.

It does not deny the differences between the Johannine text and Plato's (resp. Plutarch's) text. What is in question in the Johannine text is not seeing Beauty (but seeing God is!). Constraints on sexuality have no part in here either. They are there, but they are not prescribed. That is in a way the most essential difference. What in Greek philosophy is given as an ethic, as something which must be done, is in the Johannine text imaginarily posed as realised. Jesus and the beloved disciple do naturally what is demanded in the philosophical ethic. One could even say that the exemplary manner of behaviour of Socrates with Alcibiades is put in the shadow. When Alcibiades cuddles up to Socrates during the night, this does not evoke a sexual reaction in Socrates, notwithstanding his love for Alcibiades. It causes admiration and surprise in Alcibiades (Symp 217-218). The beloved disciple is not like Alcibiades. In the Johannine text the love of Jesus for his beloved disciple and the reaction to it from the beloved disciple himself are quite different from the way most men (in antiquity!) would behave.

2.c. the elected disciple

As far as my research and knowledge goes, the aspects of the beloved disciple as discussed so far, can be connected only to the life and culture of the Greek world. I do not know whether they play a role in the Jewish world in this explicit manner. In discourses about the love between a rabbi and his disciples, the accent is on the disciple's obligation to love the teacher. If we accept Philo as the Jewish spokesman, παιδεραστία is a veritable Greek evil. The taboo on homosexuality has probably made the difference between the Jewish and the Greek (educational) culture.

This cultural difference did not prevent affective loving relations to grow between rabbi's and their disciples. Jewish and Greek educational culture join again in another aspect of the relation between Jesus and the beloved disciple: the phenomenon that *one* is elected among the disciples: 'the one disciple whom Jesus loved'.

In Jewish culture the special relation appears rather incidentally: when on special occasions the disciple or teacher is given a specific role; or when either puts himself forward as spokesman; or shows special application. Without wanting to be exhaustive I will give four texts: two about the relation between a rabbi and his disciple(s) and two about this relation seen from the side of the disciple. The first three can be dated historically between 70 and 120 AD, —this is, at least, the story time—, the last one is much later (about 250 AD), but has an affective commitment comparable to what we are discussing.

- The relation between R.Jochanan ben Zakkai and his disciple R.Eliezer ben Hyrcanus:
Abot 2,8: "Five disciples had Rabban Jochanan ben Zakkai, and these are they: R. Eliezer ben Hyrcanus, R. Joshua ben Chananiah, R. Jose the Priest, R. Simon Nathaniel, and R. Eleazar ben Arach....He used to say, If all the Sages of Israel were in one scale of a balance, and Eliezer ben Hyrcanus in the other scale, he would outweigh them all."

- The relation between R. Akiba and his teacher R. Eliezer ben Hyrcanus:
BM 59b: When R. Eliezer ben Hyrcanus is excommunicated —because he will not accept the judgment of the majority—, someone will have to go and tell him. His most famous disciple R.

Akiba offers himself: "They said, 'Who shall go and inform him?' 'I will go,' answered R. Akiba, 'lest an unsuitable person go and inform him, and thus destroy the whole world'."

Sanh 67a: "When R. Eliezer fell sick, R. Akiba and his companions went to visit him. He was seated in his canopied four-poster, whilst they sat in his salon.... The Sages, seeing that his mind was clear, entered his chamber and sat down at a distance of four cubits. 'Why have ye come?', said he to them. 'To study the Torah', they replied; 'And why did ye not come before now', he asked? They answered, 'We had no time'. He then said, 'I will be surprised if these die a natural death'. R. Akiba asked him, 'And what will my death be?' and he answered, 'Yours will be more cruel than theirs'. He then put his two arms over his heart, and bewailed them, saying, 'Woe to you, two arms of mine, that have been like two Scrolls of the Law that are wrapped up. Much Torah I have studied, and much have I taught.....I have studied three hundred, (or, as others state, three thousand laws) about the planting of cucumbers and no man, excepting Akiba ben Joseph, ever questioned me thereon. For it once happened that he and I were walking together on a road, when he said to me, 'My master, teach me about the planting of cucumbers'. I made one statement, and the whole field was filled with cucumbers. Then he said, 'Master, you have taught me how to plant them: now teach me how to pluck them up'. I said something, and all the cucumbers gathered in one place....His visitors asked him, 'What (says the law) of a shoe that is on the last?' He replied, 'It is clean', and in pronouncing this word his soul departed. Then R. Joshua arose and exclaimed, 'The vow is annulled, the vow is annulled!' On the conclusion of the Sabbath R. Akiba met his bier being carried from Caesarea to Lydda. He beat his flesh until the blood flowed down upon the earth. Then R. Akiba commenced his funeral address, the mourners being lined up about the coffin, and said:'My father, my father, the chariot of Israel and the horsemen thereof; I have many coins, but no money changer to accept them.'"

- the relation between R. Meir and his teacher R. Elisha ben Abuja: Chag 15b: R. Meir is faithful to his teacher, notwithstanding the latter's apostasy; he wants to bring him to repentance. He lets him quote his teacher R. Akiba: "'Just as vessels of gold and vessels of glass, though they be broken, have a remedy, even so a scholar, though he has sinned, has a remedy'. Thereupon R. Meir said to him: 'Then, thou, too, repent!' He replied: 'I have already heard from behind the Veil: Return ye backsliding children —except Acher'" (= Elisha).

R. Meir then brings him to 13 different *beth midrashim* where R. Elisha makes a child recite the verse of the day. The words are always about sinners so that Acher is enraged at the end of the day.

"When Acher died, they said: 'Let him not be judged, nor let him enter the world to come. Let him not be judged, because he engaged in the study of the Torah; nor let him enter the world to come.' R. Meir said: 'When I die I shall cause smoke to rise from his grave.' When R. Meir died, smoke rose up from Acher's grave." (i.e. as a sign that he was judged and punished for his sins). When R. Jochanan dies, he achieves Acher's forgiveness.

- the relation between R. Jochanan and his disciple R. Ben Laqish:

BM 84a: "One day R. Jochanan was bathing in the Jordan, when Resh Laqish saw him and leapt into the Jordan after him. Said he (R. Jochanan) to him, 'Your strength should be for the Torah'. 'Your beauty', he replied, 'should be for women'. 'If you will repent', said he, 'I will give you my sister (in marriage), who is more beautiful than I'. He undertook (to repent); then he wished to return and collect his weapons, but could not. Subsequently, he (R. Jochanan) taught him Bible and Mishnah, and made him into a great man. Now, one day there was a dispute in the schoolhouse (with respect to the following. Viz.,) a sword, knife, dagger, spear, hand-saw and a scythe —at what stage (of their manufacture) can they become unclean? When their manufacture is finished. And when is their manufacture finished? R. Jochanan ruled: When they are tempered in a furnace. Resh Laqish maintained: When they have been furbished in water. Said he to him: 'A robber understands his trade'. Said he to him, 'And wherewith have you benefitted me; there (as a robber) I was called Master, and here I am called Master'. 'By bringing you under the wings of the Shechinah', he retorted. R. Jochanan therefore felt himself deeply hurt, (as a result of which) Resh Laqish felt ill. His sister (sc. R. Jochanan's, the wife of Resh Laqish) came and wept before him: 'Forgive him for the sake of my son', she pleaded. He replied: 'Leave thy fatherless children. I will preserve them alive' (Jer 49,11). 'For the sake of my widowhood then!' 'And let thy widows trust in me' (Jer 49,11), he assured her. Resh Laqish died, and R. Jochanan was plunged into deep grief. Said the Rabbis, 'Who shall go to ease his mind? Let R. Eleazar ben Pedath go, whose disquisitions are very subtle.' So he went and sat before him; and on every dictum uttered by R. Jochanan he observed: 'There is a Baraitha which supports you'. 'Are you as the son of Laqisha', he complained: 'when I stated a law, the son of Laqisha used to raise twenty-four objections, to which I gave twenty-four answers, which consequently led to a fuller comprehension of the law; whilst you say, 'A Baraitha has been taught which supports you': do I not know myself that my dicta are right?' Thus he went on rending his garments and weeping, 'Where are you, o son of Laqisha, where are you, o son of Laqisha?' and he cried thus until his mind was turned. Thereupon the Rabbis prayed for him, and he died."

In Greek culture the affective aspect in the stories about the relation between the teacher and his special disciple is more explicitly mentioned. It is, always, in the context of the ἐραστής and the ἐρώμενος. Innumerable pairs of lovers from all walks of life are known by name: soldiers, politicians, poets, artists and philosophers: Pisistratos and Solon; Euripides and Agathon; Phidias and Pantarces; Parmenides and Zenon; Socrates and Alcibiades; Plato and Alexis are some who are well known. There are many other stories which do not interest us here and now (see Meier 1837, 170/171; de Pogey-Castries 1930, 130ff; Buffière 1980 passim).

I still want to show, however, that this kind of love relationship played a considerable role in the succession in Plato's Academy. That takes me indeed out of the first century historically. The stories happen in the 3rd century BC and they are told by an author (Diogenes Laërtius) who lives in the 3rd century AD; but the time lapse between the story as told and the telling of the story shows something of the continuity of the tradition which went beyond the first century AD. Furthermore, Diogenes refers to Aristippus and Antigonus (of Carystus), authors from the 3rd century BC who give these stories an aura of authenticity. Even though the historical position may not be all that strong, I want to refer explicitly to them because they run parallel in many ways with what the Johannine text says about Jesus and his beloved disciple. To get the full impact of the parallel one should know that Plato left the

Academy to his nephew Speusippus. He is succeeded by Xenocrates and, then, by Polemo, Crates and Arcesilaus:

- the relation between Xenocrates and Polemo:
Diog. Laër. 4,19: "He (=Polemo) withdrew from society and confined himself to the Garden of the Academy, while close by his scholars made themselves little huts and lived not far from the shrine of the Muses and the lecture hall. It would seem that in all respects Polemo emulated Xenocrates. And Aristippus in the fourth book of his work 'On the Luxury of the Ancients' affirms him to have been his favourite (ἐρασθῆναι αὐτοῦ)."

- the relation between Polemo and Crates:
Diog. Laër. 4,21f: "Crates...was a pupil and at the same time a favourite of Polemo whom he succeeded in the headship of the school (ἐρώμενος Πολέμωνος). The two were so much attached to each other that they not only shared the same pursuits in life but grew more and more alike to their latest breath, and, dying, shared the same tomb...Hence, Arcesilaus who had quitted Theophrastus and gone over to their school, said of them that they were gods or a remnant of the Golden Age.... According to Antigonus, their common table was in the house of Crantor; and these two and Arcesilaus lived in harmony together. Arcesilaus and Crantor shared the same house, while Polemo and Crates lived with Lysicles, one of the citizens. Crates, as already stated, was the favourite (ἐρώμενος) of Polemo, and Arcesilaus of Crantor."

- the relation between Arcesilaos and Crantor:
Diog. Laër. 4,29.32: "After leaving Theophrastus he, Arcesilaos, crossed over to the Academy and joined Crantor...He was very much devoted to philosophy, and Crantor, being enamoured of him (ἐρωτικῶς διατεθείς), cited the line from the Andromeda of Euripides: 'O maiden, if I save thee, wilt thou be grateful to me?', and was answered with the next line: 'Take me, stranger, whether for maidservant or for wife'. After that they lived together....
He took over the Academy on the death of Crates, a certain Socratides having retired in his favour. According to some, one result of his suspending judgment on all matters was that he never so much as wrote a book. Others relate that he was caught revising some works of Crantor, which according to some he published, according to others he burnt."

All this can make it clear that the special relationship between Jesus and his beloved disciple is embedded in a peculiar, cultural environment. The analysis of the individual texts should clarify how the Johannine text understood it in its own way.

2.d. the texts about the beloved disciple

2.d.1. 1,35-40

Exegesis poses the question time and again whether the anonymous disciple who together with Andrew is the first to follow Jesus, can be identified with the beloved disciple. We should be aware that Jn 1,35-40 presents a scene full of mysterious silences: John (the Baptist) announces Jesus for the second time as the 'lamb of God', a title of which the meaning is revealed only at the end of the narrative; the disciples whose only interest is to know 'where Jesus is staying'; the 'staying with Jesus' on that day the meaning of which is not explained. We must see the anonymity of the 'other' disciple —who remains implied in the description of Andrew as 'one of the two who listened to John and who followed him (=Jesus)' (1,40)—, in this series of hidden meanings.

Neirynck (1990b) researched the history of the identification of this disciple. Some think of Philip, but most think only of the beloved disciple —identified or not with John the son of Zebedee, and/or with John the evangelist. The judgment is usually quite definite. One can or one can not identify the beloved disciple. Kuhn (1988, 128ff) 'proves' that the unnamed disciple is identical with the beloved disciple. Neirynck (1990b, 25ff) 'shows' that Kuhn's arguments are incorrect and that in Jn 1 there is no allusion to the beloved disciple.

Kügler (1988, 421ff) argues rather from the point of view of the reader. He points out that 13,23 —different from 19,26—, is not formulated anaphorically and that the reader, therefore, is not supposed to make any connection with the preceding text.

That may be true but, although negating any connection, by discussing 1,35-40 in this light, Kügler himself is making a readers' connection. I believe that one should make a distinction in the reading activity of the readers. In a first reading one can not assume that a reader has any idea that the unnamed 'other disciple' might have an important role to play in the story. (However, they can not have any idea either of the importance of the title 'lamb of

God'; or of the lexemes /search/ or /stay/!). Whether readers will,
then, forget such an anonymous personage I do not know. But
readers who read this passage with a knowledge of the whole book
—i.e. after repeatedly reading the book—, will surely see many
references to the coming story: Jesus as the lamb of God; the
question about 'searching', 'staying', 'staying with Jesus'. The
unnamed disciple belongs in this series and becomes more
important than Andrew whose name is mentioned. Such a reader
knows that an unnamed disciple is going to play an important role
further on in the story.

Will such a reader also come to identify the disciple? Scientific
exegesis shows that some do and others do not. It appears to me
that such a double possibility is part of the whole idea of the text. It
has, in fact, had this double effect and it is unlikely that any argument will stop the questions about who this disciple is. The text is
poly-interpretable in this respect as it is also in the question how to
divide the separate reading units or about the narrative sense of the
blanks.

2.d.2. 13,21-30

The passage where the beloved disciple appears for the first time as
such, is a narrative part of the table scene (13,1-30) which itself is
an introduction to the discourses which follow (13,31-17,26). The
table scene is in three parts: a dialogue with Peter about the
washing of feet (13,6-11); a discourse with the disciples about
service (13,12-20); a discourse about the actions of Judas (13,21-
30). The last is an impressive scene which belongs to the high
points of Johannine narration. Sticking to my topic, I will limit
myself to a discussion of the data which are relevant for the
narrative position of the beloved disciple.

Seen from the narrative characters, this position is determined by
three relationships: the relation to Jesus, to Peter and to Judas.

a/ The relation to Jesus has been given the least attention in
exegesis, while I believe that it is the most relevant relation. Two
expressions colour it: he whom Jesus loves lies ἐν τῷ κόλπῳ τοῦ
'Ιησοῦ (13,23); and when Peter nods to him to find out about
whom Jesus is speaking we read ἀναπεσὼν οὖν ἐκεῖνος οὕτως ἐπὶ
τὸ στῆθος τοῦ 'Ιησοῦ (13,25): 'he who, in this way, was lying
against Jesus' breast': in his bosom, against his breast. These are

typical expressions to be understood within a specific context. Usually not much more is said than that the narrator alludes to 1,18: 'the first born of the father who is at the father's side'. The beloved disciple has a relation to Jesus similar to the relation between Jesus and his father: in the bosom of Jesus (13,23), in the bosom of the father (1,18); Jesus loves his friend (13,23), the father loves Jesus (3,35; 10,17). The beloved disciple is the only one who is allowed to enter into intimacy with Jesus.

That is part of the expressiveness of the text, but it is not the last word. De la Potterie (1977, 228) is one of the few authors who researched the meaning of κόλπος in the LXX (cf. Meyer TWNT, s.v. κόλπος). It is important to note that the expression ἐν τῷ κόλπῳ, —if it is applied in the literal sense to the bosom of men or women—, denotes either marital sexual relations between man and woman (the woman in the bosom of the man: Dt 13,7; 28,54; 2 Kings (LXX) 12,8; Sir 9,1; the man in the bosom of his wife: Dt 28,56), or it denotes the protective love for a child in the womb of its mother (Num 11,12; 3 Kings 3,20; Ruth 4,16; Is 49,22; the sheep in the bosom of the poor man 2 Kings (LXX) 12,3).

Both references have their own expressiveness. If the expression in the Johannine text can be compared with the man-woman/woman-man relationship, the sexual connotation is very close. If it is to be seen in the context of a mother-child relationship, the connotation would be that of the protector-teacher in relation to the protegee-disciple: the teacher as father-instructor in relation to the disciple as τέκνον.

We can explicate that a little further. My position is that we are dealing here with a friendship relation which imaginary-narratively posits the classical ideal of the παιδεραστία. The love poetry from the 12th book of the Anthologia Graeca, Strato's Musa Puerilis is, then, its nearest contemporary. Obviously, these texts suggest more in the sexual field than the Johannine text wants to, but they provide a context which is contemporaneous. I give as an example 12,34 (by Automedon, an author from the 1st century BC. I use the prose translation by Loeb):

"Yesterday I supped with the boy's trainer, Demetrius, the most blessed of all men. One lay in his lap (ὑποκόλπιος), one stooped over his shoulder, one brought him the dishes, and another served him with drink —the admirable quartette. I said to him in fun, 'Do

you, my dear friend, work the boys at night too?'" (see also 12,52.
132a. 208).

How close this is to the 'child in the mother's womb' is clear from
e.g. 12,47 (by Meleager, 1st century BC):

"Love, the baby (ὁ νήπιος) still in his mother's lap (ἐν κόλποισιν),
playing at dice in the morning, played my soul away",

or, in the better translation by Peter Whigham,

"Cupid at Venus' breast
with Venus' dice
gambols at dawn:

Gambols? Gambles!
The stakes each morning —
Meleager's heart."

As is to be expected in Greek culture and as can be seen in book 5
of this Anthology, the (poetic) love for boys runs completely
parallel to the (poetic) love for girls. A poem by Meleager (5,173)
can serve as an example:

"O Morning star, the foe of love, slowly dost thou revolve around
the world, now that another lies warm beneath Demo's mantle. But
when my slender love lay in my bosom (κόλποις ἔχον), quickly thou
camest to stand over us, as if shedding on me a light that rejoiced at
my grief" (see also 5,8.16.17.25. 130.136.165).

From this poetry is made clear also that the στῆθος is not without
sexual connotations:

"Oh, would I were the wind, that walking on the shore thou
mightest bare thy bosom (στήθεα) and take me to thee as I blow"
(5,83, anonymous).

"Oh, would I were a pink rose, that thy hand might pluck me to
give to thy snowy breasts (στήθεσι)" (5,84 anonymous).

However, the στῆθος seems to have less sexual overtones than the
parallel word κόλπος (only with boys ?). That may be the reason
why the beloved disciple in patristic literature got the nickname ὁ
ἐπιστήθιος (see de la Potterie 1986, 352), and not ὁ ἐγκολπίος (cf.

the name of the famous character Encolpius in Petronius' *Satyrica* who is lying in everybody's bosom).

Taking all this together it means that, from the very first moment of his introduction, the beloved disciple, imaginarily, is given a spot which makes him the closest ally of Jesus, a two-in-one-ness of love which will prove to be unbreakable. The relation is expressed in a language which is completely ignored in a culture where men should not even touch each other.

b/ The way in which the beloved disciple relates to Peter is a constant topic in the secondary literature about the beloved disciple. It is striking that already in the first scene in which the beloved disciple appears, we hear of a kind of comparison (or, in a more distant interpretation of the text, of a kind of competition) between these two. Peter's appearance is introduced by the *aporia* of the disciples about the statement on Judas' treason. The narrator clarifies in the commentary at the end of the story that the disciples even, then, do not know what is going on (13,28.29). They understand Judas' departure in their own way and according to their own values: none of those present knew why Jesus said this (to Judas), because some of them thought that Jesus told him to go and buy something needed for the feast, because Judas carried the purse, or that he (Judas) was supposed to give something to the poor. The reader understands that the disciples had no idea of the terrible thing which happened at the table. It shows the short-sightedness of the disciples but also the lonely position of Jesus at that table. The beloved disciple alone has understood what happened.

Peter wanted to act as intermediary and convinced the beloved disciple to find out from Jesus whom he (Jesus) is talking about (13,24). He uses the love relationship between Jesus and the beloved disciple in order to end the *aporia* for himself and for the other disciples. It is part of the expressiveness of the story that the beloved disciple accedes to Peter's request. Peter takes him into his confidence and the beloved disciple acts as his friend. The real extraordinary thing is, however, that the story does not say that Peter got an answer. As reader one must believe that he did not. Only the beloved disciple knows about Jesus' answer. He is the only *intimus* of Jesus.

c/ The relation of the beloved disciple to Judas is the most specific aspect of this story. The scene opens with Jesus' prophecy about the betrayal of one of those present (13,21). This advance knowledge of Jesus has already been mentioned a few times before. It is almost a pattern, because each time Judas appears, a commentary is added to the story (see 6,71; 12,6 and 18,2.5). In this embedded story we find it in every sub-scene:

- in the introductory sentence, 'and the devil had already taken possession of Judas the son of Simon Iscariot that he would deliver him' (13,2), evoking an antithesis between the son of God and the devil;

- in the closing sentence of the first sub-scene, through an explanation of the author of Jesus' word 'you are clean, but not all', "Jesus knew who would betray him. That was why he said 'not all of you are clean" (13,11);

- in the closing sentences of the second sub-scene, as an added word of Jesus. Jesus knows what is going to happen. He knows whom he chose and he has foreseen that one of the disciples will violate the communion of the table: "I know whom I have chosen but so that the Scripture will be fulfilled 'who ate my bread will lift his heel against me'" (13,18). It is a prophetic sentence which, narratively, is further elaborated in the following sub-scene and which must make it clear that Judas' betrayal is not at the expense of Jesus' greatness.

The introductory sentences of the last sub-scene (13,22) refer to these sentences. It is striking also that the narrator uses the word 'witness', which, in the rest of the book, is reserved for the revelation of the heavenly mysteries of Jesus. Striking also that the narrator mentions that this witness of Jesus is surrounded by 'confusion in his spirit'. It is a confusion which is connected with death (see 11,33; 12,27) and which Jesus shares with other people (14,1.27). His advance knowledge does not protect him from human emotion.

These sentences determine the outcome of the rest of the story: the *aporia* of the disciples, the intervention of Peter, the question of the beloved disciple and Jesus' answer to him. Only then Judas is named explicitly (13,26). The piece of bread which Jesus dips in and gives to him is the sign as well as the end of the relationship between Jesus and Judas. With the bread Satan enters into him.

We must realise that Jesus' gesture is an act of friendship in the table culture of the time. When the host offers food to somebody, he or she receives a preferential treatment and is supposed to accept this as a sign of being selected. Apart from the beloved disciple, Judas is the only one who receives a preferential treatment. Judas is placed in the story as the anti-type of the love relationship between Jesus and the beloved disciple. Judas represents in his person the extent of hatred. Love stands beside hatred within the one group of disciples.

Kügler (1988, 155) pointed out that through the use of the word τρώγων in the biblical quote (13,18), there is a reference to the word τρώγων at the end of the discourse on the bread (6,54.56.58). Judas ate Jesus' bread and yet he lifted his heel against him. If it is possible even within the group of disciples around Jesus that one breaks the bond of love, later common meals of the Jesus-group will also not be free from hatred and betrayal. The love of one does not prevent the hatred of another.

2.d.3. 18,15-16

This is again a passage which makes the reader ask to fill in the name of the anonymous 'other disciple', this acquaintance of the High Priest who helps Peter to be present at the trial of Jesus. From various sides we find indications that point in the direction of the beloved disciple. There is the reader's question for the 'other anonymous disciple' who together with Andrew was the first to follow Jesus (1,35-40). There is this special relationship with Peter. Above all, there is the similarity with 20,2 'the other disciple whom Jesus loved'; 20,3.4.8 'the other disciple'. Neirynck (1975), especially, stands for this identification.

The identification would be conclusive, if in 18,15 it would have read ὁ ἄλλος μαθητής. The readers would, then, have been obliged to look for a specific reference. This interpretation, obviously, has left traces in the manuscript tradition. But it is too weak to pass for authentic.

It is not very useful to make a distinction between a first reading and subsequent readings of the text, as I found useful at 1,35-40. Vss 18,15.16 come narratively after 1,35-40 and 13,21-30. This means that, already at first reading, the text can be filled in variously: all these texts are about one person (the beloved disciple); they are about two persons (the disciple from 1,35-40 and

18,15-16 are the same; the beloved disciple is someone else); they
are about three persons who are all anonymous. All these possible
readings have had their place in the history of the exegesis (cf.
Neirynck 1975). The situation is not essentially different when the
reader, after a full reading of the text, also takes in consideration
20,1-10. This, certainly, is about the beloved disciple and so there
is no new personage.

Because there is no way to tip the balance one way or the other,
the text remains poly-interpretable. I believe it is proper to leave it
that way.

2.d.4. 19,26-27

This is the first time the beloved disciple is explicitly mentioned
since 13,21-30. The scene is very important in the picture of the
beloved disciple which the narrator paints for the readers.
Interpretative decisions, which mainly fill in the blank spots of the
text, mostly determine this image. In an upward scale we can see
the beloved disciple as the *kyrios* of Jesus' mother appointed by
him, as the successor of Jesus; as the adopted son of Jesus.

The way I have juridical-religiously filled in the blanks of this
concrete story in my foregoing interpretation of this text,
determines for me the more precise interpretation of the imaginary
role of the beloved disciple in this scene.

In the simplest explication, this means that the beloved disciple is
introduced by the narrator of the story as the new *kyrios* of Jesus'
mother. Jesus acts as the obedient son who absolutely fulfils the
command of *kibbud ab we'em* : in relation to his father by dying on
the cross, in relation to his mother by making sure, as her *kyrios*,
that his obligation to take care of her also after his own death will
be fulfilled. He appoints his beloved disciple to take his place as
her *kyrios*. Jesus did well, because the disciple does what Jesus
asked him: he takes the mother into his house from that moment
on.

Not many readers are satisfied with such a simple interpretation.
I do not know any. The fact that we are dealing with the 'last
words of Jesus' gives a resonance of 'last will and testament'.
Thyen (1977, 284) says it this way: 'Indem der scheidende
Offenbarer den Lieblingsjünger in die durch seinen eigenen Tod
leer werdenden Sohnesstelle einweist, macht er ihn als den
wahrhaften Zeugen zu seinem irdischen Nachfolger' (cf. Kügler

1988, 254). The beloved disciple is made the executor of Jesus' own program.

We can prove this by connecting it with the Greek practices of παιδεραστία and/or with the rabbi-disciple relations we described above. The elected disciple is given the right of succession and/or obtains that right. In the Johannine story we are not dealing with an Academy or a House of Learning, but with a μαρτυρία about the origin and destination of Jesus as we will see in the following texts about the beloved disciple. Structurally, it is not different from what is said about the succession of teacher and disciple in the Greek and Rabbinic stories (cf. the death scenes and the last will and testament stories which play an important role in these stories).

One can ask whether one can read the story also as a formula of adoption. The mutuality of the sentence 'woman, this is your son; son, this is your mother' indicates that a familial relationship is initiated. If the beloved disciple is not related to Jesus and his mother, the only possible familial relation would, then, be some kind of adoption.

Adoption was widely used in the Greek-Roman world as appears from the inscriptions on tombs in Ephesus and Smyrna where θρεπτοί is constantly used (cf. esp. Petzl 1982, 168); from the papyri in Egypt (cf. Taubenschlag 1955/2, 133ff about the *potestas patria*; 151ff about the *potestas materna*); from Roman practices culminating in the adopted emperors of the second century; even from authors like Philo and Josephus who use adoption as an imaginary possibility, even though the practice is not well developed in Judaism (cf. Schweizer TWNT s.v. υἱός, 356 for Philo about 'the sage as adopted son of God'; for Jos., see e.g. Ant 1,154 Abraham adopting Lot; Ant 2, 237 Pharaoh adopting Moses).

The sentences which Jesus speaks can be understood against the background of these practices. My problem is that, seemingly, there are no texts where adoption is settled *viva voce*. As far as I have been able to ascertain, it is done in writing through contracts. I do not know whether there is a ritual connected with this, where words are spoken which would run more or less parallel with the words of Jesus. Dauer (1972, 323) who is always cited as a kind of authority in these matters, refers only to Ps 2,7 (without regard for the problems connected with this text), and to Tob 7,12 (S) (which deals with the brother-sister relationship between marriage partners). The nearest parallel I have found is the treatment of

Clisthenes by Hippothoos in Xenophon's *Ephesiaca*. Hippothoos has fallen in love with the beautiful Clisthenes (V.9.3). At the same time he has taken care of Anthia, the heroine of the novel (V.9.13). In Rhodos they recover Habrocomes, the hero-lover of Anthia. Together they return to Ephesus. The book ends with the words: "Hippothoos decided to live with them definitively. Without delay he went to Lesbos where he erected a splendid sepulchral tomb for Hyperanthes (i.e. his first love). He adopted Clisthenes as his child (παῖς) and lived together with Anthia and Habrocomes in Ephesus." (Eph V.15.4)

However, whether the words of Jesus are understood in the context of a regular adoption contract or, less juridically, against the background of a quasi-adoption, the beloved disciple will never become the younger brother of Jesus. As a disciple he will become the adopted (or quasi-adopted) *son* of Jesus. I do not know any adoption formula which make one a brother. Firstly, the *kyrios*-regulation of the *oikos* does not allow it. And, secondly, it would be very strange because, precisely as a disciple, the beloved disciple is the τέκνον of Jesus. Now he is made the υἱός of Jesus' mother. Jesus gives his mother his own (adopted) son: 'woman, this is your son' (could this be an explanation of the peculiar γύναι?) And Jesus gives his son his own mother: 'this is your mother'. As Jesus' son he is the *kyrios* of Jesus' mother *and* his legal heir. The interpretation of the blank spots in the text shows a connection which solves some of the questions of ongoing research.

2.d.5. 19,35

The preceding scene made clear that, on Jesus' initiative, the Jesus-movement made a new start under the cross. The disciples and Jesus family who, narratively, started to be in close-knit unity but fragmented later on in the narrative, are brought together again in the person of Jesus' mother and the beloved disciple. Mary Magdalene will ensure that the group of disciples grows again. The scene looks beyond the story as it were to a future which is outside the story as told: 'from that moment on the disciple took her in his house'.

19,35 gives also a further perspective: 'the one who saw has given testimony, and his testimony is true and this one knows that he is speaking the truth so that you also may believe'. It is a difficult sentence because the communicative situation is all but clear. Who is speaking here and to whom does he speak? Is it Jesus or the beloved disciple or the narrator of the story or the implied author of the book? (see van Tilborg 1988, 19ff for the distinction between the narrator and the implied author). Should we make a distinction between the different parts of the sentence? Are some of the personages identical? I will analyse it piece by piece.

a/ 'and the one who saw has given testimony'

It seems fairly certain that this is the beloved disciple. He is the only male who plays a positive role in the scene of the crucifixion. He is, therefore, the first to be considered for this testimony. The sentence is a commentary given by the narrator. He knows of a future beyond the story as told, because the testimony is given after the facts which are narrated.

There is not much discussion about the content of the testimony. It is about the events which happened under the cross: the flowing out of blood and water; the bones which remain unbroken; the vision of the fulfilment of the prophecy that 'they will look up to him whom they have pierced'. This is not a simple seeing but a seeing filled with faith. This can be elaborated upon but for that I can refer to the existing commentaries. For my topic is important that in the formulation ('the one who saw has given testimony') as well as in the content (Jesus as the lamb of God), there is a reference to the beginning of the Johannine story, to the 'see and give testimony' of John (the Baptist) (1,34) and to the introduction of Jesus as the lamb of God (1,29 and 1,36). (cf. Theobald 1982, 168). The last Johannine text is important because it may be possible to identify the (first) anonymous disciple of Jesus. He heard from John that Jesus is the lamb of God. Now he has seen and he testifies to it as John did. If one gives up the idea that the anonymous disciple (in 1,35ff) and the beloved disciple are identical, there remains the similarity between the $\mu\alpha\rho\tau\upsilon\rho\iota\alpha$ of the beloved disciple and that of John (the Baptist): teacher and disciple of Jesus, beginning and end meet. Therefore, the implied author plays his contextual role, too, in this first partial sentence.

b/ 'and his testimony is true'

It is an evaluative sentence which comments the testimony of the beloved disciple and which, therefore, goes beyond the communication of telling a story. From a literary technical point of view this means that the implied author is speaking and addresses his readers directly. The story is truthful, because it comes from an eyewitness.

c/ 'and /ἐκεῖνος/ knows that he is speaking the truth'

This part is a real stumbling block. Several interpretations are possible. It is sometimes suggested that Jesus himself is meant (see Kügler 1988, 276; he also gives further references). This follows a Johannine mode of speaking in which ἐκεῖνος often refers to Jesus (especially in the Johannine letters) and/or is based on the presupposition that ἐκεῖνος, anaphorically, refers to a personage who is mentioned earlier on. One must, then, presuppose that the implied author used his awareness of the intimate relationship between Jesus and the beloved disciple to come to the conclusion that Jesus supports the testimony of the beloved disciple. This is not impossible (see esp. 21,17), but it would be rather unique. Nowhere else does Jesus say something about the inner attitude of his beloved disciple.

Even if this can not be excluded as a possibility for reading the text, it seems to me more probable that, with the ἐκεῖνος, the speaker of the previous part of the sentence introduces himself: 'and his testimony is true, and —he who is writing/saying this—, knows that he is speaking the truth'. This figure of speech, that the writer speaks about himself in the third person, has its own applications, especially in historiography. Kügler (1988, 406) has discovered that this mode of speaking about self in the third person can be found especially in Josephus (from Bell Jud 2,568 on; see esp. 3,202.345.351). But he does not consider this to be relevant for this part of the sentence. It is not all that extraordinary for the Johannine text. Because the author makes Jesus speak, continuously, about himself in the third person, he can do this also regarding himself.

It is much more difficult to answer the question whether ἐκεῖνος could indicate the beloved disciple identical or not with the implied author. Ἐκεῖνος, then, refers anaphorically to 'he who has seen has given testimony': 'and his testimony is true and (= because) he knows that he is speaking the truth' and/or 'I who have seen, have given testimony, and my testimony is true, because I know that I speak the truth'. If the beloved disciple is referred to without identifying him with the implied author of the text, we retain the distinction between the speaker(s) of the text and the one about whom the text speaks. If there is identification between the two, all narrators are identical with the beloved disciple. That is, obviously, not without consequences for the image of the beloved disciple. It would imply much more than the writer-identification in 21,24. Therefore, it does not seem likely, but the text itself does not exclude this way of reading.

d/ 'so that you may believe'
It is the first time in the text that the readers are addressed directly. If one asks about the speaker, part of the previous discussion comes back. The words can be attributed to the implied author, because the readers are directly addressed, but the question whether it is the beloved disciple remains open.

It may be clear that there is a lot of ambiguity and it is not simple to keep a clear head amid the confusion of so many possibilities.

If I concentrate on the reader's possibilities which affect the beloved disciple, the following conclusions are possible:
1/ the beloved disciple has given a testimony about Jesus as the lamb of God in accordance with John (the Baptist) (a.1).
2/ the beloved disciple is a disciple of John (the Baptist) and he has heard John say that Jesus is the lamb of God; now he is himself an eyewitness and he gives his own testimony (a.2).
3/ his testimony is accepted as trustworthy by the implied author (b+c.2+c.3).
4/ the implied author lets it be known that Jesus himself stands for the truth of the testimony of his beloved disciple (c.1).
5/ the implied author affirms from his own knowledge that the beloved disciple has spoken the truth (c.2).
6/ the beloved disciple testifies about the truth of his own statement and the implied author confirms that (c.3).
7/ the beloved disciple is the implied author; he testifies about himself (c.4).
8/ the implied author hopes that the readers will come to believe through his confirmation of the truth of the beloved disciple's testimony (via an awareness of Jesus; via personal knowledge; or via the testimony of the beloved disciple about himself (c.1+c.2+c.3+d.1).

9/ the beloved disciple addresses his readers as the implied
author: he gives testimony about himself about the
trustworthiness of his own words and he hopes that his readers
will also come to believe in this way (c.4+d.2).

Schematically it looks like this:

about whom	the speakers
a.1 the beloved disciple a.2 the beloved disciple = the disciple of John (the Baptist)	narrator/implied author narrator/implied author
b. the beloved disciple	implied author
c.1 Jesus about the beloved disciple c.2 implied author about the beloved disciple c.3 the beloved disciple about himself c.4 the beloved disciple = implied author about himself	implied author implied author implied author implied author = beloved disciple
d.1 the readers d.2 the readers	implied author implied author = beloved disciple

Most of these sentences deal with the post-narrative function of the
beloved disciple. In all the possible ways of reading, the text deals
with the fidelity and the trustworthiness of the beloved disciple in
relation to Jesus and what happened to him. In the reading which
makes Jesus the guarantor of the trustworthiness, there is a certain
mutuality between Jesus and the beloved disciple. All other readings
deal with the relation between the beloved disciple and the implied
author. Question is: are they the same person or not? The text is
too ambiguous to force a decision on this. Could that be intentional:
to create a confusion for the reader so that one will pose the

question whether the (implied) author might be the same person as the beloved disciple?

2.d.6. 20,1-10

The beloved disciple plays an important role also in the story of the first apparition of Jesus to Mary Magdalene. I believe, there are three aspects which are worth investigating.

a/ the introduction in 20,2

I referred to this text in the discussion of 18,15-16: 'the other disciple whom Jesus loved' is a typical expression which will make the reader recall the earlier texts about the beloved disciple (13,23 and 19,26), and which some exegetes connect with 18,15-16. The presupposition, then, is that the apposites to the lexeme /disciple/ remain unconnected: the other disciple = the disciple whom Jesus loved. This seems to be a way to read the text which has not evoked any objections, as far as I can discover.

But it should be clear that I do have objections. Let us look at the text without making an immediate connection with the foregoing and especially with the established view of the beloved disciple. The meaning, then, becomes quite different. Mary Magdalene runs away and comes to Peter *and* the other disciple whom Jesus loved, i.e. she first comes to Peter as the one disciple whom Jesus loved and then to the other. There is then a double apposite to /the disciple/. The ἄλλος is opposed to Peter and ὃν ἐφίλει ὁ Ἰησοῦς must be applied also to Peter. Does such a reading explain why instead of ἀγαπάω, now the verb φιλέω is being used, a verb that in 21,15-17 is specifically applied to Peter in his relation to Jesus, as an implicit preparation on that part of the story and as an implicit commentary on the scene of the betrayal by Peter?

Such a reading has clear advantages. Peter and the beloved disciple are put in opposition to one another without making either a loser. In this reading this is true from the very beginning of the story. Jesus loves Peter as well as the beloved disciple: the difference is that it is explicitly stated about the beloved disciple and implicitly about Peter.

b/ the contest

Jn 20,1-10 is one of the few texts in the Johannine Gospel in which there are practically no 'spoken' sentences. The announcement by Mary Magdalene in 20,2 is the only 'spoken' text; the rest are narrative descriptions. This does not mean that there is no 'discussion', but it is differently organised. The description is of a contest: together they run, one runs ahead, one is faster than Peter, one arrives first, one arrives later, one runs after the other. In this relatively short story we find many words connected with sports and contests.

In exegetical literature this contest is always placed in quotation marks as if to say that it is not really a contest in the real sense of the word. The Johannine text does not do that and that has consequences for the meaning of the text. The more serious the element of contest is taken, the greater meaning is given to the waiting and the fact that the beloved disciple goes in the vanguard (cf. the interpretation in Kragerud 1959, 29ff and the way Mahoney 1974, 245ff minimises that). I believe that the actual choice of words brings in a vital aspect which is meaningful for the imaginary presentation of the narrator. The contextualisation within the Greek cultural setting of the teacher's favourite reminds one of the language used in the gymnasium, the exercises which happen there, the results. The beloved disciple is naturally the winner, but as the beloved he gives precedence to the beloved Peter. In this way he wins once again with the readers, while Peter retains the first place.

c/ to see

This is the real topic of this narrative. Mahoney (1974, 261) points out, referring to Ramsey, that the three verbs used for /to see/ show a progression: the beloved disciple's seeing the linen cloths ($\beta\lambda\acute{\epsilon}\pi\omega$) outside the tomb is 'simple seeing' (20,5). It is the most incomplete way of seeing, dependent on an accident which the eye notices. When Peter enters he sees ($\theta\epsilon\omega\rho\acute{\epsilon}\omega$) the linen cloths and the headband rolled up by itself (20,6). This seeing takes in the total picture but does not interpret as yet. The beloved disciple makes the last step when he enters: he sees ($\epsilon\mathring{\iota}\delta o\nu$) and believes (20,8). The commentary of the narrator that they did not yet know the Scriptures that he had to rise from the dead, shows the meaning of this believing. The beloved disciple was the first to come to believe that Jesus had risen from the dead. The closing sentence is surprising: the disciples go back to their own accommodation. The story as told must be enough for the reader.

2.d.7. 21,1-24

The beloved disciple plays a role in the narrative till the very end. In the closing chapter, which has its own interpretative problems, the beloved disciple enters the story three times: as an active personage in the first scene; as one about whom Peter and the narrator have something to say; as one about whom the implied author has something to say. The distance becomes narratively ever greater while, communicatively, it diminishes for the readers. Let us look at the individual texts.

a/ 21,7

The story begins in the night. Seven disciples are gathered: some are known from the previous narrative: Simon Peter, Thomas and Nathanael. But the sons of Zebedee come out of the blue and 'two more of the disciples' remain naturally anonymous. The beloved disciple, who shortly is to make an important statement, is not mentioned. Is he supposed to be one of the four last mentioned? Neirynck (1990, 331) points out that, in that case, the beloved disciple would also 'not know who Jesus is' (in 21,4) —which seems very improbable. That seems a strong argument. The beloved disciple is a special personage who appears as if out of the blue more often (13,23;19,26). It could be like that also in this scene as well as in the introduction in 21,20. That would mean that he is not part of the group of disciples in 21,8.12. Once he has made his statement, he disappears again from the narrative.

Simon Peter really sets the pace. When he says that he goes fishing, the others follow: 'we will go with you'. It is clear from the first sentences that Peter will play a central role in the story. It did not look like that, when they were still in Jerusalem. From the meal scene till the visit to the empty tomb Peter played secondary role. The scenes were not in his favour at all. Now he is back on safe ground in Galilee: from now on things will be better.

The night comes to an end without anything happening. At first light (21,4) the miraculous events begin to play themselves out. The story is strange indeed: the unexpected presence of Jesus; the readiness of the fishermen to listen to a stranger; the unexpected catch and the unbelievable quantity; the unexpected presence of the beloved disciple and his revelation-statement which is not a surprise for the readers but which evokes in the disciples a numinous fear (20,12). The sea of Tiberias —for the narrator there is open sea and not a lake; he is not interested in geography but in events—, is surrounded with mysteries. Jesus has come to teach his disciples how to fish. They believe him on his word and the net is so full that they can not bring it in.

Having spoken his revelation, the beloved disciple disappears from the narrative. It is the last time he speaks and after 13,25 only the second time. It can be seen as a resume of his function as a witness: 'It is the Lord'. Different from the meal scene he now shares it with the disciples, first of all with Peter who honours Jesus as representative of the other disciples. The beloved disciple has fulfilled his role.

b/ 21, 20-23

Nowhere else is the distinction between the story as told and the commentary so clear as in these last sentences. The beloved disciple appears for the last time as a narrative personage —'he is the one who follows Jesus'. This brings Peter, Jesus, the brethren, and the narrator to make the beloved disciple a subject of their discussion.

Peter's question: 'what about him?' is the starting point. Again we see that the interests of Peter and the beloved disciple are central. The death of those two is in question. For Peter a martyr's death has been predicted (21,18-19). The beloved disciple hears that he may remain till Jesus comes. His special position in the story of the supper is recalled: his love-relationship with Jesus as Jesus' favourite and his relation with the identification of Judas: he may remain till I come. That privilege is not given to Peter. It is beyond his concern and responsibility. The special relation between Jesus and his favourite disciple is maintained till the very end of the narrative.

It is clear that words are attributed to Jesus which have created a good deal of confusion in the Johannine community. The implied author creates a controversy with an interpretation of 'the brethren' which he does not judge right. It is a pity that this commentary of the author can not be interpreted in one single manner. Kügler (1988, 403) points out that 21,23 can be read in two ways. It is possible to emphasise the hypothetical character of Jesus' statement. He did not mean to say that this disciple would not die, but he said; '*if* I want him to remain (alive) till I come, what is that to you?' It is not a positive statement, as if the beloved disciple would not die. It is a conditional statement to put Peter in his place. But it is also possible to emphasise the verb *remain*: Jesus wants that the beloved disciple 'remains' till he comes. Jesus did not want to say that the beloved disciple would not die. He said: he remains till I come, even if he dies (cf. 11,25-26).

The exegetes are as usual divided in two groups following one reading or the other. Kügler, rightly, pointed out that the Johannine text is not decisive. One must keep both possibilities in mind and, then, find a way to see the meaning of the text, i.e. Jesus determines whether the disciple will remain or not and not Peter, and also whether the beloved disciple dies or not is irrelevant in relation to his remaining. The teacher takes the side of his beloved disciple till the very end and beyond.

c/ 21,24-25

The closing words of the book must be understood in connection with 19,35. Vs 21,24 is an interpretation of 19,35. Anyhow, it imitates vs 19,35 in style and content. The readers' questions which remained after 19,35, are now solved positively.

Three personages play a role in this closing scene: the beloved disciple about whom is said that he gives testimony: that his testimony is truthful and that he wrote 'these things'; a group of people who are described as 'we' and who know about the truth of the testimony of the beloved disciple; and an 'I' who expresses the awareness of the author that he would have liked to write about all the deeds of Jesus but that the world would not be large enough to contain the books needed. In other words, we have two authors and a 'we'-group. The question is, obviously, how they relate to each other and who is the same as another.

It seems that, as in 19,35, the distinction between the subject spoken about and the person who speaks the text throws some light on the discussion. The text identifies the implied author with the beloved disciple: 'this is the disciple .... who wrote it'. Kügler, maybe, meant this also where he writes: "Der geliebte Jünger wird, obwohl er in der Erzählung bloss als erzählte Figur auftrat, mit dem impliziten Autor und dem Erzähler identifiziert" (1988, 406; cf. Culpepper 1983, 47). The use of the passive —'wird identifiziert'— obscures who creates this identification: the narrator, the implied author or the reader. Yet this is important to see matters clearly. The speaker of the text is the implied author and he creates the identification. The implied author says that the beloved disciple is the writer of 'these things'. Therefore, there is an explicit author.

'Writing these things' (21,24b) points, anaphorically, backwards, but how far? In agreement with their own critical view on the diachronical difference between ch. 21 and the rest of the Gospel text, commentators would like to confine this anaphorical function to ch. 21. But because of the reference to 19,35 via the lexeme μαρτυρῶν (which makes the further connection with the μαρτυρία of John the Baptist), this is linguistically difficult to maintain. Therefore, one must accept that, in the option of the implied author, the lexeme /these things/ refers back to the very beginning of the Gospel text. The implied author wants his reader to believe that the beloved disciple is the explicit author of the book so far.

Vs 21,24c, '*we* know that his testimony is true', ascribes the awareness of the truth of the beloved disciple's testimony to a 'we'-group. That is an important difference with 19,35 where it is an individual person: '/ἐκεῖνος/ knows that he speaks the truth', —with all the conflicting possibilities to interpret that text. Where the awareness of the truth is now ascribed to a group, there is no way to identify this we-group with an implied (or explicit) author (unless it would be a majestic plural which would, then, indicate again a testimony of the beloved disciple about the truth of his own statement; but that is not likely). The 'we' refers, more probably, to those sentences in the previous story which take the interest of the group of readers to heart: 1,14 especially, but possibly also 3,11; 4,22; 6,68-69 etc. The implied author is again the one who speaks and he is part of a group of people who judge the truthfulness of the beloved disciple's testimony.

In the closing sentence of the book an I-author presents himself. He is convinced that there are so many deeds of Jesus that the world is too small to contain them all. As last sentence it finally determines the narrational, (which means in this case the 'authorial') position of the beloved disciple. Seen from the viewpoint of the historiographic code of the time (cf. what we said on 19,35), it is not possible to exclude an identification of the beloved disciple as the author of the book and the I-author of this closing sentence. The historiographers of this time do write about themselves and about others in the first and in the third person. In the exemplary author Josephus, however, these quick modifications occur only in narrative texts (cf. Kügler 1988, 409). There are, apparently, no examples of descriptive texts as is the case in 21,24-25. It is, therefore, more likely —also according to the contemporary code—, that the third person in 21,24 and the 'I' in 21,25 are two different persons, i.e. in 21,25 the implied author presents himself as an I-author who is also responsible for 21,24 and thus for the whole book.

The I-character in 21,25, resp. in 21,24.25 is sometimes seen as a kind of editor who is responsible for the Johannine book based on textual material of the beloved disciple; or, somewhat less comprehensively, as the redactor who added the texts about the beloved disciple to an existing text. It is clear that 21,24 —'the beloved disciple is the explicit author'—, must be seen in combination with 21,25 —'I do not think it is possible to write everything that Jesus did'. If one does not want to enter a road which is historically impossible and which contains statements which are unlikely and/or unprovable —a beloved disciple of Jesus who as a historical personage wrote a book that belongs to the end of the first century; or who wrote a kind of basic text (a kind of 'Grundschrift') which is historically impossible to reconstruct—, one is left with one possibility: the I-character of 21,25 has identified himself with the beloved disciple to such an extent that he could write in 21,24: the beloved disciple wrote this book, i.e. not I but the beloved disciple is the explicit author of the book.

In the language used in this study, this identification of the I-character with the beloved disciple is an example of imaginative behaviour: an I-author who is guided in his fantasy by a self-identification with somebody else. Individual-personally this is not a 'falsche Verfasserschaftsangabe' (Kügler 1988, 411). It is, self-evidently, done in all honesty. It is supported also by a we-group who accepts his (i.e. the beloved disciple = the I-author) testimony as true and trustworthy.

I believe that it is probable that this identification process can be seen in connection with the self awareness of the Johannine community that it is introduced into the truth of Jesus by the paraclete. That would explain the similarity of the function of the paraclete and of the beloved disciple. (cf. Kragerud 1959, 67ff and from then on a constant topic in the literature about the beloved disciple; but see also Boring 1979, 120 about the self awareness of the author of the book —the author as prophet). Ascribing the Johannine text to the beloved disciple is, anyway, a form of pseudo-epigraphy. This can very well be compared —as far as the author's awareness is concerned—, with contemporary pseudo-epigraphical literature as e.g. 4 Ezra changing between the 'I' and the 'he' (see 1,1; 1,4; 2,10: 2,33 etc.); Gr Apoc Ezra where the story begins in the first person and ends with relating the burial of Ezra in the third person; and v.v. 2 Baruch which begins in the third person and in 3,1 switches to the first; cf. 3 Baruch and Apoc Adam. Proper to the Johannine text is the identification of the author with an *anonymous* character: 'the disciple whom Jesus loved', this teacher's favourite who gave the author the unique chance to place his book within the Jewish-Hellenistic culture.

I started this chapter with the statement that the Johannine Gospel knows a repetitive theme: as Jesus is pushed in a special way by John (the Baptist), so is the beloved disciple given a special place by Jesus. Now that we have discussed all the relevant texts, we can concretely show this in its similarities as well as its differences.

In the relation between John (the Baptist) and Jesus, John plays the active role. He testifies about himself, about Jesus, and about the reaction of the people to Jesus. He presents Jesus to his disciples, but above all to Israel. He is the 'teacher' who is prepared to learn from Jesus; he is the elder who knows to be younger; he is the earlier who takes a lower position. Jesus is the silent subject. The rare occasion that Jesus speaks about John (5,33ff), he repeats. what John has said about himself and his relation to Jesus. In the imaginary presentation John acted as the best man who led Jesus as the son of God to the marriage with Israel, his bride. In the story as told this marriage does not play a role of much importance as far as I can see. In the fantasy of John (the Baptist) it is essential, because it justifies his lower position. He is the friend of Jesus which makes him use, unknowingly, the same words and sentences as Jesus, or he is prepared to let himself be influenced and/or corrected by his friend (cf. the double interpretation of the narrative position of 3,22-36).

In the relation between Jesus and the beloved disciple Jesus is, in a way, also the active one. He is the lover. He has expressed his preference. He has elected this disciple over the others. He takes the beloved disciple into the intimacy of himself in a way which fits in the classical philosophical ideal of the teacher-disciple model. When he dies, he appoints him as *kyrios* over his mother; as his successor and as his (quasi-) adopted son. He has taken him into his love to such an extent that he will not allow anyone to interfere in letting him 'remain till he comes'.

The beloved disciple, however, becomes an active participant gradually. During the last supper he accedes to Peter's request to ask Jesus who the traitor is, but he does not share it. Something similar can be said about his believing insight that Jesus has risen from the dead. But it has, then, already been related that he took Jesus' mother into his house. And the general sentence in 19,35 shows that, sometime later, he acts as a witness about the meaning of Jesus' death. When Jesus appears at the sea of Tiberias the beloved disciple tells Peter and the others who Jesus is. And especially, he is the explicit author of the book about Jesus' deeds and words, for always hidden behind the words of the real author, but in a truthful way as the we-group in 21,24 tells us. In short, while Jesus lives, he is the passive subject of his love and after his death he is the active witness of this love.

For Jesus' social role (for the specific meaning of 'social role' and 'sense of identity' see Friedman 1988, passim) this means that the author, imaginarily, ascribes to Jesus a marriage as well as a special friendship. The difference is that the marriage is imaginary 'in the second degree' (i.e. in the presentation by a character of the narrative = John), while the friendship is narrative reality. We pointed out already that in our culture such a social role could exist only at the expense of the masculine sense of identity, while in the classical culture it reinforces the masculine code.

If we combine this with the contemporary story about the family constellation and the consequences in relation to behaviour for a son in this setting, we come to a curious conclusion. The Gospel of John tells a story, according to the code of modern discourse, about a family constellation which is positively attuned to the development of possibly homosexual behaviour. It is a possibility which we see also in the story of the relation between Jesus and the beloved disciple. But in the code, contemporary to the story as told, such imaginary homosexual behaviour is not an expression of homosexuality, but of love: Jesus as the ἐραστής of the beloved disciple. Instead of diminishing the masculine sense of identity in modern discourse, we have a reinforcement of that masculine sense

of identity in the classical discourse. In the next chapters we will
see how Jesus behaves within larger groups of men and women.

CHAPTER THREE

JESUS' DISCIPLES AS (HIS) FRIENDS

The love of Jesus for his beloved disciple is, obviously, embedded in a greater whole: the relation of Jesus to the larger group of disciples. This is presented as a love-relationship on a dual, structured level: the love-relationship of Jesus to his disciples and the love-relationship between the disciples among one another. Most typically this is expressed in the word φίλοι. Jesus calls his disciples his friends and he *demands* that they act towards each other as friends.

It is impossible to determine precisely who belongs to the group of disciples. We can say that there is a core group:

- the group of the first disciples in chapter 1: one anonymous, Andrew, Simon, Philip, and Nathanael;

- the 12 disciples in 6,70 of whom Philip, Andrew, Peter, and Judas play a role in the story as told; Thomas is also one of this group of twelve: cf. 20,24;

- the indeterminate group of disciples who are present at the last supper where the beloved disciple, Peter, Judas, Thomas (see also 11,16), Philip and Judas-not-Iscariot play a role;

- the group of eight or seven disciples in 21,1ff: Peter, Thomas, Nathanael, the sons of Zebedee; two other disciples: plus the beloved disciple (as a separate figure) or implicitly mentioned with the anonymous sons of Zebedee or with the other two anonymous disciples.

Apart from this core group which is more or less determined, there is also a larger group which is more vague. This follows e.g. from chapter 6 where the group of twelve remains out of a larger group of disciples (6,60.66), and also from the unexpected way in which Joseph of Arimathea acts —who 'is a secret disciple because of fear for the Jews' (19,38); (see also 12,42). The core group seems to be a more or less open group, varyingly composed of fewer or more persons.

One could question whether Lazarus and his sisters Martha and Mary can be considered disciples, and whether Mary Magdalene is a disciple. As I will show in the next chapter I think so, but I do not see them involved in the activities of the core group which follows Jesus geographically in his various movements. The point of departure for this chapter are the texts in which the members of that group are described in some way in their relation to Jesus and in their mutual relations to one another. It is (most probably) an exclusively male group which is narratively presented as a group of friends. It is an imaginary reality which has deep roots in the classical Hellenistic-Jewish culture. I want to elucidate some aspects of that.

1. THE IMAGINARY PRESENTATION

Such a presentation is unique in the New Testament. It is strange that this phenomenon has not been studied more deeply. Culpepper (1983, 115ff) is one of the few who devotes time to it but his analyses show some remarkable gaps and, furthermore, his only point of reference is the presentation in Mark. That is insufficient, if one wants to do justice to the Johannine texts. I realise that the following reflections do not do that either, but I believe I have made a couple of steps forward. I want to put together some more general characteristics before I enter into a discussion of the texts which bring out this mutual love-relationship. These are aspects which form the background against which other, more discursive, texts are to be understood.

1.a. the formation of the group (1,35-2,12)

The description of the contacts in the beginning of the story is already out of the ordinary. These are calling narratives of such special form that one can ask whether they should be seen as belonging to the genre of calling stories. Kuhn (1988, 209-234) denies it. He believes the text to be a mixture of several genres: 1,35-39 is a *Präsentationslegende* in which Jesus is presented to the disciples of John (the Baptist) as the lamb of God; and 1,40-42 and 1,44-50 are *Erweisungslegenden* in which it is proved that the expressed christology is correct by the description of the supernatural knowledge of Jesus (Jesus knows Peter and Nathanael without having had any previous contact). 1,43 is according to

Kuhn a redactionally added text (which he, therefore, does not discuss any further) which, however, contains the words 'follow me' and so belongs to the genre of the calling stories. This way of reading creates meaning through labelling phrases with certain codes. It strengthens the awareness of gaps in the text which can not just be bypassed (for other ways to read the text see de Goedt 1961/61; Hahn 1974; Schenke 1989; Neirynck 1990b).

The real problem is the meaning and function of 1,43: is Jesus the subject of the sentence 'he wanted to go away to Galilee and he finds Philip'? Or is it still Andrew as a sequence to the πρῶτον from 1,41 (see Neirynck 1990b for a discussion of the meaning of this)? The answer to this question is not unimportant for the vision we form of Jesus. If Jesus is the subject, he develops a certain activity. He 'finds' one of the disciples. If Andrew is the subject, Jesus remains completely passive and the story develops, independently of what Jesus is wanting or doing. It is an ambiguity in the text which can not be solved and must remain open, no matter what exegetes say about it.

The narrative structure of the scenes is determined by the notation of the time: the repetition of 'the next day' in 1,35 and 1,43, to which is added 'and on the third day' in 2,1 and which is closed off with 'and there (in Capernaum) they did not stay many days' in 2,12. These are the events of the first week of Jesus' public life. Jesus is taken from obscurity. I limit myself to what the texts say about the formation of the group around Jesus. The first two scenes (1,35-39 and 1,43-51) are double-stories (1,35-39 and 1,40-42; 1,43-44 and 1,45-51). Because 1,45-51 refers back to 1,40-42 narratively structurally, something similar seems to be the case with the relation between 1,43-44 and 1,35-39. In this sense the Cana story functions as the temporary ending.

1,35-39: Two of the disciples of John (the Baptist) go over to Jesus. John shows who Jesus is and two of his disciples draw the conclusion. They follow Jesus and are admitted to the privacy of his life. Jesus allows them to know him. The scene points to something beyond the narrative itself. It is a literary effect which is caused by the repetition of certain words: /remain/, /come/, and /see/. The mysterious character of the narrative is deepened by the fact that only one of the disciples is mentioned by name. Nothing is said about what happened that day. The only important thing is that they /remain/.

1,40-42: Only after Andrew has found his brother, the reader is informed about what the visit of the disciples has done to them: we have found the Messiah. It refers to what John (the Baptist) said about himself: I am not the Christ (1,20.25). These disciples of John are the first to know the relation between Jesus and John. The meaning of the πρῶτον is not unimportant with regard to the imaginary presentation. Most probably the meaning is 'immediately afterwards' i.e. 'immediately when the day with Jesus came to an end' (cf. Neirynck 1990b with many references). If John uses the Roman time system (cf. Culpepper 1983, 219), the two disciples have been with Jesus from about 10 AM —that explains better why it is said that they remained *that day* with him than when they would have followed Jesus only about 4 PM (according to the Jewish time calculation). In the evening Andrew right away finds his brother Peter. The group of Jesus-disciples is expanded first of all along the line of family relationships.

The end of the day is like the beginning: John looked at Jesus and said: see the lamb of God — Jesus looks at Simon and says: you are Simon, John's son. You will be called Kefas (= Rock). Maybe this is told not without irony. The lamb meets the rock. In any case the boundary between Jesus and John (the Baptist) is crossed again. Jesus knows people even before they manifest themselves to him. He uses this knowledge to win them for himself. It is probably not unimportant for the meaning of this scene that Simon's father is mentioned by name —i.e. Simon and Andrew are both free citizens—, and that the lexeme /καλέω/ is being used —i.e. the context of a calling is not completely absent.

1,43-44: In Philip is found a new candidate. It seems important that he comes from the same city as Andrew and Peter. The mention of the name of the city indicates that he has the rights of a citizen as Andrew and Peter probably did (cf. the description of Jesus in 1,45 as the son of Joseph from Nazareth).

I have said already that the text is ambivalent in relation to the subject of the 'finding': Jesus or Andrew. If Jesus is the subject, he becomes more active. If Andrew is the subject, the preceding expansion procedure goes on: the Jesus-group expands along kinship lines. Philip is, probably, not a disciple of John (the Baptist) so that another boundary is crossed. The circle of the Jesus-group is somewhat enlarged.

If I may construct an ongoing story line (as 1,40-42 is parallel to 1,45-51, so is 1,35-39 parallel to 1,43-44), Jesus' invitation to 'come and see' and the disciples' 'remaining with Jesus' (from 1,35-39) is followed by the request/command of Jesus to 'follow him'. Vs 1,43 realises, then, a more constant form of intimacy. Being close to Jesus is not tied up with a locality, but rather with his person.

1,45-51: Philip becomes active as the one who is called last. The story which is being told is a rehash with new names and new facts of the story-scene between Peter, Andrew and Jesus (cf. Kuhn 1988, 214ff). Nathanael represents, yet, another model of calling. He needs to be convinced before he will commit himself.

The logic of the argument to convince him remains rather obscure. The sentence 'here is a real Israelite; there is nothing false in him', probably, refers to 1,31. Jesus' manifestation by John (the Baptist) is complete with Nathanael. It is not unlikely that there is also a reference to Jacob-Israel, the impostor (Gen 27,35). That would, then, be a first preparation to 1,51. It is unclear how this can be combined with Jesus' mysterious knowledge that he saw Nathanael 'under the fig tree'. This phrase has loosened the imagination of many readers but that has not resulted into a univoque signification (cf. Brown 1966, 83.87.89).

The dialogue leads to the surprise of Jesus which indicates the real basis: 'Because I have said that I saw you under the fig tree, you have believed?' In question is belief, a belief so strong that the dialogue is opened up to all (readers) who listen: you will see the heavens open. The heaven in Bethany from which John saw a dove descending, becomes a heaven which is open for anyone who can believe in Jesus.

2,1-12: On the third day Jesus is in Cana with his disciples for a wedding. The lexeme καλέω is used again. The disciples are called *his* disciples although they have been with him only for a short time. A group has been formed and manifests itself for the first time in public. 21,2 shows that Nathanael comes from Cana, but at this stage it is not brought as being relevant.

The function of the disciples' presence becomes clear in the closing sentence. They are the only ones of whom it is said that they believe on the basis of the manifestation of the *doxa* of Jesus. The innumerable Jesus-titles which the various disciples used in the preceding story come to life again for them in the sign which Jesus gives.

The scene ends with the mention that Jesus together with his mother, his brothers and sisters and his disciples goes down to Capernaum (2,12). Jesus has begun his own *oikos*. The way it is expressed is significant: and they remained there 'not many days'. They do not stay together for long. That has something to do with the special structure of the Jesus-*oikos*.

John's story begins to narrate that a group of men find each other in their interpretation of the significance of Jesus. The real initiator is John (the Baptist) who sees two of his disciples go to Jesus. Jesus himself is not very active. Apart from the case of Philip, it all happens without him. He allows people to approach him and permits them, then, enter into the intimacy of himself: on the spot where he lives, and, narratively progressive: he allows them to be near to himself as individual persons. He presents himself as someone who can be 'followed'. Argumentatively important is Jesus' self presentation as someone who possesses superhuman powers. Jesus shows that he knows people, even though they have had no previous contact with him. In Cana he shows his glory. The texts are, narratively, to be read as a climax: a short sentence by Peter, a longer story for Nathanael, an even more important event in Cana. The meetings have every time a positive result. Once the individuals have been won for Jesus, they belong to his group and the outside world recognises them as such right away. The story suggests that there is some kind of link with the family of Jesus.

Notwithstanding the closeness, there is evidence in the individual stories of a remoteness. Jesus remains, ultimately, a stranger and an alien in his own *oikos*. His passive behaviour, the manifestation of his secret knowledge and power calls forth the sense of a different world to which the disciples have no access. They make grandiose professions of faith; they let themselves be described as 'his disciples'; they believe in Jesus and follow him wherever he goes but, in fact, this is true only for 'not many days'. Starting from his own family Jesus creates an *oikos* of mutual friends who have found each other on the basis of freedom and of kinship relationships. But it is not an *oikos* in which everything is shared for always.

1.b. the travels of Jesus

Without reflecting on it, we usually imagine that, during the period of Jesus' life about which his story is told, Jesus is always in the company of his disciples. I suppose that this image originates with the Synoptics. In John it is different. Jesus is alone much more often. The disciples are given some kind of freedom of initiative. They are welcome but never needed. This becomes even clearer, when one studies Jesus' Jerusalem travels more precisely.

the first journey (2,13-4,54)

The people of the original Jesus-group came from different places: Andrew, Peter and Philip from Bethsaida; Nathanael from Cana; Jesus from Nazareth. In Capernaum they did not remain together for many days. The supposition is that each went his own way, as follows seemingly from 2,13 where it says about Jesus only that he went up to Jerusalem.

It is a real question whether one can take for granted that the disciples were present at these first events in the Temple. No reaction from them is recorded. The two times that they do play a role in the story as told we find the extraordinary verb ἐμνήσθησαν (2,17 and 2,22). The first time it is a reminder of a text from Scripture which is deemed applicable. The second time it is the reminder that 'after Jesus has risen from the dead, he had said something': i.e. *if* the disciples were present the events passed them by completely and they have integrated them only later in their system of meaning.

The disciples appear, narratively, only much later, when Jesus departs from Jerusalem and enters the Judean land with them (3,22), and still later when he travels through Samaria (4,8.27.31-38). No mention is made of the fact whether they go with him to Galilee.

As a reader, one must understand from the story as told that the group of disciples has been expanded. In the discussion of the disciples of John (the Baptist) with their master they talk about 'all the people which is going to Jesus' (3,26) and John speaks of 'growing and diminishing' (3,30). And in the beginning of the journey in Samaria it is stated that Jesus has more disciples than John (4,1). These sentences are a preparation for the happenings in chapter 6.

the second journey (5,1-47)

It is most surprising that the disciples do not play any role in this second journey to Jerusalem. Jesus is completely alone. Even in the discussions about the curing of the paralytic the disciples do not appear.

the events in Galilee (6,1-71)

Back in Galilee, it appears that the events in Jerusalem have left a deep impression. The people search for Jesus 'because of the great signs which he did for the sick' (6,2). Also his disciples are now with him. The group has been considerably enlarged. As I have already shown above, chapter 6 is the dramatic turning point in the relationship between Jesus and his disciples. The expansion stops and changes into a reduction: many of his disciples go away εἰς τὰ ὀπίσω (6,66). *The* twelve remain of which Simon Peter is the positive spokesman while Judas takes the place of the devil.

the third journey (7,1-10,39)

As already described, Jesus' *oikos* falls apart. Jesus comes in conflict with his ἀδελφοί. Consequently, Jesus goes to Jerusalem in secret and alone. Only after a number of dramatic events have taken place, the disciples appear to be present, in 9,2, in the story of the curing of the blind man in which discipleship of Jesus plays an important role. In spite of a lot of resistance Jesus finds a new disciple who can see. These events take place on and shortly after the Feast of Tabernacles. On the Feast of the Dedication of the Temple, which is celebrated a couple of months later, (10,22, in the winter) Jesus is presented again as being alone. There are no disciples present, when Jesus is threatened to be stoned.

the fourth journey (10,40-19,42)

Only on this last journey the disciples are more or less constantly in the presence of Jesus. Further on I want to develop the fact that this does not lead to greater intimacy. When Jesus has retired to the spot where he encountered John (the Baptist), his disciples are with him (cf. 11,7ff). From there they accompany him to the *oikos* of Lazarus and his sisters (ch. 11) and from there to Ephraim, the spot close to the desert (11,54). When Passover nears, they are together at the festive meal in Bethany. At least Judas is there and that allows us to surmise that the other disciples were too.

When Jesus enters Jerusalem the next day, it is not so clear whether the disciples are present or not. There is a sentence similar to the one used at the first journey to Jerusalem: 'after his glorification they (the disciples) remembered that this was written about him, and that it had happened'(12,16). The last part ('they remembered that it had happened') is especially significant. The question is how one should translate the οὐκ ἔγνωσαν of the opening sentence: 'they did not know anything about it initially', or 'they did not understand it at all initially'? Against the background of the preceding story the first possibility can not be excluded. The scene in which is described how the Greeks seek contact with Jesus, would fit in with this (12,20ff). The Greeks first go to Philip who then talks to Andrew. Together they present the request to Jesus. Jesus and the disciples are in touch with each other, but there is a certain distance.

The meal scene which follows brings Jesus and the disciples together for a longer textual reality. Chronologically it is a short period only, but textually it occupies 5 chapters (ch. 13-17) and that has its own literary effect.

The notation of the author in 18,2 asks the readers to adjust the image still more. Judas knows where Jesus is because he spent the night more often with his disciples in the orchard across the Cedron. This is the last time Jesus is there with his disciples. From here he will be taken away alone. We know that Peter and another disciple follow him. The beloved disciple stands under the cross together with four women, one of whom is Mary Magdalene. Nicodemus and Joseph from Arimathea, the secret disciple of Jesus, bury him. It is the end of Jesus' journeys.

Schematically I can present it in this way:

text	place	presence of disciples	time
1,35-2,12	Bethany Cana Capernaum	present 5 people +family	*5 days* + *not many days*
2,13-3,21	Jerusalem	absent	Passover feast
3,22-3,36	Judean land	present; expansion of the group of disciples	*indeterminate*
4,1-42	Samaria	present	*2 days + travel time*
4,43-54	Galilee	absent	indeterminate
5,1-47	Jerusalem	absent	feastday
6,1-71	Galilee	present; diminished group of disciples, reduced to 12	close to Passover; *2 days*
7,1-10,39	Galilee 7,1-9	absent; conflict with family	Feast of Tabernacles
	Jerusalem 7,1-10,21	absent; present (from 9,2)	*1 day*
	Jerusalem 10,22-39	absent	Dedication of the Temple

10,40-19,42	Bethany ('of John') 10,40-11,16	present	*indeterminate*
	Bethany ('of Lazarus') 11,17-11,53	present	*1 day*
	Ephraim 11,54-57	present	*indeterminate*
	Bethany ('of Lazarus') 12,1-11	present	*6 days before Passover till evening before*
	Jerusalem 12,12-19,42	present right away or sometime later	*Passover*

The sense of community of the group of disciples is not so strong that Jesus and the disciples are constantly together. Jesus does many things alone. In any case, he does many things in a manner which for the disciples is unintelligible. Especially on the road to Jerusalem and in the city Jesus is presented as being alone. He goes there by himself. He acts independently of his disciples. He comes across disciples who, then, walk with him to Galilee via Samaria; back to the spot of John (the Baptist); to the desert; to Bethany and finally for the last meal in Jerusalem. It looks as if his disciples let themselves be surprised by Jesus time and again. He is beyond their grasp and yet he allows them to come near. In this way the disciples walk with him. Many go back 'behind' but, in their own special fashion a small group remains faithful to Jesus even beyond his death.

This is very important narratively as well as imaginarily. The conflict with the larger group of disciples and, in line with that, also with his own ἀδελφοί creates an enormous isolation. Apart from the *oikos* of Lazarus and his sisters, the disciples are the only people through whom Jesus maintains a positive contact with the world. It makes the only longer period of time in which Jesus and his disciples are together (from 10,40-18,11) into a special event: an island of love, —but Judas is also part of the community—, surrounded by a world full of hatred. One must realise that the relation of Jesus and his beloved disciple originates in this community of male friends. At the beginning of the last table dialogues we hear unexpectedly the emotionally most affective verbalisation of that. This strongly exclusive male orientation which, obviously, is culturally determined, gives again something of the imaginary sense of identity of Jesus.

1.c. the common activities of the disciples

Up to here I have looked at the texts mostly from the perspective of Jesus. One can read the story also from the perspective of the disciples. Then it becomes clear once again that the bond of community was not so intense as to make the disciples want to be together all the time. There is a form of community but the persons retain their individuality. That is most obvious in the story of Jesus' first apparition to Mary Magdalene. She goes first to Simon Peter and then to the other disciple beloved by Jesus i.e. they do not live in the same place (cf. the double use of πρός in 20,2); and at the end of the first part of the story the two disciples go back πρός αὐτοὺς: back to their own places (20,10) (cf. Neirynck 1978, 110-114). The following apparition stories also presuppose an incidental communality: on the evening of the first day of the week the disciples are together, behind closed doors (20,19.24). Eight days later they are again together behind closed doors (20,26). The repetition makes one think; in any case it shows that the disciples were not constantly together.

The text of the Johannine Gospel does not give any other hint to make us think of such a closely knit group. From time to time the disciples gather around Jesus in the manner I have just indicated. I did not pay attention to a phenomenon which, nevertheless, is surprising. Most of the time that Jesus is together with the disciples and/or they are with him, the occasion is, narratively or discursively, a meal:

- 2,1-12: the first formation of the group is concluded with the communal invitation for the festivities of the marriage in Cana.

- 4,8.31-38: on the journey through Samaria the disciples take care of the provisions. The story ends differently from what the disciples had expected, but the food which the disciples went to get determines the dialogue between them and Jesus.

- 6,1-15.22-71: during the people's meal the disciples have a special place. Philip is tested by Jesus. Andrew brings the boy with the five loaves and the two fishes. Jesus asks the disciples to invite the people to sit down and to save the leftovers. The discussion next day with the people about the manna and the bread from heaven ends with the Jesus-sentences about eating 'my flesh' and drinking 'my blood', sentences which for many of the disciples are too hard and which cause them to turn their back on him.

- 12,1-11: the festive meal at Lazarus' house serves as the conclusion of the Lazarus story. Judas is mentioned by name and also the money bag for which he is responsible. The Jesus-group apparently has a source of income which is used for communal expenses. 13,19 describes the function of this money. When Judas leaves the disciples think that he goes to buy 'what is needed for the paschal feast or that he is going to give something to the poor'. The communal money is probably used in Samaria by the disciples; it is also mentioned in the people's meal by Jesus and Philip: what money do we use to buy so much bread; 200 denarii would not be enough (6,6.7).

- 13,1-17.27: the longest story scene in the book is a story about a meal in which Jesus acts as a slave after the meal and enters into a long discussion with the disciples.

- 21,1-14: the Johannine story ends with a meal scene, fish and bread for breakfast on the beach of the sea of Tiberias. The story began with the description of the communal catch of fish. On Peter's initiative the disciples went out to fish together, the whole night, and they did not catch anything. It is the only activity which the disciples performed together in the preceding story: after the people's meal in chapter 6 the disciples got into a boat together. At that occasion too Jesus appeared to them as elusive as now in this story.

The group of disciples is composed of people who individually maintain a large margin of freedom. Jesus is the point of concentration in the story as told. The disciples join him and go with him for a time; i.e. the group of disciples meets on occasion and the composition of the group is variable. The common meals attract the most attention. Judas keeps the money which is used for

communal expenditures and for alms. After Jesus' death the
disciples go on meeting as before: twice in Jerusalem with an 8-day
interval. The last meeting takes place in Galilee.

1.d. the cultural meaning

The opening stories about the beginning of the Jesus-group set the
tone for the whole relation between Jesus and the disciples, as could
have been expected. Jesus carries an aura which has a special effect
on many men in his immediate circle. Through him they come into
contact with one another and this contact becomes constant because
he remains as the centre. But Jesus can not be put in a cadre. In his
own way he keeps the initiative. He is not really at home in this
world. His constant 'being-on-the-go' is a symbol of that. These
journeys are partly determined by the festivities in Jerusalem but
not all of them. He goes around baptising in the Judean land; he
goes away to the other side of the sea of Galilee. Especially
towards the end of the story he retires to the place where John (the
Baptist) preached and to Ephraim near to the desert. It is at that
time that his disciples are for a longer time with him
chronologically. It is a presence which narratively and discursively
comes to a climax in the last meal with his disciples.

I would like to indicate more precisely in which way this unique
imaginary reality is culturally embedded in his own time. The study
of M. J. Wilkins on the concept of $\mu\alpha\theta\eta\tau\acute{\eta}\varsigma$ (1988) is somewhat too
formalistic and, therefore, only of limited value. Starting from a
critical reflection on Rengstorf's $\mu\alpha\theta\eta\tau\acute{\eta}\varsigma$-article from the
Theologisches Wörterbuch, Wilkins checked all Greek and Jewish
texts in which the lexeme /disciple/ appears. He then comes to the
conclusion that

> "In the late Hellenistic period $\mu\alpha\theta\eta\tau\acute{\eta}\varsigma$ continued to be used with
> general connotations of a 'learner' and 'adherent', but it was used more
> regularly to refer to an 'adherent'. The type of adherence was
> determined by the master, but it ranged from being the pupil of a
> philosopher, to being the follower of a great thinker and master of the
> past, to being the devotee of a religious figure. By the time of the third
> century A.D. the term was used by one prolific writer (=Diogenes
> Laërtius) to refer to an adherent.
>
> The progression to 'adherent' in Hellenism at the time of Christ
> and the early church made $\mu\alpha\theta\eta\tau\acute{\eta}\varsigma$ a convenient term to designate the
> followers of Jesus, because the emphasis in the common use of the

term was not upon 'learning', or upon being a 'pupil', but upon adherence to a great master. Hence a 'disciple' of Jesus, designated by the Greek term μαθητής, was one who adhered to his master, and the type of adherence was determined by the master himself. The movement toward *terminus technicus* was almost complete at the time of the gospel writers....

Μαθητής and *talmîdh* appear to be equivalent terms. They were popular terms at the time of Jesus to designate a follower who was vitally committed to a teacher/leader and/or movement. The terms themselves did not determine the type of discipleship; the type of discipleship was determined by the type of leader or movement or teaching to which the disciple was committed. The types of discipleship covered the spectrum from philosophical (Philo) to technical (scribes) to sectarian (Pharisees) to revolutionary (Zealots and Menahem) to eschatological (John the Baptist). The terms were general enough to be used for all of the above. It remained for Jesus and Jamnia to make these terms specialized." (p.217.218.221).

Because discipleship depends on whom or what one adheres to, there remains a real desideratum as to content: in case the type of teacher which ultimately determines the type of disciple. If nothing or almost nothing is said about the content of the type of teacher, the imaginary aspect remains outside the consideration. I believe furthermore that the importance is not so much in questions of origin —which image comes from where—, but rather in the questions of meaning: how should one understand something in a specific context. That, at least, I would like to further elaborate on the basis of these analyses

The Hellenistic and Jewish context are not completely identical in this case. I believe that the use of the double title 'rabbi' and 'διδάσκαλος' in the first sentence which the disciples speak to Jesus is significant. The disciples call Jesus 'rabbi' —i.e. the narrator of the story lets the disciples address Jesus as 'rabbi'—; but the implicit author adds 'that means translated 'master' (διδάσκαλε) (1,38). This difference in narrative communication is true for the whole of the Gospel. Jesus is never directly called διδάσκαλος; he is called rabbi several times (in 1,49 by Nathanael; in 4,31; 9,2; 11,18 by the disciples; in 6,26 by the people; in 20,16 rabbouni by Mary Magdalene), but διδάσκαλος only indirectly (in 3,2 by Nicodemus; in 11,28 by Martha speaking to Mary; in 13,13 by Jesus about how his disciples call him, and in 13,14 by Jesus about himself). This means that on the basis of different contents, a textual identification is made.

Seen against a Jewish background is Jesus a first century rabbi:
- he does not found a school but he allows disciples to come to him. He is recognised by John (the Baptist). That is enough for his first disciples to address him as rabbi. Jesus has linked himself to John (the Baptist) and follows him in word and action. He goes around in the Judean land baptising. When things become too difficult for him in Jerusalem, he retires to the place where John (the Baptist) has preached; and when the threat of death has reached the Sanhedrin, he retires to Ephraim, an even more uninhabitable spot close to the desert. Some of the disciples of John (the Baptist) see this as a matter for conflict: 'he baptises and everyone goes to him' (3,26); not so for John (the Baptist) himself (cf. 3,27ff). There is no competition between rabbi John (for John as rabbi see 3,26) and rabbi Jesus about the disciples (see Abot de R. Natan A 3,6; 8,2; Meg 28a; cf. Stemberger 1979, 86; Krauss 1910-12, III, 220).
- Jesus possesses superhuman powers as rabbi (see 1,49; 6,25). He can be compared in this with rabbi Choni or Chanina ben Dose (cf. Fiebig 1933, 6ff; Vermes 1973, 69ff). That is not to say that there is a complete similarity between the kind of superhuman intervention or in the way that things happen (cf. Kuhn 1988, 441). It means rather that Jewish readers who know rabbis like Choni and Chanina will put Jesus in the category of rabbis with special powers (as e.g. Vermes does!).
- in Jesus' teaching the highest goal is that his disciples 'will be all disciples of God' (6,45), the theologoumenon from Is 54,13 which, in the schooltradition of Israel has had great influence (cf. Wilkins 1988, 50.91.121; Rengstorf TWNT IV, 434ff).
- Jesus admits his disciples into the privacy of his own life, but (cf. supra) he does not take them into his home as co-habitants. They join him in Jerusalem; they act as companions on the trip back to Galilee; they follow him for a short while through Galilee; they share in the last days of his life. That means: this is not the system of a rabbi who takes disciples into his house (as happens from the 2nd, 3rd century on) but rather the system of a rabbi who has disciples because of his teaching like Hillel, Shammai, Jochanan, Gamaliel.

- As disciples they are completely dependent on the teacher. If there is a conflict between the interests of one's father and the interests of the teacher, the latter is given priority. This adds meaning to the way Jesus calls his disciples τεκνία (13,33), cf. BM 2,11: 'his father brought him (=his son) into this world, but his teacher who taught him wisdom brings him into the world to come'. But it gives even more meaning to the title ἀδελφοί, which Jesus uses for them in 20,17 and the implicit author in 21,23.

- Finally something quite extraordinary. In the various stories about a meal the Johannine story often says that they are 'reclining': at the people's meal in 6,10.11; at the meal at Lazarus' place (12,2) and especially at the Last Supper (13,12.23.25.28; 21,20). In as far as these are Pesach meals the mishnah Pes 10,1 is applicable here that 'even the poorest man in Israel must not eat until he reclines'. The *gemara* explains that this is true also for the disciples in the presence of their teacher: "The scholars asked: What about a disciple in his teacher's presence? Come and hear, for Abaye said: When we were at the Master's house, we used to recline on each other's knees. When we came to R. Joseph's house he remarked, 'You do not need it: the fear of your teacher is as the fear of Heaven'" (Pes 108a).

Understood against a Hellenistic background the same data look somewhat different:

- The fact that Jesus is constantly travelling brings him close to all those Greek teachers —cynics, philosophers, sophists, orators etc.—, who go from place to place to teach; who take up residence for a short time in a place as a stranger and then take in disciples. The fact that Jesus does not accept money for his services; that money in any case is not a point for discussion, although it does create some difficulties within the group of disciples; the combination of Jesus' *Heimatlosigkeit* (having no fixed abode) and his constant influence in the political and religious centre of the country makes it possible to see the Johannine Jesus as a representative of the movement of the Cynics. I do not want to suggest that the Johannine Jesus is close to the value systems of the Cynics (cf. the few items in Downing 1988, 186), but I do suggest that he imaginary-narratively is presented as someone who belongs to this movement; or vice versa that the text calls forth this cultural reality for the Hellenistic readers.

- From the use of the title διδάσκαλος in the Lazarus story (11,28) follows that the implicit author sees Jesus as possessing superhuman powers also as a teacher. This opens the possibility for Hellenistic readers to put Jesus in the category of faith healers, magi, prophets, miracle workers, etc. whom we see in the Greek cities. Kuhn (1988, 389ff) has tried once more to combine this with the expression θεῖος ἀνήρ to arrive again at the conclusion that this is not a title for concrete persons (cf. Tiede 1972; Holladay 1977). I suppose that one can not link the phenomenon of miraculous powers to one single title or to a combination of titles. Jesus has access to powers which are beyond other people, because he is imaginarily narratively part of the divine world.

- Most distinctive in relation to the rabbinical atmosphere is the typical selection from the *oikos*-ideology. Jesus calls his disciples φίλοι. As far as I have seen the literature, disciples of a rabbi are never called 'friends'. The Johannine text deals with a special kind of friendship as I will further elaborate later on. In general one can read the text as a story in which the disciples of Jesus act as friends of an *oikos*. Remaining self reliant they are incidentally together with Jesus. Common meals and discussions play an important role. The mutual relationship becomes closer in the last period of Jesus' life and in that period the last supper and the last discussions are a climax. I will discuss that now.

2. JESUS' LOVE FOR HIS DISCIPLES

The more precise development of the texts which follows here is part of the imaginary presentation of the story as told. In that way one could say that this is not a new paragraph; it is embedded in the larger story as I have analysed it above. Selecting the appropriate texts it will explicate further the narrative-affective component of the story. This is concentrated in the scene of the last supper. It is also verbalised there discursively. The lexeme ἀγαπάω —as the specific description of the relation between Jesus and the disciples and the relation of the disciples with one another—, appears for the first time in chapter 13.

2.a. the last supper (13,1-17,26)

We now enter into a text which is, more than any other, poly-interpretable. That is so because of the content of what is said, but also —and this is more important for the reading position of this study—, because of the construction of the narrative isotopy of the text. It is the longest scene in the book. Apart from the washing of the feet and the departure of Judas there are no events that happen. The story as told is an almost endless concatenation of discourses and dialogues where the content of what is said seems more important than the formal setting as a dialogue. The remark at the end of chapter 14: 'arise, let us go' (14,31) to which in the story nobody pays attention, has been understood by exegetes as an invitation to leave the narrative framework. Only recently one has started to read chapters 15-17 again as part of the story as told; however, the attraction of the previous 'theological' reading —Jn 15-17 as a discursive verbalisation of Johannine (or post-Johannine) theology—, remains strong (see e.g. Onuki 1984, 117ff who speaks about the 'sogenannten zweiten Abschiedsrede'; Calloud-Genuyt 1985, 57ff who do not question the alternating of dialogue, discourse, dialogue, prayer).

By truly taking seriously the reading instruction of the author —especially the dialogical character of the text—, and by consistently placing emphasis on the dramatic building up of the text, I want to show that the text has its own narrative course which colours in a special way the relation between Jesus and the disciples. But before we do that, it is good to show how this long story scene is embedded in the wider structure of Johannine narrative. From 11,15 on we see a description of a last week, parallel to the opening scenes of the Gospel. The Bethany story happens 'six days before Passover' (12,1). 'Next day' (12,12) we have the entrance into Jerusalem. The last meal of Jesus with his disciples is 'in the night' (13,30) before 'the day of preparation' of Passover (18,28 and 19,14.31). So, the last meal of Jesus took place two days before Passover.

And what is happening between the fifth and the second day before Passover?
In 12, 20-36 we have the important scene with the Greeks and in 12,44-50 we have Jesus' monologue, two scenes which fit in the fourth and the third day before Passover.
Putting it all together we get:

- six days before Passover: Bethany meal (12,1-11)
- five days before Passover: entrance in Jerusalem (12,12-19)
- (four days before Passover): the scene with the Greeks (12,20-36), and the commentary of the author (12,36-43)
- (three days before Passover): Jesus' monologue (12,44-50)
- two days before Passover: (in the night) the meal, the capture, the interrogation, the betrayal by Peter (13,1-18,27)
- one day before Passover: the interrogation by Pilate, the elevation and burial (18,29-19,41)

- PASSOVER : nothing

- one day after Passover: apparition to Mary Magdalene and the disciples (20,1-23)
- eight days after the first day: apparition to the twelve (including Thomas) (20,24-28)

This list shows how chapter 12 is linked to the following chapters and how central its place is in the construction of the plot of the book. I already showed above how Jesus' being together with the disciples in this period is organised narratively. The disciples (at least Judas) are present at the meal in Bethany. At the entrance into Jerusalem it is not so clear whether the disciples are present. The scene with the Greeks expresses once again the distance between Jesus and the disciples. The scene ends with the sentence that 'Jesus goes away and hides from them' (12,36). In 12,44 follows the 'scream' of Jesus against an anonymous public. On the evening before the day of preparation follows the meal of Jesus and the disciples. Vs 13,29, the sentence which the disciples use to explain why Judas is leaving, —'they thought Jesus had told him to buy what was needed for the Feast'—, shows that the disciples believe that there will be another common meal the next evening. But they are not entirely sure of that as appears from the way the sentence continues: 'or that he was to give something to the poor'. But this does not diminish the fact of their togetherness at this meal.

2.a.1. the washing of the feet (13,1-30)

The opening sentences have created quite a bit of confusion. Grammatically these are sentences which 'carry over', a style figure which is unique for the Johannine text and which brings the readers to peculiar reading strategies. It is used as an argument to divide the book in two parts (in the Dodd tradition, a book of signs and a book of passion/glory), but also to base the division in source material (in the Bultmann tradition, more recently in Richter 1965; Segovia 1982). If one reads the text synchronically, these ways of reading the text do not offer much help. I just showed that 13,1ff is fully integrated narrative-chronologically in the story as told. The extravagant opening sentences of this new scene do not change that. The sentences draw attention because they are expressed in such a special manner: they want to prepare the reader for the special character of the story which follows. Our study focuses on the emphasis of the ἀγάπη of Jesus for his own till the very end, in relation with his journey from the world to the father.

In the discussion of the texts about the beloved disciple one aspect of the following story has already been studied: Jesus has a special friendship relation with one of the disciples. I must now show that this love relationship is embedded in a wider love relationship: the relationship between Jesus and the group of the disciples. In this pericope it is possible to distinguish two narrative levels:

- First we have the level of the story as told: the washing of the feet by Jesus as an act which is ahead of what is going to happen narratively further on in the story: Jesus is prepared to suffer the death of a slave out of love for his disciples. The link is made in the opening sentences: Jesus is aware of everything. He knows he is about to depart and yet his father has put everything in his hands. He gets up from the table and takes off his outer garment, girds himself, puts water in the basin and begins to wash the feet of his disciples. His elevated position and the lowliness of the action clarify the extremity of the road which he is walking. How far Jesus is prepared to go is expressed in a symbolic act: to the very end, as is said in 13,1 (cf. Richter 1965; Brown 1970, 565; Culpepper 1983, 118; Segovia 1985).

- But Jesus' love for his disciples plays also on another text level: on the level where the communication between Jesus and the disciples exists, in concreto in the (implicit) description of the way in which Jesus deals with Peter as the representative of the other disciples. This is the real communicative aspect of the text and in a certain sense it is more important than the content of the story as told, because it functions as a model for the readers' behaviour. Peter is the spokesman for the disciples who are surely of good will, but who do not understand what is going on. The way Jesus acts towards Peter determines, therefore, the way the reader of good will who does not understand too well, feels treated by the main character of the story. It is a level of communication of the text which lies at the base of emotional communication.

The communication between Jesus and Peter runs along three sides in fact. Jesus has taken the initiative to act as a slave, but for Peter this gesture is impossible. His protest is loud and clear. Twice even, and the second time without the title 'Master' (13,8) a title which he always uses scrupulously (cf. 6,68; 13,6.9.36.37; 21,15.16.17). Jesus rejects Peter's protest. The second time is decisive and it makes Peter say: 'Master, then not only my feet but also my hands and my head' (13,9). It is a sentence which is very surprising indeed. But even if it sounds nice to many readers and makes them smile for a short moment, the sentence makes (also) clear that Peter really does not understand Jesus at all. More important yet for the communicative impact is the following answer of Jesus, because the way Jesus deals with Peter's statement determines, according to me, the (imaginary) communication between Jesus and the disciples. How is Jesus reacting? Most surprisingly, Jesus does not object at all. He says: 'if you have taken a bath you need only to wash your feet' (13,10); it means, Jesus does not protest against the complete lack of understanding in Peter. We will meet this again and again: Jesus does not reject anyone of his disciples, however stupid, unwilling, or unbelieving they are.

The continuation of this part of the story of the meal underlines this communication. In the second sub-part (13,12-20) Jesus protects his disciples against future disillusionment evoked by Judas' betrayal; in the third sub-part (13,21-30) the beloved disciple appears unexpectedly in his relation to Jesus, Peter and Judas. These texts are beside the point of view of this part of the study, so I will not treat them here. But it is important to see that the lines of communication continue.

2.a.2. the first dialogues (13,31-14,31)

Most crucial for the interpretation of these texts is the question whether they may be looked at from a dramatic understanding: i.e. whether it is allowed to construct the text into a narrative development line, into a structure which shows some narrative progression. Johannine research is still in a different stage from present day study of Plato. There the dialogue character of the Plato text is (again) taken fully seriously, not because these dialogues show any similarity with what today is understood by the word (partners who react to each other; answers to questions posed; questions which follow a certain logic etc.), but because the text itself is structured dialogically. Plato wrote his philosophy in the form of a story and a dialogue. The modern research on Plato takes this seriously, notwithstanding problems of interpretation. It takes this linguistic form as part of the content of his philosophy (see o.a. Sinaiko 1965; Dörrie 1967; Rosen 1968; Bolotin 1979; Griswold 1986; Price 1989/90).

Johannine research is not yet that far. I do not know of any author who respects the dialogical character of Jn 13-17. One takes note that the disciples ask questions in the Johannine text, but this observation is made only to put it aside immediately and to come with a structure for reading the text which does not pay any attention to the real dialogue character of the text,

so e.g. Woll (1980) who speaks about the 'first farewell discourse' and divides the text in 14,1-3. 4-11. 12-17. 18-24. 25-31; (in 1981: 13,31-14,3. 4-11. 12-24. 25-26);

Segovia (1985) who speaks about a 'first discourse' and divides the text in 13,31-38. 14,1-3. 4-14. 15-27. 28-31;

Calloud-Genuyt (1985) who place a strong emphasis on the cognitive aspect of the text and who read according to the scheme: 13,31-38. 14,1-12. 13-20. 21-28. 29-31; etc.

It seems to be a way of reading which is attractive.

I believe that not only the modern Plato research but also the formal structure of the Plato texts can throw light on the Johannine text. This last text connects in a certain way (also) with a Plato fad of that time —as becomes apparent in certain texts of Cicero, Plutarch and Dio Chrysostom. The Johannine text is, after all, 'a meal text with dialogues'. In classical antiquity one can not then bypass Plato, a reference which is even strengthened by the presence of the beloved disciple. (It is typical that, as far as I can see, the exegetes who connect the farewell texts of John with other farewell texts never consider this meal connection, see especially the most recent and inspiring commentary by Ashton 1991, 443ff in which references to former exegetes). I think that the dialogue observations (in 13,36; 14,5; 14,8 and 14, 22) can/must be taken seriously; I believe that they determine the structure of the text which follows; and that one is invited, as a reader, to construct the narrative structure of the text from these dialogues.

Jesus enters into a dialogue with the disciples. A first (rather poor) communication has been developed. Peter's protest is silenced: the disciples have allowed Jesus to wash their feet. They have been installed by Jesus as a group in which there is a possible readiness to give this kind of slave service also to one another. The beloved disciple lies there to be loved. Judas is the appointed traitor in the group but no one knows that except the beloved disciple. Judas' departure creates confusion. There is a real need to strengthen the internal communication.

The following text deals with two mutually supportive positions: Jesus who knows everything and the disciples who do not understand anything; Jesus who is understanding towards his disciples notwithstanding everything, and the disciples who keep asking stupid but (also for the reader of the story) existentially important questions. Jesus begins with a number of 'base' sentences (13,31-35) which are rather imploring. They indicate (also) how Jesus knows himself to be united with his disciples. They refer to the opening sentences of the farewell meal (via the lexemes /love/ and /depart/, 13,1.3) and to the scene with the Greeks (via the lexeme /glory/, 12,28). The sentences make it even more clear that Jesus is alone: I am going away, and as I told the Judeans (in 7,33.34; 8,21), so I tell you: you can not follow me. The coming dialogues deal with this journey of Jesus, the separation of Jesus from his disciples. Love is indicated as the bond which will overcome the necessary separation. Communicatively the dialogues are about the necessity of the departure and about the possibility to deal with it.

It is a communication which is realised via the telling of four different verbal exchanges: Jesus with Peter, with Thomas, with Philip and with Judas-not-Iscariot, via topics which recur more or less in each dialogue.

Each dialogue opens with a short exchange between the partners; then come each time three or four themes: /faith/; the relation between Jesus and his father; statements about the helper, the spirit of truth; and, finally, sentences about the coming (back) of Jesus (and the father) which lead to the communion between Jesus and the disciples.

dialogue Jesus-Peter 13,36-14,4	dialogue Jesus-Thomas 14,5-7	dialogue Jesus-Philip 14,8-21	dialogue Jesus-Judas 14,22-31
1. the personal exchange 13,36-38	1. the personal exchange 14,4-6	1. the personal exchange 14,8-10	1. the personal exchange 14,22
2. believing 14,1	2. believing 14,6a	2. believing 14,11	5. believing 14,29
3. the relation of Jesus to his father 14,2	3. the relation of Jesus to his father 14,6b	3. the relation of Jesus to his father 14,12-14	4. the relation of Jesus to his father 14,27-28
4.	4.	4. sending the helper, the spirit of truth 14,15-17	3. sending the helper, the spirit of truth 14,25-26
5. the return of Jesus 14,3.4	5. Jesus' presence in the awareness 14,7	5. Jesus'coming in awareness; his revelation 14,28-21	2. the coming of the father and Jesus 14,23-24
			6. closing words of Jesus to the disciples 14,30-31

Taking leave, being on a journey, being absent, finding each other: these are the content of the dialogues. Together at table they speak about going away, about going on a journey and returning. Jesus helps his disciples to come to terms with his departure from this world. That comes back in each dialogue. I would like to go into that level of the text a little further.

- dialogue Jesus-Peter (13,36-14,4)

This dialogue is, more clearly than the others, filled with misunderstanding and naivety. Peter is once again the person who wants to determine grandiloquently and with too much confidence how things are with him. And Jesus is once again the one who sees through this pretence: instead of dying, Peter will betray Jesus three times. Beyond the pretences Jesus encourages the disciples. His going away is not forever. It is not good that Peter's betrayal contributes to the confusion of the disciple, but in the end all will be well. Jesus is in heaven and he will return.

- dialogue Jesus-Thomas (14,5-7)

This very short dialogue connects immediately with the forgoing scene. Thomas repeats Peter's question: 'we do not know where you are going'. His question: 'how then can we know the way?' links up to the sentence with which Jesus ended: 'you know how to get to the place where I am going' (14,4). Communicatively Thomas acts as if Jesus did not answer Peter's question, i.e. he is presented as someone who did not listen! His question then makes clear that he refuses to believe Jesus on his word: there is unwillingness and unreadiness here.

Jesus' reaction is also strange. He does not deal with the threatening break in communication. He preaches the 'good' news, even though there does not seem to be any hope for a change in attitude.

- dialogue Jesus-Philip (14,8-21)

That Thomas' position is not tied to his person is clear from the dialogue with Philip which follows immediately. One of the disciples is again introduced as not understanding, as someone who does not listen to Jesus' words. 'Master, show us the father and that is all we need', he says to Jesus. And Jesus has just said that, who knows him knows the father. Jesus' answer shows that he is not free from emotion with all these misunderstandings: 'For so long I have been with you'; 'how can you say' (cf. Bartholomew 1987, 86). This expression of impatience does not mean that Jesus is not, right away, prepared to give an answer, in sentences which are mostly a repetition of what he said already. Lack of understanding and unwillingness do not affect Jesus readiness to give an answer time and again.

- dialogue Jesus — Judas-not-Iscariot (14,22-31)

For the narrative structure of this scene it is important to notice that, although in a reversed order, the same themes are discussed as in the other dialogues. I have shown that in the scheme before. In Judas' question there is more logic than in the previous ones: Jesus will manifest himself to the disciples, but 'why to us (the disciples) and not to the world' (14,22). It seems a more 'real' question linked to the actual situation of the listeners of the story. Jesus seems not to answer directly. Important is the insight that the election of the Jesus-group is directly linked to the preparedness to keep the commandment of mutual love. It is a kind of circular argument connected with the 'message' of the story: as I have loved you, so you must love one another.

The individual dialogues develop a particular presentation of reality. Jesus helps his disciples to come to terms with his departure from the world. With regard to the content, Jesus realises this by modifying the departure theme into themes of journey, farewell and promises of returning and of helping (cf. Ashton 1991, 452.460ff). Communicatively, something different is going on. The dialogues are characterised by two almost exclusive communicative positions. The disciples are represented as characters who are incapable of understanding and believing the words and answers of Jesus. And Jesus is represented as a character who is not affected at all by this rather negative behaviour. Jesus has the task to eliminate the many barriers of understanding in his disciples. The narrator lets Jesus do this by presenting him as a speaker who patiently and understandingly (but see 14,9) is prepared to repeat again and again so that the good message can penetrate. It is from this attitude of Jesus that the content of what Jesus is saying, gets its importance. Jesus insists in promises of returning and of helping. The story as told does not imply that Jesus has any success in his trials to change his disciples' attitude. Above all, it shows that Jesus is ready to maintain the dialogue till the end.

2.a.3. the major discourse (15,1-16,4)

At this moment in the story Jesus begins a long discourse. If one can speak of a discourse in the meal-story, it begins in 15,1 and it is at the same time the last discourse (notwithstanding the authors who speak about a 'second' or a 'so-called second' farewell address; but see Dodd 1968, 409). The text introduces a particular tone in the farewell meal. More than any other text the mode of narrating fits the level of communication between the narrator and the listeners. Because it is a text which rather directly expresses the theology and the opinions of the group of John, it always receives special attention in Johannine research. More than in other parts of the text one has the conviction that Jn 15 is a later addition coming from a presupposed Johannine school (cf. e.g. Schnackenburg 1984, 153ff who wants to read Jn 15 'im Rahmen der Abschiedsreden' but who is not prepared to go beyond ,'Fragt man, wie es zu dieser zweiten Rede kam, so drängt sich die Vermutung auf, dass man in der joh Schule über die Abscheidsrede des Evangelisten (= Jn 14) weiter nachgedacht und jene Rede (= Jn 15) als Mahnung für die Gemeinde formuliert hat' (p. 162; see also Onuki 1984, 118ff).

This way of treating a text contradicts everything this study takes as point of departure. I want to try to indicate the inner dynamic of the text.

1/ First of all one sees that the text is consistently told from the communicative situation of the farewell meal. Formally, because Jesus as speaker uses in a precise way the right person: 'I' over against 'you' of the disciples who are addressed; the third person singular and plural for all persons who enter as 'discussed personages'. This does not happen frequently in the Johannine Gospel. In this text Jesus does not speak about himself in the third person and even the metaphor of the vine is told in a personified way (see how it can also be done differently in the metaphor of the good shepherd in ch. 10).

Apart from this formal aspect the content of the text refers continuously to what in the preceding part has already been discussed: the table scene of ch. 13 and the dialogues with the disciples of ch. 14. There is a similarity in content in larger pericopes as e.g. between 15,1-10 and 13,1-11 (the unity of Jesus and his disciples) and between 15,11-17 and 13,12-20 (the unity of the disciples among themselves in the commandment of love). Shorter text references also create a bond:

- the statement about the purity of the disciples (in 15,3 and 13,10);

- the sentence about the relation between a slave and the master (15,20 and 13,16);

- the inner communion between Jesus and the disciples (15,4.9 and 14,20);

- the statement about the free access to God via Jesus (15,7.16 and 14,13);

- keeping the commandments and Jesus' words and the promises connected with his words (15,9f and 14,21);

- the coming of the Spirit (15,26 and 14,16f.26).

(cf. Bultmann 1968, 365.506; Onuki 1984, 119ff; Schnackenburg 1984, 160ff).

All these references create a special effect in reading: the reader feels at home. Jesus is consistent in what he is saying.

2/ The manner in which the time scheme is handled is, of course, of primary importance in the readers' construction of the narrative unity. The preceding texts (Jn 13,31-14,31) can be summarised under the term 'farewell texts'. Looking back over Jesus life they look forward to the future in which Jesus will be absent and then present again. It is clear that the long discourse in chapter 15 is not in this sense a farewell text.

There are a number of conditional sentences: about the need to stay in Jesus and about the consequences, if one loses contact with him (15,4.5.6); about the need to keep the commandments and the words of Jesus (15,7.10.14); about the effects of Jesus' coming (15,22.24), but these sentences are not connected with a changing narrative future as in chapter 14. It is not all that important whether Jesus goes away or not. The same sentences could be used in a different narrative context as happens in fact in ch. 9, 10, 11. There is here no real looking into a future in which Jesus will no longer be present (in the same way). The text speaks as if from a present at a standstill: I am the true vine and my father is the gardener. You are clean. The world hates you because I have chosen you out of the world. After all the words about /departure/, /going on a journey/, and /returning/ in chapter 14, the topic is now /remaining/. We see some kind of description of eternity. This is the way it is, this is the way it will be and nothing can change that.

3/ The real model is Jesus' life. The text is full of remarks about Jesus' life, always in sentences which describe it as ended:
- Jesus has loved his disciples (15,9.12);
- He has kept the words of his father (15,10);
- He himself has chosen his disciples (15,16.19);
- He has come and has spoken (15,3.11.15.22; 16,1.4);
- He has performed the works (15,24);
- They have persecuted him and hated him (15,18.20.24).

Jesus' life is closed off and it serves as model and example for the future life of the disciples: as Jesus loved they must love one another; as Jesus was persecuted and hated, so they will be persecuted and hated. This persecution is the only real perspective for the future. This is clear in the text itself. At the end there are some sentences which use a real future tense: they will be banned from the synagogue. They will do that because they do not know me nor my father (16,2.3).

What is the meaning of all this for the narrative incorporation of the long discourse in the whole of the farewell situation? Jesus takes leave. He finds that his disciples do not understand (cf. 13,28) and are fearful (cf. 14,1 and 14,27; for the structural meaning of this 'fear' see Butler 1984). He tries to help them deal with it, but is only partially successful. They do not understand. They do not even listen, but Jesus is persistent. At this moment the long discourse takes place in the story. There is a continual emphasis on the 'good of today': there is contact between the father and Jesus and his disciples. It will depend on them, whether this contact will remain or not. They should know that they can not do anything without Jesus and that there will be ruin, if they lose contact with Jesus and thus with God. Jesus is their friend. He took them into his father's house as friends and not as slaves. He loves them and is even willing to lay down his life for them. They must do what he is asking of them: love each other in the same way as he loved them (cf. 15,11-17, a text to which I will come back). Jesus realises that their situation is not easy. They live in a hostile world. This should not surprise them, because that is exactly what he himself is going through. The shared hatred brings them closer together, because a slave is not above his master. They will receive the support from a helper whom Jesus will send from God, a helper who will testify about Jesus and who will strengthen their communion with Jesus. There will be persecutions and exile and even murder. Jesus has told them this before it happens.

2.a.4. the last table dialogues (16,4-33)

Jesus' discourse ends with the conclusion that the communicative situation is far from good. The narrator makes Jesus say: 'I am going away and no one is asking 'where are you going?' (16,5). The observation is not correct (see 13,36) but seems, after the many words Jesus has spoken, to be necessary to prevent a complete breakdown in communication. If it is not possible for Jesus to remain in contact with his disciples, his offer of love remains an empty offer.

1/ the answer to the question which is not posed (16,4-14)
The disciples are not given a chance to answer because Jesus gives the reason for their silence: 'your heart is filled with sorrow because I have said all these things' (16,6). Following the fear and the uncertainty (ch. 14) and the menace (ch. 15), the sorrow of the disciples is now the narrative reality. Λύπη is a theme which contemporarily is used in various forms of farewell literature (in the pseudo-epigrapha, in Josephus, in Acts, in the poetical literature). It means that the theme of the departure enters the story with new vigour. The last table dialogues resemble the first ones in this.

2/ the answer to the shared dialogue (16,16-28)
Jesus wants to diminish the force of their sorrow. Therefore, he points to the need for his departure. The story makes clear that Jesus' answers do not have the intended effect. The short sentence about 'a short time and you will not see me and again a short time and you will see me again' evokes a long discussion.

It is the first time after a long interval that the disciples are presented as speaking. They have not found much understanding of their situation. They begin to talk together and comment what Jesus has been saying. They bring in the first reproach: 'and no one is asking me where are you going?' And they question each other 'what is the meaning of that short time? We do not know what he is saying.' They do not address Jesus. Jesus knows they want to ask him (16,19) and the narrator lets Jesus repeat the sentence once more.

It is a to and fro which is unique in the Johannine Gospel. It stays in the reader's mind because of the repetitions. It is not so positive for the disciples. They even believe that they can say that they do not know something and that is, against the background of the total text, very negative indeed. Those who do not know, do not enjoy the sympathy of the narrator. But Jesus does not get rattled. He explains it once more. He is consistent in his accepting attitude from start to finish.

3/ the answer to the unexpected statement (16,29-33)
Jesus ends his answer to the disciples with the promise that he 'in that hour' will speak in a clear language about his father and not any more in images (16,25). This promise challenges the disciples to come with a final utterance. But it is a question whether it is all that felicitous. Jesus ended his answer with a very solemn sentence, a short résumé of the whole of the Johannine mythology: 'I did come from the father and I came into the world; and now I am leaving the world and I am going back to the father' (16,28).

It is nothing really new, but the reaction of the disciples seems to indicate that they only now begin to see the light: 'now you speak a clear language without using parables. Now we know that you know everything and that you do not need someone to ask you questions. This makes us believe that you came from God' (16,30). These are rather mysterious sentences which are not all that reliable. The most probable interpretation sees it as grandiloquence, parallel to the pompous words of Peter in the beginning of the table dialogues. The rest of the text shows this. Jesus does not take his disciples on their word. 'Do you believe now? The time is coming that you will be scattered and that each one will return to his own home'. He foresees a time, when the group will disintegrate. The formulation refers back to what happened at the Passover celebration in Galilee when 'the disciples' turned their back on Jesus and were no longer prepared to follow him (6,66). The content points ahead to the future. To the events surrounding Jesus death? In the following story this is not stated expressly, but Peter will deny Jesus three times and, apart from the beloved disciple, none of the disciples will be under the cross. Is he the only disciple who is faithful to Jesus till his death?

This desertion does not have any influence on Jesus. He remains. He is not even alone, because his father remains with him. The disciples must know that Jesus is not perishing. He is the victor over the world. 'Do not be afraid; I have defeated the world'. Fear and sorrow can be kept in check against the backdrop of this victory.

2.a.5. Jesus' prayer (17,1-26)

If the proposed interpretation of the meal story has any basis —as far as I can find in the literature, it is really terra incognita—, the text has a dramatic structure, not paralleled anywhere. Jesus uses all possible means to win the love of his friends. He is an active lover who is leaving no stone unturned with these men, but ultimately he remains alone with his offer of love. His disciples keep asking the wrong questions. Their last statement about their own insight and their knowledge of Jesus sounds pretty good, but Jesus does not trust it. He sees no other way than to go back to his father: i.e. to his own imaginary world from which he can again face reality.

Jesus' prayer is an act of communication with his father who is, obviously, addressed as God-father, but also with those present who are addressed and about whom he speaks. If one wants to show how the text of chapter 17 is embedded in the communicative situation of the story as told, it is not enough to show which farewell themes still play a role in the text (see Onuki 1984, 167ff). One must look at the whole of the communicative context. In question is the imaginary contact between Jesus and his father and how this is brought up at a moment, when the dialogue between Jesus and the disciples is finished. In question is also the contact between Jesus and the disciples which they want but which Jesus judges impossible for them, and how it is still offered from Jesus' side.

Jesus' prayer is the concluding climax of the meal story. It is a text which is surrounded by mutually contradictory commentary texts. I can not go into this now in all its implications, but I would like to take a few points which are relevant for the narrative development of the relation between Jesus and his disciples.

1/ the name of God is manifested (17,6-8)
Following the opening sentences which evoke the relation between Jesus and his father, Jesus begins to speak with his father about 'the people from the world whom you have given me' (17,6), i.e. the

disciples who are with Jesus. In the total context of the prayer it is not strange that Jesus talks about the disciples. It is different, however, when one realises the content of what Jesus says. The disciples are presented as the perfect listeners and the perfect followers of Jesus:

- Jesus manifested to them the name of the father (17,6);
- they have kept the word of the father (17,6);
- they know now that everything-in-Jesus comes from the father (17,7);
- they have accepted the words of the father (17,8);
- they have recognised that Jesus comes from the father (17,8);
- they have believed that Jesus is sent by the father (17,8).

These are statements about the disciples which are really beyond belief. Nothing in the preceding story justifies such a conclusion. The discussion between Jesus and the disciples certainly does not give any basis to speak about them in this way. It is arguments like these which bring exegetes to take the whole prayer out of the communicative story context. One says that chapter 17 is the climax of the theology of John (cf. Ritt 1979) or that Jesus is speaking in the midst of the Johannine community as the glorified one (cf. the Bultmannian expression 'nicht der 'historische Jesus' spricht, sondern historisch gesprochen: die Gemeinde; aber in der Gemeinde spricht ja er selber als der δοξασθείς' (1968, 401). Without denying this, I think one should accept also the context of the story. The disciples have not understood anything about Jesus so far. They have not yet given any real confession about Jesus and yet, Jesus now speaks in these extraordinary sentences about their insight, their knowledge and their faith. Presupposing that the narrator is not trying to present Jesus as a liar or a dreamer, this means communicatively that *Jesus* accepts his disciples no matter what. In all their failed attempts, he realises that they have come to faith and to insight. The sentences show an impressive accord with the message of the author which has been discussed widely in the meal story: seen from the point of view of Jesus, his disciples can not do wrong. He knows them to be better than they are in fact. He loves them till the very end. The narrator of the story presents this attitude of Jesus to his listeners: whatever is the matter with you, Jesus will stand by. It anticipates in a way the last story of Peter where Jesus keeps asking Peter whether he loves him; the story which ends with the statement by Peter: 'Lord, you know everything, you know that I love you' (21,17) (cf. more or less Okure 1988, 218 who distinguishes from another perspective the two standpoints upon which the text is composed: "From the father's standpoint, therefore, these verses are intercessory, but from that of the disciples who are listening they are hortatory").

2/ Jesus prays for his disciples (17,9-19)
If ἐγὼ περὶ αὐτῶν ἐρωτῶ of 17,9 next to οὐ περὶ τούτων δὲ ἐρωτῶ μόνον κτλ of 17,20 can be seen as reader instructing pointers, —many authors do this; for a résumé of the older ideas, see Becker 1969; supplemented by Ritt 1979, 92-146, but, obviously, nothing can be said to be obligatory here—, then the text is organised in a tripartite way: 17,1-8. 9-19. 20-26. In the middle part (17,9-19) Jesus becomes active in his role as intermediary for the disciples. He distinguishes between his disciples and the world, because they have been given to him by his father from the world. The farewell sounds, therefore, more clearly than before:

I am no longer of the world (17,11);
I go to you (17,11);
when I was still with them (17,12);
now I go back to you (17,13).

Jesus foresees a difference between now and the time to come, a difference which has to do with his departure, not with the situation itself. Because, as the disciples are in the world, so it was with Jesus: in the world but not of it, supporting each other against the hatred of the world. It is a very special bond which the disciples must forge, a relationship which belongs to the relationship between the father and Jesus himself. The heavenly things are a model for the group of disciples.

The formulation of verse 15: 'I do not ask that you take them from the world, but that you protect them from evil' creates a division in the text: the first part is about living in the world, the second about the separation between the holy and the evil. In both passages we find a proper prayer imperative:

keep them in the name which you have given me (17,11);
sanctify them in the truth (17,17).

These are two rogatory sentences which —cf. de la Potterie 1977, 721ff—, are structural-narratively and semantically closely interrelated.

Jesus spoke already about the name of God. In the preceding prayer sentences he said: 'I have made your name manifest to the people from the world you have given me' (17,6). He returns to that in a slightly different setting. Jesus now says that a name has been given him and he asks his father to keep the disciples in that name. Which name can that be? De la Potterie (1977, 724ff) advocated that John meant the name 'father'. Jesus would have manifested the name 'father' and he would be asking the father to protect his disciples in the name 'father'. I think de la Potterie under-interprets the expression ᾧ δέδωκάς μοι. Vs 17,11 is about a name of God given to *Jesus* and this name is so powerful that it becomes a place of asylum for the disciples, a safe place where they will be protected against the hatred of the world.

I believe then that it can only be the name of God I AM (cf. Brown 1976, 764ff). First of all it is a name to which Jesus has a right; which he manifested to his disciples as a proper name of God; and thirdly, which did give protection and will give protection against the powers of the world. One could think of the story of the walking on the water (6,6-12), but even more of the story which follows immediately, the capture of Jesus in the orchard of the Cedron (18,1-11). The soldiers ask for Jesus from Nazareth, and Jesus answers them: 'I AM'. They move back and fall to the ground. The disciples are all saved, 'because the word must be fulfilled: of those you have given me no one is lost'. Precisely that is expressed in this prayer: 'I kept them safe in your name and not one of them was lost except the son of perdition' (17,12; even in detail it is clear the prayer belongs in this context). It is about this name of God that Jesus asks his father that it may protect and save his people, because in that name they will recognise that Jesus and the father are one.

The second part of this passage fits perfectly. It is about Jesus' request that the father may 'sanctify the disciples in the truth', the truth which is nothing else than the word of the father. Ἁγιάζω evokes in biblical language the opposition between /the holy/ and /the evil/ (cf. 17,15). Sanctification means to set something apart for God, take something out of the profane world to dedicate it to the divine. Whether a relation should be created with sacrificial practices, in conjunction with ὑπὲρ αὐτῶν in 17,19, —Jesus who sanctifies himself on the cross for his father; who places himself, as victim, completely at the disposition of the divine—, has been denied rightly by de la Potterie (1977, 756ff). The connotation with 'Holy Israel' i.e. Israel which belongs exclusively to God, is far more important. Jesus asks his father that the disciples may be 'holy' i.e. 'like Israel, exclusively belonging to God': while remaining in the world to be free from evil. The last rogatory sentence (17,17) is a pendant of the previous one (17,11). When the name of God I AM is as a wall around the group of disciples and protects and guards them, they are God's own exclusive property. Jesus has been sent by God into the world as a foreign element, a heaven on earth. In the same way he sends his disciples into the world, as 'sanctified by God', as people who are cloaked with the name of God.

3/ an unending perspective (17,20-26)

Rather unexpectedly Jesus broadens the actual narrative context in the third and last part of the prayer to the future as well as to the past. Jesus looks forward to the people who will believe in him because of the word of the disciples and he looks back to the time before the foundation of the world. The perspective widens in such a way that 'the faith of the world' (17,21) and the 'knowledge of the world' (17,23) appear on the horizon, in connection with the activities of the father-God himself, his benevolence towards the world which he demonstrated by sending his son into the world as an expression of his love for his own.

This is about a future which is based in the past: the oneness of father and son as the model for the future oneness of God and world, mediated by the bond between the Jesus-group and the God-father of Jesus. Jesus looks ahead and sees that the disciples will go around announcing the word and that they will gather co-believers. The sentences are directly linked to the vision of the future which is the vision of the narrator of the story. There is a link with the commentary which he gave in connection with the session of the Sanhedrin about the prophecy of Caiaphas: 'because Caiaphas was the High Priest for that year he prophesied that Jesus would die for the people, and not only for the people but to bring all the scattered children of God together' (11,51ff).

Jesus' death opens a future which is important for all God's children. It will bring these people together in a unity which, as the text says, is modelled on the unity between the father and the son. Jesus has recourse to heavenly realities once again to move his father to action. The unity between father and son is origin and end for the Jesus-group in this world. On his journey towards the world Jesus showed this bond between him and the father. That was his task; it was also his honour. Through this bond he was able to hold his own in the world. Therefore, he wishes this also for his followers. In the far future there is the perspective that the world will believe in the divine origin of Jesus and that it will come to the knowledge of the mutual love between father and son. If the Jesus group becomes one, part of the oneness of father and son, the world will no longer be able to resist. It will desist from its 'anti'-attitude and be open for the word of liberation and eternal life.

Referring to the opening sentences of the meal story (13,1-3), the word ἀγάπη falls in this context for the last time, but now against the perspective of the love which Jesus showed in his words and actions. Desire for eternity plays a major role here: the love of the father for Jesus who exists from before the foundation of the world (17,24); the love of the father for the disciples as the ultimate aim of the knowledge of the world (17,23); the presence of the love of the father for the son in the disciples as the aim of the manifestation of God's name (17,26).

I think that readers who till now have been led by the proper meaning of the meal story will not be too surprised by this emphasis on love at the end of the story. That proper meaning is, precisely, to be found in this love of Jesus for his own. Jesus stands by them till the end, even though they let him down and fall short in understanding, but not in readiness. He has taken them into his love and he is faithful to that. He bases himself on the eternal love of his father for him. That love kept him alive and it is the basis of his relationship with the disciples in the hope and the expectation that they will, therefore, also love one another; that even the world will be convinced of the power of love: the heavenly love which takes in even the world, the heavenly love as the origin and the ultimate aim of the world to wit the world which originated from the love of God and is destined to be taken up into that love again.

2.b. giving his life for his friends (15,12-17)

Jesus has bound himself to his disciples unconditionally. His not so active role in calling them does not prevent him from being the active one when it comes to love. In the imaginary presentation

Jesus saves this love: without his active role little more than misunderstanding, incomprehension and unwillingness would have been left. In his fidelity in offering his love Jesus wins victory over all the deficiencies of the disciples.

To close this description of the love-relationship between Jesus and the disciples I would like to look into 15,12-17 a bit more. I believe that it is a text which refers, discursively, to all the previous themes and which, in any case, shows their ultimate consequences. I want to distinguish two levels of interpretation.

2.b.1. the basic metaphor

Jn 15,12-17 is an extraordinary text which has not been given much attention by the exegetes (see esp. Dibelius 1927/1953; Grundmann 1959; Stählin TWNT s.v. φίλος; Thyen 1979). Apart from Stählin who, at any rate, brings in the *amicitia* literature, no one mentions the importance of the basic metaphor, the specific relation between the text and the, then, current *oikos* ideology. Jesus imaginarily accepts one of the conditions for a complete *oikos*, because he calls his disciples 'friends'. Apart from possessions (house, land, slaves) and wife and children, 'friends' are seen as part of an *oikos* (Callicratides, 'it is fitting for an important man not only to have a lot of possessions and relatives, but also to have a large number of friends' in Stobaeus IV.28.16 p. 683; and cf. Perictyone, in Stobaeus IV.28.19 p. 688; connecting with the more elaborate *amicitia* literature of Cicero, Seneca and Plutarch, following the classical treatises by Plato, Aristotle and Xenophon). A man's friends are part of his *oikos*. They determine the social position of the *oikos* and are determined by it. The greater and more important the *oikos* is, the more numerous and important are the friends; but also the more important it is to be a friend of the *kyrios* of such an *oikos*.

Jn 15,12-17 presupposes imaginarily a powerful *oikos* with a father-*kyrios* who heads a household in which the son plays an important role as mediator between selected friends and the absolute sovereignty of the father. Let me put the data together:

- the son loves his father and is obedient to all the commandments of the father (15,9.10);
- the son is prepared to select some people and to make them his friends. He allows them to enter into the intimacy of his father:
  - he does not call them slaves but friends (15,15);

- he tells them everything he has heard from his father (15,15);
- they know everything that happens in the house and esp. they know what the *kyrios* does (15,15);
- they are allowed to approach the father and if they ask him something in the name of the son, the father will give it to them (15,16).

- the love of the father for his son serves as the model for the love of the son for his friends (15,9),
- in the same way the obedience of the son to the father serves as a model for the obedience of the friends to the son (15,12.14.17).

Because Jesus himself is speaking, we are narratively in the imaginary order of the second degree. Jesus knows that he is in the service of the *oikos* of his heavenly father. Choosing disciples and making them his friends he enlarges the *oikos* of his heavenly father. He allows these people to enter into the covenant of love and obedience which exists between him and his father. As far as he himself is concerned he is willing to lay down his life for his friends to prove this. That is the most typical sentence of the whole text. It is also the sentence which connects the narrative-*real* situation of Jesus and his friends with the narrative-*imaginary* situation of Jesus in relation to his heavenly father.

2.b.2. *the ethical philosophical embedding*

The sentence about 'the greatest love' is spoken narratively by Jesus on the eve of his death. The narrator thus places the death of Jesus in the perspective of this saying: Jesus' death is an expression of the highest which is attainable in loving. He does not make Jesus speak in the first person, but lets him use a kind of adage which evokes a feeling of self-evidence: everyone knows that greater love is not possible than that someone lays down his life for his friends.

As far as I have been able to verify in my research, this is a literary fiction. Stählin supposes that it is a topic from the *amicitia* literature as are expressions like μία ψυχή; κοινὰ τὰ φίλων; ἰσότης φιλότης (cf. Arist Eth Nic IX.8.2). But that is not the case. Jn 15,13 seems to be rather a kind of résumé by the author on the basis of a philosophical ethic which is common to almost all philosophy schools in Greek-Hellenistic antiquity. I will put the data together:

Plato:

Plato introduces the topic of dying for friends in two places: in the discourse of Phaedrus in favour of Eros in the *Symposium* (Symp 178a-179c) and in the *Apologia* of Socrates (Apol 28b-c). Phaedrus wants to prove the magnificence of Eros and he does it by pointing out that only Eros can make people die for one another: Alcestis for her beloved husband and Achilles for Patroclus. Plato is interested in the imaginary possibility that someone would be willing to lay down his life for someone else. Love for each other can make people do it: 'to die for one another is only possible for people who love, not only men but also women' (Symp 179b).

In the *Apologia* text love has no place. Achilles is again used as an example, but now as a model for Socrates' death whose deeds are just and good, even if they can cost him his life. The male courage in battle is the real point of comparison: "For thus it is, men of Athens, in truth; wherever a man stations himself thinking it is best to be there, or is stationed by his commander, there he must, as it seems to me, remain and run his risks, considering neither death nor any other thing more than disgrace" (Apol 28d)

Aristotle:

In Aristotle's text (Nic Eth IX 8.9) these two things come together. He says: "Truly, the honourable person does many things because of his friends and his country; if necessary, he will even die for them." The πατρίς joins the friends. The saying is in the context of the problem of the well understood love of self (cf. Price 1989/90, 118ff who explains the philosophical problem). The good person is capable of giving up everything for the sake of a friend. The better he is, the greater is his willingness to give up things, because he strives for the good. This enables him to strive for a short and intense pleasure instead of wanting the little but long lasting joy: better to live one year honourably (καλῶς) than many years without honour. In Aristotle's view the acquisition of such honour is necessary because of the need of proportionality between giving and receiving. Love demands some form of equality. The giving of one's life is proportionally set off against the receiving of the honour (cf. Jn 15,7; 13,31?).

Epicurus:

Three texts, where friendship is at stake, can be attributed to Epicurus with some probability (cf. Long-Sedley 1987, I, 126/127/ 133; II, 132/133/141).

- from Plut., Against Colotes 1111B: "Though choosing friends for the sake of pleasure, he (Epicurus) says he takes on the greatest pains on behalf of his friends."

- Vatican sayings nr 28: "Neither those who are over-eager for friendship nor those who are hesitant should be approved, but it is also necessary to take risks for the sake of friendship."

- from Diogn. Laër., X.120: "Epicurus on the wise man: And he will on occasion die for a friend."

From the context from which I bring these text the most amazing thing is that Epicurus does not connect the demands of friendship and the demands which come from the $\pi\alpha\tau\rho\acute{\iota}\varsigma$ or $\pi\acute{o}\lambda\iota\varsigma$. (cf. the Jn text where this is absent too, in contradistinction to Plato, Aristotle and Epictetus). Long-Sedley write:

> "It is tempting to think that the necessary connection between living pleasurably and living honourably is best illustrated by the activities of friendship ... Living honourably ($\kappa\alpha\lambda\tilde{\omega}\varsigma$), in ordinary Greek, has a powerful political ring (cf. Aristotle, Eudemian ethics I.5.1216a25). In Epicureanism that resonance is rejected in reference to conventional public life, with the value of friendship correspondingly enhanced. Thus in microcosm the Epicurean Garden community anticipated the time when 'everything will be full of justice and mutual friendship' (Diogenes of Oenanda new fr 21.1.4)" (Long-Sedley 1987 I,138).

Stoa:

It is well known that from the very beginning the Stoic authors contributed to the *amicitia* literature. Only minor texts have been preserved and they do not speak about friendship being at stake. In fact only two texts are known from the Hellenistic-Roman period:

- Seneca, Ep I.9.10: "Why do I seek someone's friendship? So as to have someone for whom I would be willing to die. So as to have someone whom I would be willing to follow in exile, against whose death I would protest and for whom I would sacrifice myself."

- Epictetus, Ench 31,1: "Hence, when it is your duty to share the danger of a friend or of your country ($\pi\alpha\tau\rho\acute{\iota}\varsigma$), do not ask of the diviner whether you ought to share that danger. For if the diviner forewarns you that the omens of sacrifice have been unfavourable, it is clear that death is portended, or the injury of some member of your body, or exile; yet reason requires that even at this risk you are to stand by your friend, and share the danger with your country."

In both texts there is a connection between friendship and the situation of the πατρίς: in the Seneca text negatively via the mention of exile and the enforced death (the text is written in 63/64 under Nero!); in the Epictetus text also positively.

Pythagoreans:

We do not have to worry here about the problems of dating Pythagorean texts. The story of the Pythagorean Damon, ready to give his life for his friend, is contemporarily told in many different versions. We may take it that in the period which is relevant for us, this exemplary story is well known as part of the Pythagorean heritage. I give the version which Cicero uses:

"They say that Damon and Phintias of the Pythagorean School, enjoyed such ideally perfect friendship, that when the tyrant Dionysius had appointed a day for the execution of one of them and the one who had been condemned to death requested a few days' respite for the purpose of putting his loved ones in the care of friends, the other became surety for his appearance, with the understanding that if his friend did not return, he himself should be put to death. And when the friend returned on the day appointed, the tyrant in admiration for their faithfulness begged that they would enrol him as a third partner in their friendship." (De off 3,45; for the other versions see Cicero, Tusc Dis 5,63; Diod Sic X.4.1-6; Val Max IV.7 ext 1; Hyginus Fab 257 —using the names Moerus and Selinuntius; Jambl. Vit Pyth 33.234-236).

The context of the story is explicitly political, but, as with the Epicureans, love for one's country does not play a role.

Returning to the Johannine text a couple of things seem to me important for the meaning of the text:

- The main difference between the Johannine text and all other texts is the fact that the Johannine text deals with a narratively 'real' event which is not true in any of the other texts: i.e. Jesus does what the philosophical ethic demands. The intention of the sentence runs parallel with the description of the love relationship between Jesus and the beloved disciple. As the highest ethical ideal becomes reality in the relationship between Jesus and his beloved disciple, so Jesus realises in relation to his disciples the highest that can be found in the ethical field as ideal behaviour.

- It seems to me also important that the Johannine text does not mention the love for the πατρίς. In this the Johannine text follows the movement in the Epicureans and especially the Pythagoreans. There is a political context —Jesus' death happens in the centre of political power—, but the love for one's country does not play a role. As I will develop in a moment, discussing the mutual love in the circle of friends, this does not mean that there are no political implications. Far from it. The group of friends will function as the real πόλις (cf. the explanation of Long-Sedley of the Epicurean Garden). The devaluation of the one political reality creates the re-evaluation of the social reality which supplants it.

- Jn 15,12-17 is the affectively most poignant statement about the relationship between Jesus and his disciples. This has nothing to do with soldier heroics (contra Dibelius 1927/53, 204ff, cf. Thyen 1979, 467ff), but it has everything to do with the readiness of Jesus to commit himself totally, in obedient love for his father, to gather the scattered children of God in unity (cf. 11,52). The text imaginarily determines —obviously in connection with all that precedes—, in a way as happens in the relation between Jesus and John (the Baptist) and between Jesus and the beloved disciple, the affect of Jesus' social role in his relation to his disciples. Jesus is prepared to put his life at stake for this group of men-friends knowing that this is the highest form of love. He actively loves men. In classical culture this reinforces the male code. In the culture in which I live such a culture of male friendship is brushed aside —except in gay circles. The silence of the exegetes on this phenomenon is again symptomatic: it runs parallel with the silence within this culture of the positively evaluated male friendships.

2.c. Peter's love for Jesus (21,15-19)

The scene at the end of the book in which Jesus asks Peter three times whether Peter loves him, belongs in a way to the transition between the description of Jesus' love for the disciples and the mutual love of the disciples among themselves. It is a special scene in the whole of the NT. As Bartholomew (1987, 77ff) shows, there is an intrinsic connection with the pericope about laying down one's life for one's friends, which we just discussed. Because Jesus' triple question 'do you love me?' points back to Peter's triple negation (in 18,15-27), the scene refers also to 13,36-38 where Peter assures Jesus that he will lay down his life for him, while Jesus predicts that Peter will deny him three times. Jesus' love has made the high stakes come true. Peter's love has failed. That does not mean that all is lost. Three times Peter is appointed as shepherd over the flock, an assignment which carries with it the demand that one be ready to lay down one's life for the sheep. If we place the Greek sentences in line is becomes clear how the same line of thought determines the thinking:

13,37: τήν ψυχήν μου   ὑπὲρ σοῦ   θήσω
13,38: τὴν ψυχήν σου   ὑπὲρ ἐμοῦ   θήσεις
15,13: τὴν ψυχὴν αὐτοῦ θη   ὑπὲρ τῶν φίλων αὐτοῦ
10,11: τὴν ψυχὴν αὐτοῦ τίθησιν ὑπὲρ τῶν πρωβάτων

Jesus opens the future anew for Peter. The failure to lay down his life for Jesus out of love for him, is not definitive. Peter is given a new chance. The closing sentences of this scene (21,18.19) make clear that the narrator speaks from a perspective 'post factum', knowing the end of Peter's life. In a solemn sentence Jesus predicts how things will be with Peter. The very precise contradistinction /young — old/, /fasten your own belt — someone else will fasten your belt/, /go where you wish — go where you do not want to go/, is mysteriously broken by the addition 'you will stretch out your hands'. Because this sentence has no parallel, it is a key expression for the listeners. Jesus does not speak about the opposition young man — old man, but there is some 'deeper' meaning.

I am not so sure whether the listeners to the story would manage to see this meaning without further commentary of the author. Anyway, the author does explain in 21,19 that Jesus meant to speak about the death of Peter. The description of the old man which is not really correct —there are not many cultures where old people are constantly brought to places where they do not want to go—, is an allegory of death on the cross. Stretch out one's hands is the main signal: the crucifixion itself. What, textually, follows —the tying and being led to a place where one does not want to go—, precedes in the reality of a crucifixion (cf. Brown 1970, 1107).

The writer's certain knowledge indicates that he knows about Peter's death. He uses the same expression as in Jesus' death (see 12,3;18,32). In the story as told this means that Peter in fact followed Jesus in his death and that he fulfilled what Jesus asked of him: follow me (21,19). Peter's love for Jesus has not failed him any more after the apparition in Galilee.

But in the story as it has been told up to 21,19, things are different. If my interpretation of 20,2 is correct —Peter as the one disciple whom Jesus loves, apart from the beloved disciple as the other disciple whom Jesus loves—, Peter is the only disciple, apart from the beloved disciple, of whom it is said, at least indirectly, that the love of Jesus is personally directed to him. Peter is in any case the only one in whose love Jesus has an interest.

In contradistinction to the beloved disciple who remained faithful to Jesus till his death, Peter 'earned' Jesus' interest because of his failure in the house of the High Priest (18,12-27). This is a scene which has a unique structure in the Johannine Gospel. Nowhere else the narrator interweaves his story as in this episode: question-denial-question-denial. Probably it is an attempt to set the synchronism of the events: while Jesus is being interrogated and gives his testimony, Peter gives his counter testimony.

Every reader will unravel this simultaneity again, although that is not really correct. For the two narrational fragments are not only in time but also in content related. While the High Priest interrogates Jesus about his disciples (18,19) and Jesus tells him that he spoke in public and that the High Priest can ask anyone about it, Peter says immediately upon entering to the portress that he has nothing in common with Jesus. Peter's denial makes Jesus' testimony untrue.

This is even more distressingly true in the second answer Jesus gives. One of the High Priest's servants has slapped Jesus in the face because of his answer. Jesus says then: 'if I said something wrong, find a witness; but if I am right, why do you hit me?' (18,23). Immediately after Jesus says this, Peter negates the statement: I am not one of his disciples; I was not in the garden. The only one who is asked to testify, refuses to answer and even denies that he has anything to do with it. There are no witnesses who speak for Jesus. He stands alone. The crowing of the cock shows that Jesus knew it beforehand (cf. 13,38).

This interpretation colours 21,15-19. Jesus and Peter have shared an experience which is still not finished. Bartholomew (1987) points out that, for the interpretation of the scene about Peter's love for Jesus, the way the emotional quality is understood, is decisive. The dialogue gets a different meaning, whether Jesus is supposed to be angry or to be sad. Peter's sadness when Jesus asks him for the third time whether he loves him (21,17), brings me to an interpretation which supposes a certain sadness also in Jesus himself. Anger evokes anger or fear or uncertainty in the partner. The table dialogues, the last sentences Jesus spoke to his disciples, somehow play a role: 'do you believe now; see the hour will come ... that you will leave me alone' (16,31.32), a prophecy which refers especially to Peter. And its fulfilment will not be a cause for joy. The love of Peter to which Jesus now appeals, points to a need in Jesus (cf. a similar need in God who 'searches' for people who will honour him in spirit and in truth 4,23), to a desire for the love of another, concretely here Jesus' desire for the love of his friend Peter.

In his answer Peter appeals three times to the 'knowledge' of Jesus. That must be a knowledge as expressed by Jesus in 17,6-8, a knowledge which, bypassing actual behaviour, sees more deeply a communion in love which is present notwithstanding shortcoming and failure. The continuity of mutual love depends on the imaginary knowledge which is prepared to overlook actual incongruous behaviour. In his answer Peter appeals to that knowledge which is better, because it is based on love. We could think of a text like 1Jn 3,20 in the interpretation which sees expressed here the mercy of God: 'and before Him we shall calm our heart as to whatever our heart might condemn us for, because God is greater (in forgiving) than our heart and knows all things' (cf. Brown 1983, 459), a sentence which is placed in the context of laying down one's life for the brethren! (1 Jn 3,16) and in the context of the saying that in loving not the word and the mouth are important but the acts and the truth, 'let us not give lip service to our love with words but show its truth in deeds' (1 Jn 3,18). I am not interested to prove any form of textual dependency. I am interested in a parallel thought structure. What in the letter is attributed to God, is presupposed by Peter to exist in Jesus: a knowledge which accepts the presence of love even if the deeds do not prove it. The closing sentences in 21,18.19 show that Peter as well as Jesus, at least post factum, are right.

3. MUTUAL LOVE

As I pointed out in the beginning of this chapter the love relationship between Jesus and the disciples has a layered reality. Jesus calls his disciples friends and he acts accordingly as I just showed. At the same time Jesus *asks* that his disciples will behave in mutual friendship. This mutual love has, therefore, narratively a quite different structure. It plays mostly on the level of an imperative, the level of what Jesus imposes as a command/task/law. That is also a narrative reality, but it points towards a future beyond the story itself; a future which in the story is only inchoate. In a final paragraph I will describe this onset of mutual service. I start with a description of the narrative structure of the Jesus-imperative itself.

3.a. the commandment of mutual love

From what has been said, one could draw the conclusion that the command of Jesus about mutual love is only expressed discursively, in sentences which prescribe in the imperative that the disciples must love one another. That is only true up to a point. The first time Jesus pronounces this commandment, it is part of an explicit narrative context which gives it a special colour.

It is the scene of the washing of the feet (13,1-30), specifically what in my way of reading is the second part of this story: 13,12-20. This sub-story has been a bone of contention for a long time in scientific exegesis. The transition from the first scene to the second is, indeed, confusing. While the dialogue between Jesus and Peter indicates that the act of the washing of the feet is indeed unique, an act of humiliation which can be understood only after the exaltation of Jesus, here in the second dialogue we find an act which can be repeated and which is given by Jesus as a commandment to his disciples —'you must wash each other's feet'—, vs 13,14 as a model whose meaning is immediately accessible —, 'as I did to you, so you must do to one another'— (13,15) (cf. Segovia 1982, 46).   Linguistically speaking it means that after the indicative form which the first part of the story is told —Jesus presents a sign (13,1-11)—, an imperative follows in the second part of the story —the sign must be seen as a model (13,12-20). This combination of indicative and imperative is well known in Pauline literature. As a narrative phenomenon it is unique for John. Discursively, however,

we can think of those καθώς - οὖτως sentences which imply a
future tense: as I (am), so you must (be):
- 13,34:as I have loved you,
           so you too must love one another.
- 15,4 :Just as a branch can not bear fruit by itself without
           remaining on the vine,
           so neither can you without remaining in me.
- 15,10:Just as I have kept my father's commandments and remain
           in his love,
           you will remain in my love, if you keep my
           commandments.
- 15,12:Love one another
           as I have loved you.
- 17,11:That they may be one
           just as we.
- 17,21:That they all may be one,
           just as you, father, in me and I in you.
- 17,22:That they may be one,
           just as we are one.

A similar καθώς sentence is central also in the story of the
washing of the feet: 'I set you an example so that you may do just
as I have done for you' (13,15). Immediately it is about the
washing of feet. Jesus appeals to the actual mutual relationship:
'you rightly call me Lord and Master and I am'. But he uses this to
point to the future: 'as I did, so you too must wash each other's
feet' (13,14). The text suggests, according to me, that there is more
to it than just the washing of feet (although, see 1 Tim 5,10). The
narrator makes Jesus return to the opposition between slave and
master, between the sender and the one sent. With that he intends
(at least) to say that the mutual conversion structure is also part of
the task set. The narrator makes Jesus say: if I, although I am your
teacher and Master, have made myself a slave, then you must also
be prepared to be each other's slave, because you are not higher
than I am. Jesus makes his disciples each other's slave: a story of
instalment which has no comparison in world literature. Indirectly
the first part of the story comes back. Jesus is prepared to die the
death of a slave. If the slave is not greater than his master and the
sent one not greater than the sender, this must be true also for the

disciples as slaves and sent by Jesus. The μακάριος sentence (13,17) is meant to clarify this.

The closing sentence of this part (13,20) shows that one can not always have one's focus on infinity. Hospitality (see again 1 Tim 5,10, but esp. 3 John) is an essential part of mutual love. It is an important reality for the narrator as is shown by the fact that he makes Jesus speak about it at this point. In the story itself it is bracketed between two Judas sentences (13,18.19 and 13,21ff). Whoever abuses hospitality, can be compared to Judas (and separates himself from the community of friends?).

It is clear that the story of the washing of the feet has a special place in the Johannine Gospel. It is in a way the basic story of the *oikos* of Jesus and his friends: the washing of the feet as sign of the high stake of his love, but also as an act of hospitality; the disciples who need to behave themselves as mutual friends: ultimately ready to lay down their lives for the brethren, but in the meantime ready to be guest-friends of each other; Peter as the spokesman of the people who claim to be ready for this but who have their shortcomings; Judas as the representative of the worst that can happen among friends: doing evil, notwithstanding the fact that friendship has been offered; the presence of the beloved disciple shows that all of this does not necessarily harm the perfection of love.

In two other texts Jesus returns to this commandment of mutual love. They are real discursive sentences which express the commandment/the wish and not much more.

In 13,34.35 it is explicitly called a new commandment. The construction of 13,34 is elliptical and is, therefore, very difficult to translate. The ἵνα ἀγαπᾶτε ἀλλήλους which comes back twice, indicates that the installation of the group of friends as a group of people who truly love one another, does not have such a solid base. Linguistically it is an optative sentence, i.e. there is a wish but there is as yet no corresponding reality. The closing sentence (13,35), which again brings in a future tense —'all will know'—, makes clear how much being a disciple is linked to this mutual love in the opinion of the narrator (resp. of Jesus). The sentence posits an exclusivity which did have an ideological effect. Jesus gave his disciples only one commandment. If the disciples keep this commandment, it refers exclusively to Jesus. Such a pretence has had to prove itself and this did not go without discussions and competition as appears from the *amicitia* texts of the philosophical movements of the time which I quoted, and to which can now be added the commandment of mutual love as practised in the Qumran group.

Finally, in 15,12.17 the relationship between the commandment of mutual love and Jesus' willingness to lay down his life for his friends is most explicitly established. Vs 15,13 is in fact a concrete development of the 'as I have loved you' from 15,12, a love which serves as a pattern for (again) the optative sentence about mutual love. The whole idea of mutual love is linked to this concept: 'you are my friends if you do what I commanded you' (15,14). What was developed, narratively, in the two interrelated sub-stories from the scene of the washing of the feet (13,12-20 after 13,1-11), is discursively verbalised in 15,12ff. One can even wonder whether the closing sentence in 15,17, parallel to the closing sentence in 13,20, might have intended to say that, previous to the high stake of the laying down of one's life, many other acts of love are demanded, a love in fertility with fruits which will remain with the heavenly father (15,16).

3.b. *the socio-political implications*

So far and especially in the discussion of 15,12-17, I have pointed out several times that the love relationship between Jesus and his disciples and the commandment of mutual love is imaginarily linked by Jesus to his own love relationship to his father. That means that we have in the Johannine Gospel a triple structure when it speaks about love: Jesus in his love relationship to his father (and v.v. the father to him) as a narratively-imaginary reality; Jesus in his love relationship to his disciples as a narratively-'real' reality; and the love relationship of the disciples among themselves as a narratively-imaginary-future relationship. Globally —without speaking about the structural narrative differences in these relationships—, this tripartite division is a constant topic in Johannine research. Modern studies use drawings to visualise the various relationships: concentric circles, squares with hooks and arrows, overlapping triangles. I do not want to reproduce them here, because they do not really add to what has been said in words.

I want to add, however, that different triads are used on various levels within the theoretical discourse of the *amicitia* literature. This is certainly true for Aristotle.

For him the distinction between friendship which is based on the good, on the pleasant or on the useful is basic: "It seems that not everything is loved, but only what is lovable, and that this is either what is good, or pleasant, or useful (ἀγαθὸν ἢ ἡδὺ ἢ χρήσιμον)" (Nic Eth 8.2.1). Only that friendship is constant and essential which is based on the good. The friendship which is based on the pleasant stops, when nothing pleasant can be achieved any more (as with the erotic attraction which diminishes). The friendship which is based on the useful is the most common, but also the most complicated of the three. Though it is a lesser form of friendship, it is a very important one, because it is the root of cooperation within the *polis*. "The political association, it is believed, was originally formed, and continues to be maintained, for the *advantage* of its members" (Nic Eth 8.9.4; for the totality of Aristotle's way of thinking in this and for the changes which Aristotle introduces in himself —in the *Politeia* he seems to think that the *polis* presupposes a friendship of benevolence—, see Price 1989/90, 193ff).

This insight brings Aristotle to speak about various forms of πολιτεία and the ways in which the *polis* can be organised. We see again a triad: kingship, aristocracy and timocracy (in which people govern on the basis of a property classification) which can turn into their opposites: tyranny, oligarchy and democracy (Nic Eth 8.10ff). Aristotle does not hide the fact that he is a fervent proponent of the kingship and, therefore, a clear opponent of timocracy, or even worse, democracy. For our topic it is important that he links these three constitutional forms with the three forms of friendship:

> "One may find likeness and so to speak models of these various forms of constitution in the household.
> The relationship of father to sons is regal in type, since a father's first care is for his children's welfare. This is why Homer styles Zeus 'father', for the ideal of kingship is paternal government.(...)
> The relation of husband to wife seems to be in the nature of an aristocracy: the husband rules in virtue of fitness (κατ' ἀξίαν), and in matters that belong to a man's sphere; matters suited to a woman he hands over to his wife. (...)
> The relation between brothers constitutes a sort of timocracy; they are equals, save in so far as they differ in age." (Nic Eth 8.10.4-6).

The *polis* and the *oikos* are not hermetically closed off compartments. They are comparable; they are interdependent etc. Friendships which originate from the *oikos*, therefore, have a political implication linked to their social function. And above all, the *oikos* itself realises the fullness of the *polis*.

I am not introducing this Aristotelian doctrine, because I think that there was a direct influence from Aristotle on the Johannine vision. That could be the case if, with some probability, such doctrine would be visible contemporaneously in the culture. But that does not seem to be the case as far as I can see. All the elements appear separately in the various authors: as to the division of friendship in three motives see (a.o.) Plut., De Amic Mult 94B; for the discussion about the constitutions, and especially the discussion about which is preferable, see (a.o.) Plut., De Monarchia, Democratia et Oligarchia 826B; Ps-Arist., De mundo, from 397B9 on; Dio Chrys., Or 3, 45ff; Philo, De Spec Leg I,13-20; for the various forms of friendship, see esp. Callicratides, in, Stob. IV.28.16 p.681, but e.g. also Philo, De Spec Leg II,224-241 (about parental love); De Virt 51-174 (about philanthropy). But I did not find a text which brings together all the elements as the text of Aristotle does.

I do introduce the text of Aristotle, because it can serve as a theoretical cadre for the whole of the Johannine vision regarding the love relationships as they have been discussed so far.

Jesus' relation to his father and —via Jesus who introduces his disciples as his friends in the *oikos* of his father—, the relation of the disciples to the father are *regal* in character: God as the Father-King who cares about the wellbeing of his children-subjects. The advantage of this friendship goes, in a way one-sidedly, to the recipients of this love, to the subjects who, in their very existence, are dependent on their Father-King-God. The proportionality which all love demands requires that the recipients of this benevolence are prepared to return their love as honour: concretely, as respect and obedience (cf. the Johannine use of the lexemes /glory/, /honour/, /knowing God/, /obedience to the word, commandments of God/ etc.).

Jesus' relation to his disciples is *aristocratic* in character. In a way we might even apply the aristocratic paradigm of Aristotle to the Johannine vision: Jesus as the groom-man who loves the group of disciples —the Israel of the covenant—, as his bride-woman (cf.

1,34.47.51; and esp. 3,29 cf. the explanation I gave of this mashal). Anyway, this love relationship of Jesus for his disciples is based on a relationship which is κατ' ἀξίαν: the Loeb edition translates 'in virtue of fitness', i.e. in proportion to what is fitting. The love relationship between Jesus and his disciples is based on an inequality of positions. Jesus can prescribe, in a way which fits this relationship, what the disciples must do without determining their life to such an extent that they would lose their independence. While honour plays a role because of the inequality (cf. the demand to obey Jesus' commandment; the mode of address for Jesus as *kyrios* and rabbi), the possibility of mutuality in love is greater now because of nearness. We can think of the stories about the beloved disciple and about Peter.

The mutual love relationship of the disciples among themselves, finally, is *timocratic* in character. This comparison is more abstract than the others. The love relationship among the 'brothers' is based on an equality with differences. There is a fundamental equality, because everyone has the possibility to take a leading role, but there are differences in preference and in actual potential. We can think of Jesus' command that the disciples must love one another, i.e. the command is the same for everyone. Everyone has also the same right to speak up in the group. Nobody is ever 'punished' on account of his contribution to the group itself. But there are differences: the different roles and tasks between the beloved disciple and Peter; Peter as the constant spokesman of the group; the relation between Andrew and Philip; the anonymity of several people. The fundamental equality does not take away individual differences.

Theorising from Aristotle about the narrative reality of the Johannine Gospel clarifies also something else. The *oikos* of Jesus with its various love relationships is in itself autonomous. It realises in its totality the whole of the *polis*. It is enclosed in itself and does not need extension. Understood from the background of the actual political situation in which this *oikos* must be realised, there are serious political consequences. Jesus' *oikos* must prove itself in a society which is organised extremely hierarchically, with a pyramidal structure which has an emperor-god at the top; in a society where power is determined by the Roman army and by those who have the legions on their side; a society where money and possessions determine who will be its leaders. In Aristotelian terms this means that the *oikos* of Jesus with all its good aspects must prove itself in a society which is in opposition to this, in an empire as it happens which is oligarchically organised and which easily takes on tyrannical traits (as for example under Nero and Domitian). The fate which Jesus had to undergo because of his total commitment to shape his *oikos*, shows that the actual world does not accept this autonomy of an alternative life style. The Johannine Gospel promotes the tendency to retreat from the world. The reason is the idea that the *oikos* of Jesus possesses everything necessary for life (in this vision, even everything necessary for eternal life). The outcome of Jesus' life (and Peter's cf. 21,18.19) shows that the actual world can not allow this. The alternative of love evokes the hatred of the world. It is part of the most fundamental message of the Johannine Gospel that love ultimately wins victory.

3.c. mutual service

As I said already, the commandment of mutual love is given in the story as told only indirectly and in principle. To end this chapter I want to put together all the data which, with some interpretative benevolence, can be understood as a narrative fulfilment of Jesus' commandment. It is a last concretisation of the more general vision of this group of friends: to strive for a common interest on the basis of a good deal of independence.

When 'the disciples' appear in the story they are presented mostly as an undifferentiated group: the disciples who are present at the marriage in Cana (2,2ff); who remember what happened in Jerusalem (2,17.22), etc. (see 3,22; 4,1.2.8.27.31.33; 6,3.12.16. 22.24.60.61.66; 7,3; 9,2; 11,7.8.12.54; 12,16; 13,5.22.23; 16,17. 20; 18,1.2.19; 20,10.18.19.20.25.26.30; 21,1.2.4.12.14). Some time we read that individual people have a contribution to make: Philip and Andrew in 6,6-9; Thomas in 11,16; 20,24; Peter who acts several times as spokesman for the group (in 6,66ff; 13,6ff; 18,10ff; 21,3.7); the beloved disciple who has his own special place (in 13,23); and Judas as the traitor (in Jesus' words in 6,70ff; 13,10.18; in the words of the narrator in 12,6 and narratively in 18,1ff). These appearances have their own narrative function. They clarify something of the complicated relationships within the group, but they do not say that people treat each other lovingly.

However, these stories clarify indirectly that there is some sort of group feeling. This happens most explicitly in the stories about the events following Jesus' death: in the story about Mary Magdalene who actively calls on Peter and the beloved disciple, 'because *we* do not know where they have put him' (20,2); in the story about what happened on the evening of that same day. The disciples are, then, gathered behind closed doors. There is a supposition here that someone placed his house at their disposal (20,19ff). As a group the disciples then tell Thomas that they have seen the Lord. And eight days later Thomas is present, behind closed doors, in the house (20,24ff). In Galilee the disciples are also together as a group, along the seashore, and on Peter's initiative they go fishing together, although unsuccessfully (21,1ff). The stories indicate a sense of community. They link up with expressions earlier in the story of such a sense of community which makes Peter say in 6,68: 'to whom would *we* go. You have words of eternal life'; and which make Thomas say in 11,16: 'let *us* go (to Judea) too to die with him'. The group of disciples is a group which experiences a sense of community.

That the mutual relations are based on love or on benevolence is, narratively, most clearly expressed in a very special phenomenon. The Johannine Gospel presupposes that the disciples fairly often act in pairs who are internally serving each other. The pair Peter and the beloved disciple is the most outstanding and the most often mentioned. There is a discussion in the exegetical literature about the question whether their relation must be seen as competitive or rather as collaborative (see Maynard 1984; Kügler 1988). To evaluate this correctly I think it is important to realise that there are other pairs apart from this one in the Gospel:
- Andrew and an anonymous disciple (1,37-39);
- Andrew and his brother Peter (in 1,40-42 and cf. the indication with Andrew that he is the brother of Simon Peter in 6,8);
- Andrew and Philip (in 1,43 as Andrew wins Philip for the Jesus movement, but also in 6,6-9 and esp. in 12,20-22);
- Philip and Nathanael (in 1,45-46);
- Peter and the other disciple, an acquaintance of the High Priest (in 18,16);
- Joseph of Arimathea and Nicodemus (in 18,38-39);
- I should mention also the peculiar list in 21,2 in which 'the sons of Zebedee' are mentioned —if one may suppose from the Synoptics that there are two persons involved here—, and also 'two others of his disciples';

- in a way Thomas belongs in this series: three times it is said that he is also called 'Didymus' (in 11,16; 20,24 and 21,2).

The appearance of these pairs of disciples signifies most concretely the mutual love relationships of the disciples. Generally speaking we can say that these people are prepared to help one another.

In a more derived sense this is true for the stories of the calling of the disciples in which one disciple convinces another to accept the confession of Jesus.

It is true in a more direct sense for the other relations:
- regarding the relation between Peter and the beloved disciple, the texts have been discussed already. The interpretation of the relationship of these two disciples is closely linked to the option from which one reads these texts. Whoever reads this Gospel as a possible source of information for (later, ecclesiastical) positions and discussions, will understand the relationship as competitive. Whoever stays closer to the narrative reality of the text, will see that a comparison is made between the two personages: Peter as the one who leads the group of disciples and the beloved disciple as the one who guarantees the 'tradition of the $\mu\alpha\rho\tau\upsilon\rho\acute{\iota}\alpha$ of the death and resurrection of Jesus'. Such a reader will not see their combined action as competitive. Narratively it is really more a friendly relationship. Peter asks the beloved disciple whether he is willing to speak to Jesus about who will betray him. The beloved disciple does that right away, even though the story does not tell us whether he also passed on Jesus' answer to Peter (13,21-30); in the story about their search for the body of Jesus the beloved disciple lets Peter precede him, even though he arrived first (20,1-10); in the story about the catching of fish the beloved disciple says only to Peter that the man on the beach is the *kyrios* (21,7). And even though Peter does not receive a positive answer from Jesus, he is the one who sees that the beloved disciple follows Jesus and he speaks to Jesus about it (21,20ff). Peter and the beloved disciple are linked together through the love of Jesus (cf. 20,2).
- regarding the relations between Andrew and Philip: when Andrew wins Philip for the Jesus movement, Philip owes his discipleship to Andrew. There is clearly a special relationship between these two. When Philip is tested by Jesus in the beginning of the popular meal (6,5-7), Andrew comes to his aid. In the scene of the Greeks (12,20ff) we see something similar. The Greeks ask

Philip to be their intermediary with Jesus. He then goes to Andrew
and together they go to Jesus.

- regarding the relation between Peter and the other disciple: as an
acquaintance of the High Priest he helps Peter to enter the house of
the High Priest (18,15ff). If we can identify this acquaintance of the
High Priest with the beloved disciple, this scene would belong in
the relation between Peter and the beloved disciple.

- regarding the relation between Joseph of Arimathea and
Nicodemus: they take care of Jesus' burial together: one takes care
of the body, the other of the spices (19,38-42).

The narrative impact arises from the repetition of the
phenomenon. The mutual relations of the disciples are kept alive
and are reinforced through personal relations. They can call on each
other and the reaction is always positive. The word 'love' is not
used here. But, because there is always a relationship between two
persons which develops in a positive sense, a kind of mutual
benevolence is at least not absent. Maybe we can even say, against
the background of the multiplicity of these friendly relationships,
that the narrator of the story has seen Jesus' relationship with his
beloved disciple less exclusively than people mostly think.

CHAPTER FOUR

LOVING WOMEN

This study is organised in such a way that the circle of the addressed widens continuously. Having described the relations in the more intimate situation of family and school, I want to trace now how Jesus' ἀγάπη is realised outside of these realities: in the meetings with men and women which develop in a positive sense. I realise that this argumentative continuation of my study is in fact a reader's construction. The study follows a biographical narrative *parcours* which does not immediately connect with the narrative parcours of the story as John tells it. In a biography the restricted intimacy of family and school is followed by the confrontation with the openly conflicting world. In the Johannine Gospel the story is told from the viewpoint of fully grown adults and the biographical notes remain implicit. This reader's construction functions thus as a code which opens a vista on what is implicit in the story. In this way it shows its selfinterest. The focus remains the imaginary representation of reality and, because there is a significant difference in the relations of Jesus with men and with women, I will treat them separately. Having discussed men so far, it will be good to see how women fare in the Johannine story.

It is well known that a number of women play an important role in the progression of the story: Jesus' mother who activates him in Cana and who is present when he dies; the Samaritan who makes his trip to Samaria a success; Martha and Mary who take care that Jesus becomes active again after the failure in Jerusalem and who play their special role in the resurrection of their brother Lazarus; Mary Magdalene who is present when Jesus dies; who, after his death, brings the disciples together and who is the first to see Jesus and who is appointed messenger (/ἄγγελος/). Part of the larger story we have the presence of four women who stand at the foot of the cross: with Jesus' mother and Mary Magdalene, his mother's sister and Mary the wife (or daughter) of Klopas. The narrative-communicative meaning of the relation between Jesus and his mother was discussed in chapter 1. Here I want to treat the stories of the other women, the stories with a happy ending about the Samaritan woman, about Martha and Mary and about Mary Magdalene which, each in their own way, say something about the imaginary presentation of love in the Johannine Gospel.

Research about the role and position of women in antiquity and especially in the first century A.D. is developing steadily. Many different positions are expressed. Brooten's plea (1985 cf. Pomeroy 1975; Blok 1987) to finally begin to look at women from a woman's perspective can be honoured by me only indirectly. More or less aware of my male perspective, I can try to show the imaginary space given to women (and subsequently to men) as seen from the specifically male perspective of the author of the Johannine Gospel. Feminist criticism within the world of exegesis has shown that this double male perspective has often worked negatively in evaluating the man-woman relation in the text. A remedy is only possible, if one is prepared to be a participant in this discussion.

1. THE IMAGINARY PRESENTATION

In the same way as I did when discussing the beloved disciple and the disciples, now too I want to discuss the cultural background of a couple of particulars in the man-woman stories of the Johannine Gospel before I enter into discussion of the texts themselves. We find a freedom of action and behaviour which only partly fits what the existing *oikos*-ideology imposes on women. It is quite extraordinary in fact. All texts which deal positively with the patriarchal *oikos*-mentality (as the treatises of Philo and Plutarch, the Greek, Rabbinic and Christian *oikos*-treatises, the women's stories in Josephus etc.) are, therefore, not of any real interest in dealing with the Johannine stories. Because the focus of this study is the imaginary presentation, I have added to what models presentday-research offers (the studies e.g. of Pomeroy 1975; Lefkowitz-Fant 1982 and Bremen 1983 about the (richer) Hellenistic women; Mayer 1987; Archer 1990 and Fander 1990 about the Jewish women) a study of the Hellenistic-Roman romance literature: i.c. Chariton's *Chaereas and Callirhoe*, Longus' *Daphne and Chloe*, Xenophon's *Ephesiaca*, Achilles Tatius' *Clitophon and Leucippe*, Heliodorus' *Aethiopica* and Apuleius' *Metapmorphoses*.

This is love-literature; it belongs, globally, to this era (from the first century B.C. till the third century A.D.), and women play a role here in much the same way as in the Johannine story contrary to the cultural code of the *oikos*-ideology. Especially the women in the sub-stories find themselves in this role —as is true in the Johannine Gospel—, where the cultural code is broken also especially in the sub-stories.

1.a. the stories in the Johannine Gospel

I want to put together in a few points the data of the Johannine Gospel:

1. the independence of the men

Central in the *oikos*-ideology regarding women is that they never have an existence independent of men. Women are always linked to men: to a father, a guardian, to brothers, to a husband or their own male children. I discussed this reality before. It is therefore quite extraordinary that in the Johannine Gospel women act without any kind of *tutela mulieris*.

The introduction of Mary as ἡ τοῦ Κλωπᾶ (19,25): Mary the wife or daughter of Klopas is conform the *oikos*-ideology. This is true also, more implicitly, for Jesus' mother as I have explained (also for her sister?). But the situation of the sisters Martha and Mary is already more complicated. They are linked to their brother Lazarus in some way, but their own *oikos* —no parents, no husbands, no children—, is special and when the brother dies, there does not seem to be a male successor. Mary Magdalene is even more independent. We hear only of the name of a place, an indication that she is not from Jerusalem. The Samaritan woman is the most independent. She defines herself as 'someone who has not a husband' (4,17): a definition which Jesus prophetically knows and affirms.

This textual reality can, obviously, be explained partially from the narrativity of the text. John tells a story in which the lineage of the persons is not always important, but this is surely not true for Martha and Mary or for the Samaritan woman. There must be something special here.

2. the freedom to act

We see a freedom to act which, apparently, is linked to this independence from men. The activities of these women are partly linked to the factual role division between men and women: the Samaritan woman goes to draw water; Martha and Mary fulfil the prescribed death ceremonies at home; Martha serves at the table during the festive meal after the resurrection of Lazarus; the group of four women standing under the cross, —although they had to travel to get there—; Mary Magdalene takes care of the body of Jesus after his death. But these people also do a number of things beyond this role: the Samaritan woman successfully fulfils her role in the city proclaiming the good news; Mary embalms Jesus feet with precious nard against the objection of Judas; Mary Magdalene, a woman from Magdala, knows herself responsible for what has happened in Jerusalem. The public nature and the naturalness of their actions are striking. In John's imaginary presentation of things, the women fulfil a public function which is very important for the progress of the story as told. I will return to this later.

3. the openness to men
The focus of this study sees this freedom of action specifically in the openness to. men which is something one would not expect.

In the story of the Samaritan woman it is a topic in the discussion: the five husbands which Jesus tells her about, determine the content of her message to the people in the city: 'he told me everything I did' (4,29 and 4,39 referring back to 4,17.18). Neither Jesus nor the woman add any critical remarks to this. Jesus only wants to say that the woman is right, when she says she does not have a husband, and the woman correctly interprets it as a statement from someone who has secret knowledge. This statement makes Jesus later on, for the woman and for the city, a prophet and Messiah.

In the story of Martha and Mary this openness to men is limited to the special relation which these women have with Jesus. Their behaviour is, therefore, more intimate, more direct and more physical. They take the initiative to send him a message when Lazarus falls ill; independently of each other they address Jesus with a freedom which confuses many exegetes. In the closing scene of the story Mary acts as a true intima, when she pours the balm over his feet: is it an act of love of a slave, of a prostitute, of a lover, of a spouse? Jesus interprets it as a burial ritual, but it is not so clear whether this explains the event completely.

The story of Mary Magdalene realises this openness to men in a different manner. She can, without evoking comment, go to the house of Peter and the other disciple whom Jesus loves in the early morning. She can go to the (male) disciples to tell them that she has seen the Lord. The μή μου ἄπτου (20,17) indicates that at least she herself does not want to avoid physical contact with Jesus. It is a short version of a recognition scene which finds a fuller expression in Hellenistic romance literature.

4. Jesus' openness

Jesus behaviour is organised symmetrically to the behaviour of the women. Their openness to men determines his openness to them. He begins the discussion with the Samaritan woman by saying, 'give me something to drink' (4,7). That initiative amazes her but she accepts Jesus. The amazement of the disciples that Jesus is talking to a woman makes it clear not only that Jesus acts in an extraordinary way, but also that the responsibility for such a discussion in public lies with the man.

In the relation between Jesus and Martha and Mary the amazing thing is that we read: 'Jesus loved Martha and her sister and Lazarus' (11,5). The ἀγάπη which is attributed to Jesus is as shocking, culturally speaking, as the love he has for the beloved disciple. The love of a man for an unmarried woman belongs in a context which exegetes would rather not discuss.

In the story of Mary Magdalene, finally, the disciples play a kind of passive role. Peter and the beloved disciple investigate the disappearance of Jesus' body when she tells them about it, and the story suggests that the disciples believe her statement that she has seen the Lord. Again, Jesus takes the initiative. While Mary Magdalene still believes him to be the gardener, he asks —as did the angels earlier—, why she is crying. Here we do not see any amazement that a man addresses her, a woman, but we have a direct answer which leads to the scene of recognition.

1.b. The Greek-Roman romance literature

I want to try to place this mutually related cluster in the context of some stories about women in the Greek-Roman romance literature. I am well aware that in this way I enlarge the imaginary character of the stories of the Johannine Gospel. Yet, the typical differences will also be highlighted. In this way it will be possible to create a real vision on the narrative reality of the Gospel, on what is imaginarily possible for the narrator of the text.

In order to make the comparison clear I will proceed step by step, even though this does not do justice to the narrative embedding of the stories. It seems to me to be the only way to proceed in this study.

1. freedom of behaviour

I already pointed out that the main story is usually not the most interesting part for any real comparison. This is certainly true for this topic. The main personages in this story —a nice young man and a beautiful woman from the better echelons of society who are destined for each other from the beginning of the story, but who will come together only at the end—, do not have much freedom of movement. Usually events are determined by external circumstances. Bandits, pirates, a war, a storm on the open sea determine how the story will proceed. Sometimes the main characters take the initiative: e.g. in the escape from the city of Clitophon and Leucippe, because Leucippe's mother has discovered that someone (=Clitophon) has spent the night in the women's quarters together with Leucippe (Ach Tat II.26ff); or when Theagenes and Chariclea escape from the pirates as Heliodorus relates the story (Aeth I.31 — II.1ff) etc. In the execution of these plans, the male partner is essential and these initiatives are always part of the main plot of the story.

Real freedom of action, especially where women are concerned, is given only to the minor characters. Remarkable is the naturalness in the freedom of travel (understandable, though, because it is in accordance with the main plot of these stories as travel stories). The jealous sisters of Psyche who, because of their marriage with foreigners live far away, do not need to convince their husbands to travel time and again to visit their parents and their sister by boat (Apul V.7.9.14.16.27). Rhopodis, the Thracean woman in the full bloom of her age who manages to convince the priest Calasiris to leave Memphis, travels around Egypt with a large company (Aeth II.25.1ff). Melite, a woman from Ephesos who remains in Egypt for four months because of her love for Clitophon, determines for herself when she will return to Ephesos (Ach Tat V.11ff).

Still other ways of freedom of action are ascribed to women. Byrrhena, the aunt of Lucius, who himself is the main character in

Apuleius' story, is a good example. In the beginning of this sub-story about the relation between Lucius and his aunt, when she is introduced as matron, there is still mention of her husband: 'an old man weighed down with years was clinging to her side'. But once this man has introduced Lucius to his aunt, he disappears completely. Byrrhena organises everything: the festive meal, the invitation for the guests, the nocturnal events connected with it etc. (Apul II.2ff.18.19.31; III.12). Byrrhena determines her own life. It is much the same with Pamphile, Milo's wife and Lucius' hostess. She knows how to reach her Boeotian lover through magic and sorcery (Apul II.11; III.15.21ff). The writers use different material, but everywhere we find independent women who determine their own life.

2. sexual freedom

Such freedom is most explicitly exhibited in the sub-stories which narrate the sexual desires and lusts of women. With the exception of Chariton's narrative the heroes of all the stories are subject to the desire of at least one, sometimes more than one woman: Daphnis is desired by Lycaenium (Longus III.15-19); Clitophon by Melite (Ach Tatius from V.11 on); Lucius by Photis (Apul II.7ff.16ff); Habrocomes by Manto (Eph II.3.1-9.4) and by Kyno (Eph 12.3ff); Theagenes by Arsace (Aeth VII.2ff).

The evaluation of such love is closely connected with the main plot of the story. In Daphne and Chloe, Lycaenium's love for Daphnis is placed in the context of sexual *paideia*. Because Daphnis and Chloe do not know how to behave —apart from what they have seen the goats do—, Lycaenium gets a chance with Daphnis. Once she has taught Daphnis how humans practice sex, the story can proceed (but see Winkler 1990, 101ff). In Achilles Tatius' story the main characters do their utmost to remain faithful to each other. Leucippe manages to come through the Pan-test and proves thus that she is a virgin. But when Clitophon must tell his future father-in-law what happened, he skips the one time that he and Melite had intercourse: 'I related the story of Melite's love for me, my own chastity with regard to her ... Only one thing I omitted in all my adventures, and that was the somewhat delicate matter of my connection with Melite after the events just mentioned; but I recorded my dinner with her etc.' (Ach Tatius VIII.5). In the *Ephesiaca* and the *Aethiopica*, which constantly deal with the mutual fidelity of the main lovers, the women who threaten this fidelity are given all kind of evil attributes: they are ugly, untrustworthy, vicious and liars. However, this is also true for the men who desire the heroic women in these stories: they are always seen as brutes, barbarians and bandits. Lastly, Lucius' relation with his Photis, clearly, has the approval of the narrator. But Lucius has no obligations and Photis is an unmarried slave and thus available. It is a nice story because she enjoys it (something which is not true any more for the erotic stories of book IX and X in the *Metamorphoses*).

Eros holds everyone under his spell, men and women alike. That this can bring about strange and awful situations is clear from the main plots of these novels. It can also lead to love affairs which sometimes have a happy ending and sometimes not. If women take the initiative, it is supposed that their husbands are somehow absent: he is old or on a journey or dead. We could be tempted to think that the narrators see a causal relation between the absence of the man and the desire of the woman. That might be true in some cases (esp. in the erotica in the *Metamorphoses*) but it, certainly, is not always so. That would not really be possible either, if we consider the necessity of the σωφροσύνη of the heroines of the story. In final analysis the stories portray how love, coloured by desire and lust, can be faithful under trial and absence.

The female characters in Hellenistic romance literature represent a whole range of human possibilities. They are linked to a male community which largely determines their mode of behaviour but, within this restriction, many women find a way to stand for their own rights.

In this way we see a strong resemblance between these women and the women in the Johannine Gospel, but there is also a real difference in two respects.

The public function which the Samaritan woman is given and which Mary Magdalene takes upon herself, is completely absent in the romance literature. There women belong to the private realm and the men are supposed to take care of public functions. When Chariclea is asked to speak publicly, she begins by saying: 'It would be more fitting for my brother here, Theagenes, —who is in fact her lover—, to be the speaker; for I think it proper for a woman to be silent, and for a man to make answer, before a company of men' (Aeth I.21.3 cf. X.18.2). Here we find verbalised what is culturally seen as desirable (cf. the mock-scene in Apul III.9 where an old woman speaks in a popular meeting). It is clear that the women in the Johannine Gospel act in an extraordinary way.

On the other hand the sexual freedom, ascribed to the women in the romance literature, is absent in the Johannine Gospel (although the five husbands of the Samaritan woman are no barrier for her to be in touch with Jesus). Generally speaking, we can say that eroticism is absent in the Johannine women. The narrator of the Johannine story uses a language, however, in a manner parallel to the texts of the beloved disciple, which connects very closely with the eroticised Hellenistic culture. When we come to these texts, I will show this more explicitly for the two relevant scenes in John: the anointing scene in Jn 12 and the recognition scene in Jn 20.

2. THE TEXTS

This rather global textualisation is not the last word. Other realities play a role in the story as told, realities which need to be considered in the process of signification. In the following analysis I want to deal with a number of them.

2.a. the story of the Samaritan woman (4,1-42)

Modern research pays ever closer attention to the narrative construction of the story (Olsson 1974, 115f; Hudry-Clergeon 1981; Lenglet 1985; Rebell 1987, 177ff; Ritt 1988; Okure 1988). One can see a certain consensus. The text must be read as a narrative, in which the beginning and the end differ in a way which is significant for a story. Since the different authors have varying views on narrativity, they come to different and varying conclusions: Jn 4 is a meaningful succession of events (Olsson); a dramatic spiral and elliptical structure (Rebell); the acquisition of an object by a subject and the narrative programs which this implies (Lenglet) etc. The evaluation of the scenes in 4,27-30 and 4,39-42 determines the difference between these narratologists and the older exegetes like Schnackenburg, Brown and de la Potterie. They qualify the scenes as resp. *Überleitung und Abschluss* (Schnackenburg 1967, 477.488); *introduction and conclusion* (Brown 1966, 181.184); *transition et conclusion* (de la Potterie

1962, 35), because they find the meaning of the text in the content of the two discourses: between Jesus and the Samaritan woman (4,7-26) and that between Jesus and the disciples (4,31-38). It seems that there is a kind of reader's decision here. One can read the story from the viewpoint of a double structure of the two discourses: with the woman about the water and with the disciples about eating. But one can also read it from the viewpoint of the active input of the woman: the woman as the representative of the city who convinces many people to accept Jesus. This last aspect has surfaced only in the last ten years. It is obvious that I go along with it.

Because I see the focus of my research in the narratively presented man-woman relation, I want to look at the text from this perspective. I make a distinction. I want to start with a description of the relation between Jesus and the Samaritan woman. This relation is coloured because, apart from Jesus, various other men and male figures play a role: 'our father Jacob' (4,5 'and his son Joseph'; 4,12 'and his sons'); the (male) disciples of Jesus; her own five husbands (4,16-18); 'our fathers who worshipped on this mountain' (4,20); God as 'father' (4,21.23); the (mixed) group of the inhabitants of the city. The single woman is surrounded by many men and male figures. In as far as this is important for the focus of this study, I will discuss it later.

2.a.1. the Samaritan woman and Jesus

The relation between the Samaritan woman and Jesus belongs to the narrative topic of the story. On this level exists the interpretative choice I just indicated: the decision of the reader to insert the discourse between Jesus and the Samaritan woman in the construction of the narrative plot.

A discussion with the Pharisees has forced Jesus to travel through Samaria. About 'the sixth hour' he reaches Jacob's well (4,6 πηγή, only the Samaritan woman calls it a φρέαρ, a pit or hole 4,11). The determination of this time indication is not without importance for the interpretation of the text. There is a real difference whether one follows the Jewish or the Roman mode of telling the time. For the Jewish mode 'the sixth hour' is about noon. This is stressed with the known addition that that hour is the heat of the day: Jesus is tired from the journey and the heat; and the fact that the woman is there to draw water on this strange hour, makes clear from the beginning that there is something out of the ordinary with her (see the attempts by Olsson 1974, 150 and Okure 1988, 87 to find, nevertheless, a coherent interpretation). In the Roman mode 'the sixth hour' is six P.M. (and for those who see Jn 19,14 as an argument against —as e.g. Brown 1966, 169; Olsson 1974, 150— 'the sixth hour' in Jn 19,14 is six A.M. which fits in with the πρωί in 18,28 and with the schedule of a Roman procurator who is available only in the morning). Six o'clock in the evening is the time to prepare food and drink which is what the disciples do when they go to buy food, and what the woman is also doing when she comes to get water. This way of reckoning the time also clarifies better how it is possible that the inhabitants of Sichar come running to Jesus and also why they invite him to stay with them. It is almost dark, the appropriate time for social gatherings and for the preparation of the night. My supposition is, therefore, that the Johannine story places the discourse with the Samaritan woman in the beginning of the evening; not in the night as in the discourse with Nicodemus, but in the twilight of the day when man and woman find time for each other.

The discussion functions, communicatively, as the transition from the original resistance of the woman to her complete commitment and from the indirect self expression of Jesus to a self definition. Jesus wins her over to the Jesus-movement and the woman has the effect that Jesus speaks about himself in the first person singular for the first time in the story. Jesus has the initiative, but it is not without gaining something for himself.

The discussion itself can be divided in three parts which each have their own communicative meaning: 4,7-15 where misunderstanding has the upper hand; 4,16-18 where communication is restored; and 4,19-26 which leads to the self definition of Jesus. We can be even more precise how this works. In this analysis of the communicative process of the text, it is presupposed that every deviation from the σύ — ἐγώ scheme has meaning for the mutual communication.

4,7-15: Initially, the partners in the discussion address each other in the I-you form. Jesus introduces himself as a questioner (4,7). But the woman says that she can not really do what he wants. It is impossible to accede to the request because of the broken communicative man-woman *and* Judea-Samaria relationship (4,9).

Jesus, therefore, redefines his request in new terms in which he is no longer the one who asks but the one who gives (4,10). The woman does not follow him in this transition, but remains on the first communicative level. She points out that Jesus lacks something: he does not have a water bucket and Jesus can not be greater than our father Jacob (4,12). Jesus clarifies his offer, but at the same time he begins to speak to the woman in the third person singular about 'whoever drinks from this water', a sign that the communicative relationship is disturbed (4,13.14). The woman accepts the offer apparently. The δός μοι of Jesus in 4,7 has become a δός μοι of the woman in 4,15; yet the answer shows there is a misunderstanding: is it irony or is it a last word to close the conversation?

4,16-18: Whatever, it is for Jesus a reason to begin a new topic: Jesus' command/request that the woman will go and fetch her husband (4,16), is an absolute break in the communication seen from the viewpoint of the woman, because with this command, Jesus ends the conversation between himself as a man and the Samaritan as a woman. Communicative-narratively the sentence refers to 4,9, to the first problem which the woman raised: how can you, as a man, address a woman. She corners him with her self description ('I do not have a husband' 4,17). He must speak with her or he should not speak with anyone. In fact, the woman saves the conversation by her honesty. Because Jesus tells the woman what he knows (4,18), he accepts the challenge she puts to him. There is now communication between Jesus and the woman.

4,19-26: The position of 4,19 is a double one: on the one hand, it is the closing of the previous discussion indicating that Jesus and the woman have found a common ground: after Jesus has defined the woman, she tells him what she thinks of him: you are a prophet. On the other hand, the verse is also an introduction to the last conversation. By restoring the communication new communication can begin. The woman now introduces the new topic (4,20). Communicative-narratively it refers again to 4,9, to the second problem which the woman indicated: how can you as a Judean speak to a Samaritan. The woman still speaks from an opposition point of view, the opposition between we-Samaritans and you-Judeans. Jesus denies this opposition, because in the third person plural, in a group which is beyond the opposition we-you, a higher unity can be found (4,21.22/23/24). Because Jesus uses the future tense, the woman can agree with him. It is the beginning of the personal expression of faith of the woman (4,25). It is also an answer which brings Jesus to act in a different way: he speaks about himself in the first person singular (4,26): I who speak with you am the Messiah whom you expect. Narratively, this is the first time Jesus speaks about himself in such a direct way. The first person singular refers directly to the opening sentence of the conversation 'give me to drink' (4,7) and especially to the sentence 'if you knew who it is ὁ λέγων σοι' (4,10). The dialogue of Jesus and the woman has come to an end.

The single initiative of Jesus has effected a multiplicity of subtle reactions. Most determining for the positive ending of the conversation from Jesus' point of view is the apparent refusal of Jesus to continue talking with the woman (4,16) and from the woman's points of view the readiness to commit herself completely (4,17a). The interpretation of the communicative meaning of this exchange is, therefore, not unimportant. Okure (1988, 109) who sees the behaviour of the Samaritan woman —up to 4,17a—, as quarrelsome and annoying Jesus, writes about 4,17a: 'the woman is telling the truth, but with her tongue in her cheek, because she wants to get rid of Jesus. If so, she is caught in her own trick.'

It should be clear from all this that I do not agree with this interpretation.

On the one hand, it does an injustice to the narrative-communicative position of the woman. Verse 4,9 poses a real problem; even the narrator of the story identifies with it as is clear from his commentary in which he explains for the reader why the woman speaks as she does; the verse is also programmatic for the whole sequence of the conversation (cf. the reference in 4,16 and 4,19); and verses 4,11.12 are full of respect for Jesus notwithstanding the sense of distance and misunderstanding, cf. the question about the πόθεν which is central to the whole of Johannine theology and the term 'our father Jacob' with which the woman is the first to bridge the opposition between Samaritans and Judeans via the common father Jacob.

On the other hand, such an interpretation honours Jesus too much. Notwithstanding the enigmatic sentences (in 4,10.13.14), his indirect way of communication (in 4,13.14) and his apparent rejection of the woman's feelings (in 4,16 —although this comes after the ironic statement of the woman in 4,15 —), Okure ascribes to Jesus a consistently positive communicative attitude. Where the woman keeps trying to get rid of Jesus according to Okure, Jesus is consistently patient and only wants the continuation of the conversation.

I showed already that such an image of Jesus is true in the last meal of Jesus and the disciples. But here it is different. The Samaritan as well as Jesus take a constant gamble with the whole of the communication, but it is the woman who creates the positive communicative contact. Because, even if one accepts that 'Jesus knows everything that goes on in men's hearts' (2,25) and that he, therefore, with the request to the woman to go and fetch her husband only wants to test her (cf. 6,6), it remains true that the Samaritan woman passes this test with her answer in 4,17a and that she, therefore, saves the conversation. Only when she has answered him truthfully is the sting, which hinders this man-woman conversation, removed. The story has opened up again; a positive relation between Jesus and the woman is created; the conflict Judea-Samaria can be discussed; for the first time in his narrative existence Jesus can make a statement about himself; and the woman becomes an active propagandist for the whole city; when the disciples return she leaves her jar and goes to the city.

This is elaborated in two mutually related scenes.

4,27-30 relates how the woman tells her story to the inhabitants of the city. Following the above analysis she concentrates on what was essential communicatively in the conversation: 'he told me everything I have done.' (in reference to 4,17-18) and 'could he be the Christ?' (in reference to 4,25-26). Her question is enough incentive for the inhabitants to go out to Jesus.

4,39-42 describes the success of the woman. Her word (λόγος) brought many to believe in Jesus. She won over a whole group of people for him. Even more, she did what Jesus predicted: she got the Judeans and the Samaritans together in one group. On the invitation of the Samaritans Jesus and his disciples remain in the city for two days. There is again a reference to that part of the conversation where the communication between Jesus and the woman was restored (4,39 and 4,18). Her success is surpassed only by the word (λόγος) of Jesus. Hearing Jesus himself makes the witness to his word secondary (4,41-42). That is not negative towards the woman. It belongs to the very nature of witnessing that it is subject to hearing and seeing directly. In fact, it underlines the truth of the witness of the woman: we now heard it with our own ears.

2.a.2. *the one woman and the many men*

The relation between Jesus and the woman is embedded in the relations she maintains with many other men. I want to elaborate on this in as far as it colours this relation.

2.a.2.1. *our father Jacob and his sons*

Exegesis has expanded on the idea that the Samaria story in mentioning Jacob and his well recalls the way in which the patriarchs obtained a wife (Jaubert 1976, 58; Neyrey 1979; Dagonet 1979, 33ff; Rebell 1987, 189ff). A woman and a man near a well is an erotic setting. Later on in the story the disciples, returning from the city, interpret the situation in this manner. (4,27). Not many readers of the story will dare say that all manner of attraction between the man and the woman is absent. The question is whether this is put in terms which refer directly to the biblical stories about the patriarchs.

Okure (1988, 87ff) has shown that this is not the case. She writes: 'while there are some broad similarities in all the stories combined: the meeting at the well itself, some connection with marriage, and, in the case of Jacob and Moses, a possible persecution to a foreign country, there are no real parallels between the OT stories and the Samaritan narrative as it now stands.' Literarily-theoretical we are dealing with allusions, a technique which John uses extensively (cf. ch. 6 and the story about the manna; ch. 7 and 8 about the Feast of the Tabernacles; ch. 10 and the story about the shepherd; ch. 14 and the story about the covenant; ch. 15 and the allusions about the vine).

As far as I can see in the secondary literature, two references seem sufficiently clearly based in the text to be seen by several authors as intertextual references intended by the author.

There is first of all the reference to TJ I Num 21,16-20:

"And from thence was given them the *living well*, the *well* concerning which the Lord said to Moses, assemble the people and give them water. Then, behold, Israel sang the thanksgiving of this song, at the time that the *well* which has been hidden was restored to them through the merit of Miriam: Spring up, o well, spring up, o well! sang they to it, and it *sprang up*: the *well* which the fathers of the world Abraham, Isaac, and *Jacob*, digged; the princes who were of old digged it, the chiefs of the people, Moses and Aaron, the scribes of Israel, found it with their rods; and from the desert it was given to them for a *gift*",

referring to the lexemes:

well	spring up	gift	Jacob
well	spring up	gift	Jesus

> (cf. Olsson 1974, 164ff; Jaubert 1976, 58; Neyrey 1979, 422ff; Okure 1988, 89).

Then there is, more specific maybe, a reference to TJ I and Neoph Gen 28,10; 29,10.22; 31,22; TJ II Gen 28,10; 29,22; 31,22. This last one says in the translation of Klein (1980 II, 106 in the Vatican ms Ebr 440; see parallel the Paris ms Hebr 110, p.19ff):

> Gen 28,10: "Five miracles were performed for *our father Jacob* at the time that he left Beersheba to go to Haran....The fifth miracle: when *our father Jacob* lifted up the stone from upon the mouth of the *well*, the *well surged up*, and continued to *surge up* for *twenty years*..."
> Gen 29,22: "And Laban gathered all the local people, and he made a feast; Laban began by saying to them: 'These seven years, this righteous man is here; ever since he came to us, our troughs were not lacking water, and our springs have increased; and now, come give me advice....'"
> Gen 31,22: "And when his (=Laban's) shepherds gathered together, in order to water the sheep, but they were unable, then they waited two or three days, perhaps the *well* would *surge up*; but it did not surge up; and thus Laban was told on the third day that Jacob had fled,"

referring to the lexemes:

our father Jacob	well	spring up	twenty years
Jesus	well	spring up	forever

> (cf. Neyrey 1979, 422; more hesitantly Olsson 1974, 169 and Okure 1988, 89, because the dating of these targum traditions is less sure).

2.a.2.2. *the five men and the one man who is not her husband*

These intertextual references change the meaning and the position of Jesus. This son of Jacob is greater than Jacob himself. The water which Jesus gives as a free gift —resp. Jesus himself as the gift of God—, is a well of living water for everlasting life. Against this fullness, the position of the woman becomes more and more insignificant.

This is even more so, because of what the narrator tells his listeners and, narratively, what Jesus tells the woman in 4,17.18. She has had five husbands and the man she has now is not her husband. Even though Jesus does not judge her, the text makes clear that this daughter of Jacob has a socially quite special position; more probably, even an extraordinary one. Apart from the possibility that the five husbands have a symbolic meaning as the five gods which are worshipped in Samaria (cf. Jos Ant. 9,288), the story demands narratively that her five or six husbands are seen as real. Jesus' revelation makes sense only, when one accepts that they are real physical persons; and only then, it can become the main argument of her witness in the city.

That means that while Jesus moves up in the course of the conversation, the Samaritan woman moves down. She is not Rachel and not Leah. Because almost nothing is said about her relations with her husbands, one should maybe also not think of Dina the dishonoured and revenged daughter of Jacob. It is simply stated that her present man is not her husband. It means that this man is her lover. Could she have something of Ohola, the adulterous and over-sexed woman from Ez 23 who symbolises Samaria?

2.a.2.3. *our fathers who worshipped (God) on this mountain and the father-God who looks for people*

As I showed above, the narrative program of the Samaria story realises the transition of the opposition between the cult in Samaria and Judea to a higher unity where Samaritans and Judeans worship God in spirit and in truth. The Samaritan woman is the main character in this transition, because she convinces the inhabitants of the city to believe in Jesus and to receive him and the disciples as welcome guests. She makes it possible for Jesus to manifest himself to her as a prophet; she begins the Samaria-Judea discussion and she gives witness in the city on her own initiative, thereby giving

hospitality its chance. It means in fact that through the activity of
this woman, Israel is restored to its old glory ; that there is a return
to the time when the sons of Jacob were not yet divided; that, most
of all, we have a preview of the future foretold by the prophets: the
reunion of the Northern and Southern Kingdom (see Jer 3; 31; Ez
37,15-27; 48,5.6; Am 9,11-15; Za 9,10 - 12,17). As far as I know,
this aspect of the text has not been treated in exegesis. The Samaria
story participates in this direct narrative manner in the covenant
theology which the Johannine Gospel puts forward in a variety of
ways.

Maybe we can be more precise. The implicit reference in Jn
4,36 to Am 9,13 :—'the one who ploughs follows the mower and
the one who squashes the grapes the sower'—, as an eschatological
promise in the restoration of the house of Jacob and the tent of
David, and the reference in Jn 4,37 to Mic 6,15 —'you will sow
but not reap'—, as an announcement of the punishment for all who
follow the practices of Omri and Achab, the kings of Samaria (cf.
Brown 1966, 182), are the textual indications that the Samaria
connection is also intertextually conceived. It is, then, not unlikely
that Jer 31,22 also plays a role in the text:
    'how long walk back and forth,
    backturning daughter;
    see, JHWH creates something new on earth:
    a female courts a male.'
Jer 31 is a text where the house of Israel and the house of Judah are
as equals, both enjoying the mercy of God. God is surprised that he
has mercy on Ephraim but he has to do it. Ephraim is addressed as
'first-born' (31,20), as 'virgin Israel' (31,21) and also, —cf. the
quote above—, as 'backturning daughter', in a pun which looks
forward to the end of the sentence —the שׁובבה will be made by
God into a female who courts a male, סבב cf. Gesenius who gives
as meaning 'das Weib wird sich umtun (werbend) um den Mann';
Zorell, 'cum amore et fide femina circumdabit virum, sponsum
suum JHWH; Koehler-Baumgartner, 'encompass (with protection)'
(cf. Jer 3 in which the behaviour of the two sisters Israel and Judah
is described and where the concept משׁובה plays a central role).

Applied to the Samaria story this means that God, who searches
for people who will worship him in spirit and in truth, found one in
the Samaritan woman. Through this woman, who in her own way
stands for the whole of Samaria and who, because she is actively

involved with Jesus, makes the transition from שׁבב to סבב, God creates something new on earth: the restoration through Jesus of the covenant between God and all of Israel.

2.a.2.4. the disciples

Inspired by God and under the influence of the Jesus' words this woman with her socially special position, is given this important role. She acts as a woman. The action of the (male) disciples and especially, the lack of it indicates how strong the man-woman opposition remains till the very end of the story. The disciples went to the city during the conversation between Jesus and the Samaritan woman. When the conversation is ended, they return and play their own role in the story as told.

From the perspective of the narrator, it is said that they are surprised that Jesus talks with a woman (4,27). Culturally this surprise fits in the system of norms of the time: a man alone does not speak to a woman alone. The remarks in the story —'but no one said what are you looking for? or why are you talking with her?'—, clarify something else. The disciples did think these things but they did not say them. They did not dare express these misogynous remarks. These now turn against the disciples, because they remain without comment from either Jesus or the woman. *They* had these judgmental thoughts without reason.

While the woman is in the city, the disciples offer Jesus from the food they bought. This is the opening of the second conversation of the Samaria story in which Jesus uses the food as an occasion to clarify for the disciples what has happened between him and the Samaritan woman (including the Samaria connection as I have shown). Different from the first conversation, this remains stuck in misunderstanding. The two occasions in which the disciples say something, and especially the second one, 'could somebody have brought him food?' (4,33), make it clear that they have no idea of what Jesus is trying to tell them. It is not denied but neither is it said that they have come to understanding, when the conversation ends.

The text makes clear in its concrete structure that there is a real difference between the Samaritan woman and the disciples. Jesus' conversation with the disciples is framed by the two scenes which relate the witnessing activity of the woman. While Jesus and the disciples discuss witnessing, discuss sowing and reaping, discuss effort and fulfilling one's calling, the Samaritan woman is doing it and doing it successfully. The active woman prevails over her male opposite characters in every respect.

The Samaritan woman is a loving woman. She acts publicly in reaction to what she has experienced with Jesus. She commits herself to his interests. She gains (regains?) thereby the respect of her fellow citizens. Whether Jesus loves her too, is apparent only indirectly in the sentences which he speaks —in an indirect narrative interpretation of 4,31-38—: that she is reaping and gathering fruits so that the sower may find joy together with the reaper, and that one sows while another reaps; —in relation to the Samaria connection as we explained earlier. Jesus touched her and through her response it has become a true event. Indirectly Jesus expresses his admiration and makes her a model for the disciples. The indirectness indicates a distance as do the closing sentences which Jesus speaks to his disciples: 'what I sent you (plural) to reap was not something you (plural) worked for. Others have done the hard work, and you (plural) have come for the fruit of their work'. The Samaritan woman is then at most one of the hard workers. From the stories of the other women it will have to become clear whether this kind of reaction in which the woman becomes an anonymous, indicates some kind of pattern.

2.b. The story of Martha and Mary (11,1-12,11)

Jn 11 is often called the story of Lazarus. That is, obviously, not wrong and I will return to it under this aspect. But in reality Lazarus only plays the role of the one discussed. The story is composed of a multitude of conversations between Martha — Mary and Jesus, and once between Jesus and his disciples. I use these conversations as reader's cesurae to explicate the various aspects of the man-woman relationships in the story.

2.b.1. the message of Martha and Mary to Jesus (11,1-6)

The sub-story as well as the setting is dramatically structured. There are three narrative realities.

First of all, the story of the resurrection of Lazarus is the end of a climax, the end of a series of sign-miracles which are ever more impressive: the double events in Cana, the cure of the lame man, the popular banquet, the cure of the blind man, and now as the climax the resurrection of Lazarus. The relation with what happens before is made in the text itself (11,37.47) and has thus the approval of the author.

Secondly, Bultmann (1941, 299) has pointed out in one of his few narrative remarks that 11,1-52 is framed by 10,40-42 and 11,54, two texts which relate how Jesus retired to a quiet place. In 10,41 there is still a great surge of people; in 11,54 it is in a region close to the desert. These are chronologically the periods where Jesus is alone with his disciples for a longer time. We are not given any further information. They are interrupted by Jesus' grand appearance in Lazarus' Bethany. In between the two periods of quiet, Jesus makes himself heard even in the realm of the dead.

Thirdly, in 10,40-42 Jesus has retired 'to the place where John used to baptise' i.e. Jesus has returned to the place where he himself —and the story— began, Bethany across the Jordan. After all that has happened, Jesus is back at the beginning. It is literally a dead end of the story —a reason why some commentators want to finish the book here, cf. Brown's 'at one time the Johannine sketch of the public ministry came to a conclusion with X 40-42' (1966, 414). The threat of death has come very close for Jesus. On the feast of the dedication of the Temple he had been threatened to be stoned and they wanted to grab him (10,31.39), but Jesus walked away. He retired to the place where it all began. It is no longer clear how the story should continue.

There is, therefore, a narrative cesura between 10,42 and 11,1, an empty space which textually is filled by the special introduction of the new personages. Lazarus, Martha, and Mary are people who have been known to Jesus for quite some time. Even before the narrator tells us that Jesus loves Lazarus (11,5), his sisters have stated in their message to Jesus that 'he whom you love, is sick' (11,3). Mary is given a very special introduction. She is proleptically introduced as the one 'who anointed the lord with balm and dried his feet with her hair', in an abbreviated version of the story which is still to come and which, therefore, has its own importance. Martha has a more simple position in the beginning. She is Mary's sister (11,1), but in 11,5 their roles have been reversed. In this sentence, which explains Jesus' relation to the family, Martha is mentioned first and Mary remains unnamed. Whatever the meaning of all this is, each sentence of the introduction shows that an —as yet unmentioned—, intensive relationship has developed between Jesus and this *oikos* which consists of only a brother and two sisters, in which the two sisters are in a special relationship to each other and, together, to their brother. The socially difficult situation in which Jesus finds himself is softened by this place which is for him a safe place.

This is the setting from which the sisters send Jesus their message. They use a form which is like a letter: short and with a precision which evokes wonder and emotion. The sentence is just a statement; it is not a request for him to come but only a message. Are the sisters keeping this in hand? In his answer (directed to the hearers of the story) Jesus foresees certain events: that this sickness will not lead to death, but is for the glory of God and for the glory of the son of God. The sisters' concern seems not to touch Jesus. He remains two days in the place where he is: a delay of which the meaning is not yet clear.

But in the meantime, something important has happened narratively. The message of the sisters puts an end to Jesus' inactivity. Because Lazarus' sisters have taken the initiative, the story proceeds —with important consequences as is known. The action of these women —based on the love which Jesus has for them and apparently without consulting the brother—, brings Jesus out of the isolation in which he placed himself or to which circumstances had condemned him. Martha and Mary are the women who make sure that the deadlock is removed and the story can proceed.

2.b.2. *the conversation of Jesus and Martha (11,17-27)*

After a conversation between Jesus and his disciples to convince them to come with him to Judea, a conversation which is filled with allusions to dying, Jesus arrives in Bethany which is near Jerusalem. Martha and Mary now begin to play their own individual roles. As is well known in exegesis, Martha is given the role which is linked more directly to the language, the style, and the theology of the Johannine Gospel (cf. Seim 1987, 71). For the moment she is the most active. While Mary remains at home, she runs to meet Jesus.

The conversation opens abruptly. Martha takes the initiative. There is no sense of wonder that a woman publicly addresses a man. The relation between Jesus and this *oikos* is apparently known and accepted. In 11,11, Jesus spoke to his disciples about 'our' friend Lazarus: his disciples are at home with the family too.

The opening sentence itself, 'Lord, if you had been here, my brother would not have died' can be compared with what Jesus' mother said to him in the Cana story, 'they have no wine'. It is an affirmation which does not imply a question but which, at the same time, makes an appeal to Jesus. Martha expresses this concretely: 'but even now I know that whatever you may ask of God, he will give you.' It does not sound very logical, but it is not without importance for the continuation of the story. At the end of the narrative Jesus will publicly pray to God and that will be the first time he does so in the Johannine story. Although in the story no connection is made between this affirmation by Martha about Jesus' special relation and God —as we will see Jesus will even deny the content—, Martha effects as woman and as the first in the story a behaviour of Jesus which he has not yet shown.

The sequence of the conversation is not without surprises either. Martha gives concrete expression to the future time of Lazarus' resurrection about which Jesus speaks (11,23), with the addition, 'it will happen on the last day' (11,24). That is a misunderstanding as becomes clear from Jesus' answer. The future which she expects, is here already: 'my brother will rise on the last day' over against 'I am the resurrection and the life'. Martha's misunderstanding is thus of a different order than the misunderstanding of Nicodemus, of the Samaritan woman, or of the disciples. Martha does not wrong Jesus in any way. In his closing response Jesus helps her to make the transition from present to future. He does so by changing her *knowing* about the future resurrection in a *believing* in him who is the resurrection and the life. 'Martha's knowing' (11,22 and 24) will change into 'believing in Jesus' (11,26: 'do you believe this?'; 11,27: 'I believe'), a faith which in Jesus' statement is twice connected with 'life' (11,25 and 26). Faith in Jesus brings life, because it wins victory over death.

The conversation between Jesus and this woman ended again, from his side, with a self-disclosure. Because Jesus has used ἐγώ εἰμι-sentences before, it is not a new narrative reality, different from the conversation with the Samaritan woman. Jesus already said about himself that he is the bread, the light, the door, the good shepherd. On the other hand, (cf. Neyrey 1988, 88) 11,25 is an I AM statement which is totally different from all other ἐγώ εἰμι-statements. Neyrey writes: 'In 11,25 Jesus does not replace any obsolete or false Jewish cult object or expectation —as in the other I AM proclamations—, for Jesus does not merely revive Lazarus, replacing prophets of old who could do the same act of power. He claims to have an eschatological power that belongs to God alone'. And even though I do not believe that one should speak —from the Johannine (and also Christian!) point of view—, of 'obsolete and false Jewish cult objects', —it is clear that Jewishness is set up anew by God in Jesus; God is, through Jesus, even more intensely faithful to his covenant with Israel, since in the person of Jesus God commits himself to Israel—, this does not deny that 11,25 is about a more comprehensive re-installation than the other I AM sentences. Jn 11,25 refers to 10,28, to 10,17-18 and, especially, to the great discourse in 5,19ff which started from the conflict about Jesus as God's equal. That Jesus is the resurrection and the life, makes him equal to God as the absolute source of life.

The content of 11,25 is about the transference of God's power to Jesus to bring the dead back to life. Jesus exercises this divine royal function in God's name (cf. 11,41ff). Dan 12,2, probably, played an important role in the Johannine theology (cf. 5,29). When the rabbis are to prove that the doctrine of the resurrection can be found in Scripture, they find that quite difficult (see the base text in Sanh 90b). Dt 31,16, Is 26,29, and Cant 7,10 are rejected, because they are open to a different interpretation. The common ground is Dt 11,9 and Dt 4,4, texts which play a role also in the Johannine theology (cf. Beutler 1984, 55ff) and which, even more importantly, bring the resurrection from the dead in line with the promises of covenant which God makes to Israel. Therefore, I believe that, as in the story of the Samaritan woman, the covenant theology plays a role also here, even though it remains more implicit.

The confession of faith with which Martha closes the conversation (11,27), indicates that she (at least) understood what Jesus was speaking about. There is a double reason why one should judge this profession positively. Her statement is completely in line with the intention of the writer in writing his book (20,31), i.e. before any of the readers, Martha achieved what the writer intended. She is the perfect reader model. Secondly, and narratively maybe even more important, her profession is a precise summary of the scene which has just been told of the feast of the Dedication of the Temple (10,22-39). In contradistinction to the inhabitants of Jerusalem, Martha understood that Jesus is the Messiah who works in the name of his father and from whose hand no sheep is lost (10,24-25); and also that Jesus is the son of God, not because he makes himself equal to God, but because he is in truth God's son (10,33.36.38). Martha's faith is clearly contrasted by the unbelief of the Judeans. She listened carefully to Jesus and showed that she belongs to the sheep of the shepherd-Jesus. Of all the people in the Johannine Gospel Martha is the only one who claims for herself this honour in such an explicit manner and so in conformity with the author's intention.

2.b.3. the meeting of Mary and Jesus (11,28-37)

Mary has a totally different role from Martha. She gives body and substance to what has happened (cf. Genuyt 1986, 28). She does not say much, but expresses her sorrow bodily. She brings other people to take a positive or negative stand in relation to the events. For us the most interesting part is the change in behaviour she effects in Jesus.

In the opening scene Martha is the intermediary. Immediately after expressing her profession, she brings Mary into the scene. While Jesus remains stationary, the women walk back and forth: talking secretly, getting up quickly, expressed as ἐγέρθη. Martha calls Jesus 'teacher', opening the question whether Jesus was 'their teacher' and they 'his disciples'. The use of the title alone does not prove much. Even if Jesus is the teacher only of male disciples, it is still possible for others to call him teacher. But it also said that Jesus 'calls' Mary, an other word that functions in the relation teacher-disciple. It is this typical combination that makes it probable that the two sisters indeed belong to the circle of disciples.

The Judeans who are present are, for the time being, only companions. In fact they will become commentators. When they see Jesus cry, they split into two groups which react positively or negatively to Jesus. The event is not a family affair. It becomes ever more important and public.

The one sentence which Mary speaks is, as far as content is concerned, identical with what Martha said to Jesus. But there is a subtle difference in formulation which changes the tone of the communication. The possessive μου comes earlier and expresses thus a stronger affectivity. Martha says 'my brother', while Mary says 'that brother of mine', indicating that she is herself affected by his death.

She expresses that also bodily: 'crying', 'at the feet of Jesus'. This is positively or negatively evaluated, dependent on the individual values of each exegete. The narrator gives it such importance that he shows Jesus in sympathy with this behaviour. It is one of the few times that Jesus reacts bodily. After Mary and the Judeans he now also cries himself, a crying Jesus open to the comments of the people around him. Seeing Mary's grief, it becomes possible for Jesus to express his own grief based on his love for his friend Lazarus. A woman has again helped Jesus to be closer to whom he is and has made it possible for him to express himself.

2.b.4. the scene at the tomb (11,38-44)

The story progresses. Jesus nears the tomb over which he will eventually win victory. It does not go so well with the relation between Martha and Jesus. At least, that is the way I read this text, be it with some reservations.

Martha is introduced anew, now as 'the sister of the dead person' (11,39) which brings her forward as the spokesperson for Lazarus. She objects to Jesus' command to open the tomb. There is a certain sense of reality here: 'he smells', a negative reference to the glory: stench against glory. In his answer Jesus deals with this, but communicatively less unambiguously than most of the exegetes seem to think. He asks Martha: 'Did I not tell you that, if you believe, you will see the glory of God?' (11,40). The simplest answer to this question is 'no', but Mary is silent and the stone is taken away. How should we interpret this narratively empty space in the text? One could say that the protest of Martha is refuted by Jesus. Exegesis takes this option unanimously as far as I know: Jesus rightly resists Martha's remark.

In this interpretation the open gap of the text is filled up in three different ways:
- From the viewpoint of the narrative progression of the story:
The hearer of the story is introduced in 11,40 into a part of the conversation between Jesus and Martha which is not mentioned before. Something similar happens in 11,28 where Martha says to Mary: 'the teacher is here and calls you'. That had not been said before either and yet one can not say that Martha is lying. It is not

that the narrator has forgotten something, but he is making up for something. Jesus refutes Martha's objection on the basis of a previous conversation: the stench of the body can not stand against faith, because the stench will become the glory of God: a pun which in Greek is even recognisable phonetically: ὄζει against ὄψῃ.

- From the viewpoint of the interpretation of the conversation in 11,17-27:

Martha's profession of faith in 11,17 must have been defective, because Jesus accuses her in 11,40 of a lack of faith. The supposition is that she did not express a personal profession of faith and that this breaks up now; or that the misunderstanding between her and Jesus is not fully solved. The open gap is placed on Martha's side and the text says about Jesus that he shows her this deficiency (e.g. Bultmann 1941, 311; Genuyt 1986, 31).

- From the viewpoint of the textual totality of the story of Lazarus:

In the totality of the text the content of what Jesus says here has been mentioned twice: as Jesus' answer to the message of the two sisters in 11,4 and, more indirectly, in the answer Jesus gives his disciples, when he has convinced them to come with him to Judea (11,15). In this interpretation the beginning of Jesus' sentence in 11,40 —'did I not tell you'—, is put aside. Just as the hearers of the story have heard everything Jesus said, it is accepted that Martha has heard everything too and that she now does not make use of it (e.g. Brown 1966, 436).

Although these readers' strategies are mutually exclusive, their individual impact is quite strong. They fit in with the writer's perspective that Jesus is always right. In line with this, these exegetes construe a simple narrative isotopy. I ask myself whether it would not be more correct to accept a narrative break in the text. Martha's protest is put aside by Jesus in a manner which is not in line with what happened in 11,17-27. She is silenced abruptly and in a way which we do not understand. It is a narrative preparation for what is going to happen in 11,41.42, in the prayer in which Jesus speaks, demonstratively, about the way God listens to him, and about his awareness of this listening. In this prayer Martha is silenced in an even more literal sense. Jesus leaves out completely what Martha said about this to him (in 11,22). While, in 11,40, Jesus accuses Martha of not having heard what he said —without any proof of this in what went before—, Jesus acts in 11,41.42, as if he did not hear what Martha literally told him.

I can not but see a parallel here with the story of the Samaritan woman. As the Samaritan woman is evaluated at the end of her story by Jesus only indirectly (interpretatively by readers who want to read 4,31-38 narratively) and inclusively anonymously (in 4,38), so also Martha in this story. In a certain sense she is even worse off, because she is made completely anonymous.

2.b.5. the scene of the anointing (12,1-11)

One more time Martha and Mary play a role in the story, in the sub-story of the meal in Lazarus' house. After the judgment over Jesus has been passed that he is to die, and he retires with his disciples to Ephraim, he comes back to Bethany in Judea, six days before the Passover, back to Lazarus' family where an evening meal is prepared in his honour. The multiple connection with the Lazarus' story (the same people; the introduction of Lazarus as 'he whom Jesus had recalled from the dead'; Mary is going to do that which the readers already know she has done cf. 11,2), inevitably, bring the readers to see this meal as a meal of thanksgiving. Lazarus' family repays through this meal the gratitude they owe Jesus. Martha is the one who makes the meal possible for the guests.

For our context the scene of anointing is important, because it determines definitively the relation between Jesus and Mary. The anointing is also important for the narrator of the Johannine Gospel. In a way he relates it twice: in Jn 11,2 introducing Mary in the story of Lazarus as a personal description of Mary, and in 12,3ff as a narrative. There is a double reality: the anointing of the feet with nard and the drying of the feet with her hair. The scene reminds one of the story in Luke about the woman which is known as a sinner and who washes Jesus' feet with her tears and dries them with her hair, kisses them and anoints them (Lc 7,38), a story which explicitly tells about the $\dot{\alpha}\gamma\dot{\alpha}\pi\eta$ of the woman. (In the parallel stories of Mt 26,6ff and Mc 14,3ff the woman anoints the head of Jesus and does not dry anything).

The mention at the end of 12,3, 'that the house was filled with the smell of the perfume' is special. De Merode pointed out that the expression $\dot{o}\sigma\mu\eta$ $\mu\dot{\upsilon}\rho\sigma\upsilon$ is the same lexeme as used in Jer 25,10 (LXX). The 'smell of perfume' there is connected with the 'voice of the groom and the voice of the bride' (1982, 61), an implicit indication that the anointing by Mary has sexual connotations.

I would like to expand on this somewhat, because it seems to me that this possibility of understanding the text is not talked about at all in exegesis. In a certain sense I agree completely with Coakley's conclusion : 'Her (= Mary's) act was an extravagant gesture of love which, when criticised, Jesus reinterpreted in terms of his impending death' (1988, 254), but I think this statement needs some addition and explicitation. In the same way as in the description of the behaviour of the beloved disciple, the narrator of the Johannine Gospel uses in this narrative a language which suggests more than exegesis usually explicates. I need to return here to the Hellenistic romance literature.

That the anointing of feet evokes an erotic connotation as preparation for sexual intercourse according to the cultural code of the time, is very clear from a text of Athenaeus who provides us with a collection of places in Greek literature where this custom is mentioned:

"So Eubulus says in Sphinx-Cario: '(You should have seen me) lying at ease in the bed-chamber! and all about me luxuriant demoiselles, very voluptuous and mincing, will rub my foot with unguents (μύροις) of amaracus'.

And in Procris someone tells how Procris's hound is to be cared for, always speaking of it as it were a human being: 'A. So then, you shall spread a nice soft bed for the hound; underneath you will lay cloths of Milesian wool, while over him you will spread a soft robe. B. Apollo defends us! A. Then you will soak for him some wheat groats in goose milk. B. Heaven above! A. And smear his feet with Megallus scent (μύρῳ).'....

Anaxandrides, too, says in Protesilaus: 'Perfume bought at Peron's shop, some of which he sold yesterday to Melanopus, and expensive Egyptian too (μύρος; πολυτελοῦς); with it Melanopus is now anointing the feet of Callistratus.'" (Deipnosoph XII.552-3).

In the romance literature I found this custom described only in the absurd story at the end of the *Metamorphoses*, when Lucius still has the appearance of an ass and is used as a circus performer: to sit at table, to answer questions, to copulate. The story is similar to what Athenaeus relates about the hound of Procris. A bed is prepared with lots of pillows and precious covers. Candles are lit:

"Then she stripped herself of all her clothes, including the band with which she had bound her lovely breasts. Standing next to the light, she anointed herself all over with oil of balsam (*oleo balsamino*) from a pewter jar, and lavishly rubbed me down with the same, but with much greater eagerness. She even moistened my nostrils with frankincense. Then she kissed me intimately...Next she took me by my halter and made me lie down, as I had learned to do. I obeyed readily, because I did not think my task would be anything new or difficult, and especially since for the first time in a long while I was about to enjoy the passionate embraces of a very beautiful woman. Furthermore I had saturated myself with a generous quantity of the finest wine and aroused my desire for sex with the heady fragrance of the ointment." (Apul X.21).

Mary uses her hair to dry the feet of Jesus. That is a gesture for slaves as is evident in (e.g.) Petronius:

"Trimalchio cracked his fingers. One eunuch came up at this signal and held the jordan for him as he played. He relieved himself and called for a basin, dipped in his hands and wiped them on a boy's head." (= 'in capite pueri tersit') (Satyrica 27); and "I redeemed my wife to preserve her from indignities "(= 'ne quis in capillis illius manus tergeret') (id 57).

Corresponding to this Jn 11,2 speaks about Mary who anointed 'the *kyrios*' and dried his feet with her hair. Together with Martha's service, Mary serves as a slave.

Drying his feet with her hair presupposes that she loosened her hair. Women do that either as preparation for sexual intercourse or in ceremonies of mourning. That loose hair brings sexual connotations is easily understandable. Apul., Metam II.9 and II.17 elaborates this literarily, but the same can be found everywhere in love-poetry. In the Johannine story Jesus takes the second connotation: the loose hair —untended— as a sign of mourning for a dear departed person.

All this helps me to discover a pattern in the stories about women of the Johannine Gospel. Where Jesus initially reacts positively to what women have to offer and even sometimes takes the initiative, at the end women are always put in their place so to speak. Sometimes almost literally as in the story of Martha and here with Mary, sometimes more implicitly by making their merits anonymous as happens with the Samaritan woman and with Martha. Now we want to look at how this happens with Mary Magdalene.

2.c. the story of Mary Magdalene (20,1-18)

Ashton (1991, 501ff), recently, pointed out through a whole series of, in his own words, 'insensitive questions' that there are many narrative problems in this story. I believe that he, afraid of having wandered into an Alice-in-Wonderland world, forgets that the Johannine narrator is not afraid of realistic absurdities in the rest of his story which would not be misplaced in a story like Alice-in-Wonderland: a whole cohort (and that means at least 600 soldiers cf. Jos BJ 3, 67) which as one man steps back and falls to the ground as reaction to a simple sentence of Jesus' ἐγώ εἰμι (18,6); Jesus who dines with Lazarus just out of the tomb, surrounded by a curious multitude who wants to see (and hear?) Lazarus (12,9); Jesus who simply walks away, when a large group of people want to get hold of him to stone him (10,39); Jesus who walks on the water and the boat reaches the shore immediately afterwards (6,16ff) etc. The narrator of the Johannine Gospel confronts modern readers with a different idea of narrative realism than we are acquainted with. In short, I think that, narratively speaking, a modern evaluation of narrative realism can not be used to prove the presence or absence of a narrative logic of a story.

This is an unexpectedly polemical opening to my discussion of the story of Mary Magdalene. This is necessary, however, because the narrative unity of this story is in question here and Ashton is, in a way, the exemplar of many exegetes (cf. Mahoney 1974, 171ff which gives an overview of this way of reading; Ritt 1983, 117ff; Witherington 1988, 177ff). When does a story break in two parts so that one has a double point which can not be combined in a higher narrative isotopy? Concretely for the story of Mary Magdalene: is it necessary for the unity of the story that it is told that Mary Magdalene, after her visit with the two disciples, goes back to the tomb (as the Johannine narrator does in 1,38.39 in the sequence of words: 'where are you staying — come and see — and they came and saw where he stayed'); is it necessary for the unity of the story that Mary Magdalene experienced what happened to the two disciples at the tomb (as e.g. in 3,26 is related how John the Baptist experienced from his disciples what happened with Jesus). Is it necessary that Mary Magdalene looks at the tomb in the same way as the disciples and that she sees the same things (as e.g. in 6,1ff Philip and Andrew look at the multitude in the same way as Jesus does, or in 7,45ff the servants of the High Priests and Nicodemus look at Jesus)? Mary Magdalene stands, narratively unprepared, before the tomb in 20,11; it is not said in the story that she is present, when the two disciples arrive, but is that important? Mary Magdalene sees two angels in the tomb, and the disciples see the linen cloths, but is there a conflict here? A story is not improved by the fact that it is repeated, when there are no open gaps and no surprises. The preceding questions are, for me, rhetorical questions and should be answered with an unequivocal no! There will be a break in a narrative, when the storyline is broken irreparably as e.g. in the story of Cana, when Jesus has said, 'my hour has not yet come' (2,4) or in the story about the conflict between Jesus and his brothers and sisters when Jesus says: 'I am not going to the feast' (7,8); or in the story of Lazarus —as explained above—, when Jesus says to Martha: 'did I not tell you?' (11,40). The story of Mary Magdalene does not show such a break. I realise that the determination of such a broken storyline is a reader's decision or a reader's construction, but I realise also that the arguments about it are on a different level than the examples just mentioned. Therefore, my supposition is that 20,1-18 is a coherent story which has a continuous storyline. In connection with the focus of this chapter, I want to link the discussion of the story with three topics: the search, the recognition, and the mission.

2.c.1. the search

To judge the narrative position of Mary Magdalene it is important to remember that together with the beloved disciple, she was present when Jesus died on the cross. With him she is a witness to Jesus' death. The story in 20,1ff connects with that. In the early hours on the day after Easter, she goes to the tomb, sees that the stone has been rolled away and runs back. Her search has started.

I discussed above how the two disciples fare in this situation. For this chapter it is important to see how again a woman is the active participant who activates others. The two narratively most important male disciples are literally awakened by Mary Magdalene. Her 'running' (20,2) is finally imitated by them and ends in a contest which they win together.

The communication is found in the sentence which Mary Magdalene speaks to the two disciples (separately?): 'they have taken the Lord away and we do not know where they have put him' (20,2). There are a number of things, we can say about this sentence:

- The use of the plural 'we' indicates that Mary Magdalene speaks from a sense of solidarity. This can be linked to the fact that she speaks about 'the Lord', implying that Simon Peter and the beloved disciple recognise Jesus also as 'the Lord'. Mary Magdalene's message to these disciples is communicated in the context of a cohesive group which is not very clearly defined, but some names are known.

- Mary Magdalene has seen more than the narrator has communicated so far. In 20,1 it is said only that the stone was rolled away. Now she appears to know that the body of Jesus has disappeared. Mary does not speak about theft or robbery. Her supposition is that some people who are not part of the group of disciples, have taken the body and deposited it elsewhere. The text probably tries to make a connection with 19,41, where it is said that Nicodemus and Joseph have placed the body of Jesus in the nearest tomb because they were in a hurry.

- Finally, it is a declarative sentence which implicitly contains a request. It is the same kind of message as in the sentence of the two sisters Mary and Martha to Jesus (in 11,3), or as in Cana with the mother of Jesus (in 2,3). Here the request is something like: could you check this and/or do something about it? The male disciples do not do much more than confirm the statement of Mary Magdalene for themselves. If the faith of the beloved disciple is related to his faith in the resurrection of Jesus, he gives the absence of the body a different interpretation, but Mary Magdalene does not know about this interpretation or such an interpretation is unintelligible for her.

The choice between the last two mentioned narrative possibilities depends on the way one fills in the empty space in 20,11, the introduction of the second move in the search of Mary Magdalene: 'Mary Magdalene stood near the tomb, outside, crying'. The time element is left open narratively. It could be 'meanwhile', i.e. while Peter and the beloved disciple were near and in the tomb, or 'later', i.e. when the disciples have gone back home. In the first case Mary Magdalene's crying is a reaction to the blindness of the disciples; in the second case —more intelligible—, it is the result of her frustrated search. The disciples have not been able to help her.

The second way finds support in the sentence which Mary Magdalene speaks to the two angels: 'they have taken my Lord away and I do not know where they have put him' (20,13). The similarity in content with what she told the disciples makes it clear that she holds on to her search. Two small changes indicate the difference in communicative meaning: 'the Lord' has become 'my Lord' and the plural 'we' has changed into the singular 'I'. Mary Magdalene does not have the same relation with the angels as she has with the two disciples. She does not simply accept that Jesus is their Lord too and she does not have the same communitarian solidarity with them. The angels are not disciples who are part of the group she knows.

The simple sentence they speak to her, 'woman, why do you cry?' (20,13) evokes sometimes surprise with exegetes and it is surely not a heavenly message; it has literary-communicative meaning, because Jesus —as the supposed gardener—, begins with the same sentence (20,15). It is the opening sentence of the third move in the ongoing search of Mary. The failure of the contact with the angels makes her turn around, away from the tomb towards Jesus. It is a scene in which the Johannine misunderstanding appears in its most appealing form: searching for a dead body Mary can not recognise Jesus in this living person. At least, it seems that this is the interpretation one must give to this scene from the perspective of the personages involved. She can not recognise Jesus, because she can not imagine him as 'living'. One could call that a defect. Culpepper seems to do this when he writes: 'Although she sees how he dies, discovers the tomb empty, sees the angels, and even sees the risen Lord himself, these experiences do not enlighten her' (1983, 144). One can also see the narrative as the process of change: a reversal in perception which comes about through frustrations.

What is important in any case is that Jesus takes the initiative to show himself to her. That is naturally also the introduction to the climax of the story: the progressive seeing of Peter and the beloved disciple and now the seeing in phases of Mary Magdalene. Against the background of the last sentence which Jesus speaks in this chapter: 'Happy are those who do not see and yet believe' (20,29), one must say that the beloved disciple is the happiest of all and is the proto-type of all future believers. Mary Magdalene is given the first place as the one who witnessed the resurrection of Jesus. This woman is the first elect among all the disciples (cf. Hengel 1963, 243ff). The story suggests that it is the reward for her searching, the fulfilment of her desire to be in touch with Jesus even after his death.

2.c.2. the recognition-scene

The real recognition occurs when Jesus speaks Mary's name, in Hebrew, making it even more realistic. For its interpretation exegetes pointed to Jn 10,8.16.27: the sheep who recognise the voice of the shepherd (Brown 1970, 694; Thyen 1977, 291). Mary Magdalene recognises the voice of her shepherd, (but Jesus spoke to her already before!). She addresses Jesus as Rabbouni, a mode of address which is sometimes seen as insufficient (e.g. by Witherington 1988, 179: 'she still thinks of Jesus in terms of her past relationship with Him'). It shows, in fact, that Mary considers herself a disciple of Jesus, a discipleship which goes beyond his death (cf. 20,18.19.24.30).

The conclusion of the scene with the famous $\mu\acute{\eta}$ μov $\check{\alpha}\pi\tau\text{ov}$-sentence is striking as is the rather incomprehensible reason for it: 'because I have not yet gone back up to the father' (20,17). The first part of the sentence is in the context of this chapter the most relevant. There are two ways to translate it (cf. Feuillet 1963, 100; Dodd 1968, 443; Brown 1970, 992ff): 'do not touch me', or, 'do not cling to me'/'stop touching me'. In the second case Mary touches Jesus, but Jesus forbids/prevents her from continuing to do so.

As became clear to me in the study of the Hellenistic romance literature, this conclusion belongs in a certain way to the specific genre of a scene of recognition. It is part of the main plot of the romance literature that the two lovers find each other after a long absence and many difficulties. Literarily, it is expressed in a scene of recognition which is typically comparable with the scene of recognition between Mary Magdalene and Jesus in Jn 20.

Let me give the relevant texts:

Chariton VIII.1.7ff: Chaireas has taken possession of the harem of the king of Persia. His beloved Callirhoe is there without his being aware of it. At the moment that he decides to return the harem, Callirhoe is brought to him:

> "He (=Chaireas) stepped across the threshold and saw the young woman stretched out, covered with veils. He was touched right away because of her breathing and her shape. He would have recognised her immediately, if he had not been convinced that Callirhoe had been given to Dionysios (by the king). Very delicately he approached her and said: 'Courage, woman (γύναι) whoever you are. I do not want to harm you. You will have the husband you desire.' While he was still speaking to her, Callirhoe recognised his voice and threw off her veils. Immediately they called out together:'Chaireas — Callirhoe!'. They threw themselves into each other's arms and fainted ..."
> —Polycharmus, their friend, tries to bring them round—, "but the two, as if sunk into a deep well where the voices from the top can hardly penetrate, came to only very slowly; they saw each other anew; they covered each other again with kisses and again they fainted; twice, three times without saying anything else than:'I have you, if you are really Callirhoe —if you are really Chaireas.' "

Eph V 13.2ff: The recognition of the two lovers Habrocomes and Anthia knows several stages. To begin with Habrocomes is recognised by his slaves Leucon and Rhodos (V.10.6ff). When these slaves recognise Anthia a couple of days later in the temple (V.12.3 - 13.1),

> "only one thing was lacking to their happiness. Habrocomes did not yet know! Without further delay they ran home (τρέχω) to fetch him. An inhabitant of Rhodos had told him in the meantime that Anthia had been found. Shouting the name of Anthia he ran as crazy through the city. In front of Isis' temple he meets her. An enormous crowd followed her. When they saw each other, they recognised each other right away. This was what they had always wanted. Embracing each other they fell to the ground. All kinds of emotions were going on inside them: happiness, sorrow, fear, the memory of the past, the thoughts of the future. The crowd of inhabitants of Rhodos shouted loudly in their honour."

Aeth II.6.3: Theagenes and Chariclea have lost sight of each other in the battle in the village of the pirates. They find each other again in the cave where Chariclea had been kept:

"She, having clambered up with hands as well as feet to the light, came running (προσδραμοῦσα) to Theagenes and clung round his neck. 'I hold you, Theagenes!' and 'I have you alive, Chariclea!' they said to each other, again and again, and ended by falling both at once to the ground, where they lay clasping one another in a mute embrace, yet seeming to have become but one person, and were at a point very near to death...." —Cnemon, their friend, brings them round by sprinkling water over their faces and by tickling their noses—. "Then they, suddenly finding themselves prostate in attitudes so different from those in which they met each other, at once stood upright and blushed —Chariclea especially—, for shame that Cnemon should have witnessed such a scene, and besought his pardon. But he smiled at them." (transl. W. Lamb, see also V.11.1ff en VII.7.5).

For the sake of completeness: Feuillet (1963, 102ff) pointed out that the Song of Songs 3, 1-4 knows a similar structure. The girl finds her beloved after a long search:

"Scarcely had I left the watchmen behind me or I found my true love. I seized him (ἐκράτησα) and would not let him go (οὐκ ἀφήσω) until I had brought him into the house of my mother, in the room of her who conceived me."
(Song of Songs 3,4)

It is clear that in this kind of story one can not think there would be a difference between Jewish and Hellenistic literature. The Jewish novel Joseph and Aseneth, however, does not have a recognition scene so that this literature is not important under this aspect.

The stories about the recognition of the two lovers show a clear narrative structure: the delay in recognition, the calling of the names, the embrace, and the emotions which even bring them to faint, and the end of the greeting. The recognition story in Jn 20 corresponds in details to this narrative structure. The use of the words τρέχω, γύναι and ἅπτομαι, and the story line developed from the delay in recognition, the recognition, the calling out of the names, and the closing with the greeting make clear that the Johannine story belongs to this genre.

Dependent on the translation of μή μου ἅπτου from Jn 20,17 —'do not touch me', or, 'stop touching me'—, follows the distance or the nearness of the Johannine story and the other recognition scenes. In the first case it is an absolute prohibition in which Jesus prevents Mary Magdalene to vent her emotions which are suited to the situation for her. In the second case Jesus ends the affectively presented greeting. The Johannine story participates then more fully in the love literature: the physical contact between Jesus and Mary Magdalene comes to an end but the contact itself is not broken.

2.c.3. the mission

In fact, the text continues reinforcing the contact. That supports the second interpretation of the text. Jesus gives Mary Magdalene the task to tell 'the brethren' that he is going to go 'to my father and yours, to my God and yours.' It has been made clear in exegesis that this is the language of covenant (cf. Feuillet 1963, 101; Brown 1970, 1016ff). Jesus' word reminds of the promise which God made to his people: they will be my people and I will be their God; reminds of the answer of Ruth to her mother-in-law who does not want Ruth to go back to the land of Judah: 'where you go I will go, where you remain I will remain. Your people are my people; your God is my God' (Ruth 1, 16). In the name of the disciples Jesus enters into a covenant with God the father, a covenant which lasts beyond his death and beyond the telling of the story.

For the relation between Jesus and the individual women, it is important to note that the theology of covenant of the Johannine Gospel is again activated in this context: in this case most directly in a formula which comes straight from the language of covenant. Through this woman Jesus lets us hear for the first time and definitively that his presence with the father is the guarantee of the continuing reality of the covenant between God and Israel.

Mary Magdalene is given the task to tell 'the brethren' about it. It is a mission which she fulfils immediately: Mary Magdalene, as the *apostolos-aggelos*, the angel-messenger who as the first says, first of all, that she has seen the Lord; and only after that she tells the content of what she heard from Jesus. That belongs together: the content of the words is guaranteed by the seeing, and the seeing is given its content by the message.

Does the story of Mary Magdalene follow the pattern of the other women stories? We have the 'rejection' of Mary Magdalene by Jesus in Jn 20,17. In the translation (and interpretation) of μή μου ἅπτου as 'do not touch me', there is a literal conformity. Mary's own emotional response is literally rejected more or less parallel to what Jesus does to Martha and Mary, and to his own mother. More probably, however, one should translate 'stop touching me', and then the sentence is only the end of the bodily expressed greeting scene, a gesture necessary for the progression of the story and in line with the genre of recognition scenes. But even in this interpretation Mary Magdalene does not survive as her own person. Even then the woman is made anonymous and put in second place. This is done through two narrative manipulations: by telling the progression of the story —where Mary Magdalene completely disappears—, and by the closing sentence which is spoken by Jesus.

It is quite possible to suppose that Mary Magdalene is present among the 'disciples' in the following two scenes —in the story of Jesus' apparition to the disciples (Jn 20,19-22) and to the disciples together with Thomas (Jn 20,23-29)—, but even then her presence is totally anonymous. The narrator's interest is only for Thomas as 'one of the twelve', and the text in 20,24 —'the other disciples'— even seems to suggest that on the evening of the first day only eleven disciples are present (including Judas?). Mary Magdalene has disappeared completely.

The last sentence which Jesus speaks —beginning as addressing Thomas, but ending more generally: 'because you have seen you believe? Blessed are those who have not seen and yet believe' (20,29)—, gives a strange twist to the story of Mary Magdalene after the story itself. Applied to the story the beloved disciple —who does not see and yet believes—, is given an honour much greater than Mary Magdalene —who only after seeing comes to belief. According to the vision of the implied author —and maybe it must be reminded that this is imaginarily the beloved disciple—, Jesus prefers the beloved disciple above this loving woman.

The relation between Jesus and the women in the Johannine Gospel is quite special and, as should be clear by now, it is also somewhat ambiguous. The beginning and the end of the stories show quite a difference. In the beginning of the various stories Jesus is inviting and open; he opens the conversations and listens to them; he helps the conversation to progress. He also receives a lot: personally, because the women make it possible for him to express himself in a way which in other situations is not given to him or not yet given; and beyond the personal, because the women win people time and again for the Jesus movement and in this way make the covenant between God and Israel visible and open for new possibilities.

But each time there is a phase in the story where this openness is closed off: the active Samaritan woman is made anonymous; the theological Martha is accused of not having faith; the affective Mary hears an interpretation which is surprising; the radiant Mary Magdalene with her message that she has seen the Lord is rated lower than the beloved disciple who does not see him and yet believes. The implied author developed imaginarily a vision of Jesus which rather closely fits what has been said at the end of chapter 1 and in chapter 2. At decisive moments Jesus retreats from this relation to women: he finds refuge in his relation with the male disciples (in the case of the Samaritan woman); he retires into himself (in the case of Martha and Mary) and, in the closing stories, he goes back to his relation with the beloved disciple (in the case of his mother and Mary Magdalene). One can surmise that the women are left empty-handed even though the story does not say so. The return to the male partner(s) is in the story something self-evident and demonstrates once again that the social role of Jesus in the Johannine Gospel is clearly circumscribed.

CHAPTER FIVE

BELOVED MEN

Men play a significant role on several levels of the story: groups are identified as male even though they are composed of men and women —the Galileans, the Judeans, the inhabitants of Jerusalem, the Samaritans, the Jews, the Greeks, cf. 6,10 where only the men are counted—; the exclusively male groups —the group of the male disciples as we explained, the Pharisees, the High Priests and their cohorts, the soldiers of Pilate; as individuals who react positively or negatively to Jesus: Nicodemus, the king's official and his son, Annas, Caiaphas, Pilate, Joseph from Arimathea; and finally as the men with whom Jesus is actively involved: the paralytic in ch. 5, the blind man in ch. 9 and Lazarus in ch. 11 and 12. Jesus' active involvement with these men makes these stories relevant for the description of the imaginative love in John because of the focus of this study. Three men, three stories which are comparable with the way in which Jesus deals with women. As I said above, the stories about these men are significantly different from the stories about the women. In the men's stories Jesus is much more actively recruiting all the time. Conflict and crisis are uppermost. Jesus' position is clarified, not primarily through his self expression, but via processes which involve life and death. When men are touched by the gracious preference of Jesus, they apparently need to justify themselves before a hostile audience.

1. THE NARRATIVE-IMAGINARY CONTEXT OF THE STORIES

Discussing the Cana story, I asked the question whether for the meaning of the story it is relevant that precisely his mother is the one who points out the need. In these men-stories this question is even more relevant: is it relevant for the meaning of the story that John's Jesus only cures men? That he acts in a special manner towards some of them? That the 'effects' of his action are quite special in some cases and how that is related to their maleness? These questions are not posed in the secondary literature as far as I can see. Yet, they might be important considering the special preference of Jesus for men.

His preference is not for everyone in the same way. Sometimes men search him out as the king's official because of his sick son; Nicodemus comes with his questions; his brothers, some Greeks. A lot happens then, but there is no spark coming from Jesus. He cures the son of the official, but he does not enter into any personal relationship with the man or with his son. Nicodemus appears to be more and more involved with Jesus as the story progresses, but one can not really read that in the story itself. The request of the Greeks to see Jesus is probably granted, but the story is not very clear about it.

In the story of the paralytic, the blind man and the dead man it is different.

- Jesus takes the initiative: he 'sees' the paralytic and he knows that this man has been an invalid for a long time (5,6); he 'sees' the blind man in passing and he knows that he has been blind from birth (9,1); he also knows what is going to happen to the man (9,3.4); even before Lazarus falls ill, 'Jesus loves Lazarus', a love which gives the sisters reason to get Jesus to move (11,3.5). Even though Jesus does not answer the implicit request of the sisters, he lets it be known where the events will lead (11,4); and he acts as the one who has taken the initiative. 'Seeing' the crying of Mary and the Jews prepares the closing phase of the story (cf. the use of εἶδον in relation to Jesus: only in 5,6; 9,1; 11,33, and in 11,29 where Jesus 'sees' his mother and the beloved disciple).

- When the stories end, Jesus takes the initiative again, something he does not even do for his disciples (in as far as the paralytic, the blind man and Lazarus are not disciples). He searches for his people and he 'finds' them. While the paralytic is asked by the Judeans who the man is who cured him —in the narrative supposition that he goes to search for Jesus—, Jesus 'finds' the paralytic in the Temple (5,14). When Jesus hears that the blind man has been thrown out, he goes after him and he 'finds' him (9,35). In the case of Lazarus it is not so much a question of 'finding' (see however 11,17: 'he found that he had been four days in the tomb') as it is a question of returning. Six days before Easter Jesus returns to Lazarus and his family, notwithstanding the death threats, and there is a festive meal to close off the event of Lazarus' resurrection and to introduce Jesus' passion and death cf. the use of εὑρίσκω in relation to Jesus: only in 5,14; 9,35; 11,37 and in 1,43 (? Philip); 2,14 (the cattle and the sheep in the Temple); and 12,14 (an ass).

- Narratively special in these stories is the fact that in the main story we find several retrospective references: Jesus refers to the cure of the paralytic (in 7,21-24); the people who see Jesus cry because of Lazarus refer to the cure of the man born blind (in 11,37); the narrator of the story refers to Lazarus several times in his narrative (12,1.9.17). These retrospectives do not occur in other stories.

7,21-24:
During the Feast of the Tabernacles Jesus teaches in the Temple. His teaching is under discussion: its origin and its relation to the teachings of Moses. Jesus says he has done 'one' work, the cure of the paralytic on the sabbath. The cure is compared to circumcision: as work or sign of the covenant? Because the cure on the sabbath is again put into question, the story of the cure is given more space narratively.

10,21; 11,37:
While 10,21 still fits more or less in the story as told of the cure of the blind man —chronologically-narratively there is no new scene—, there is a real referring back to the story in 11,37. Different from 10,21 the point of view in 11,37 is negative. The signs of Jesus are ambivalent and can be used to prove or disprove the point. In both cases are the Judeans the speakers, a group of people who are ambivalent themselves.

12,1.9.17:
In connection with the story as told of the resurrection of Lazarus we find references to this all through chapter 12. The sentences refer back to it because they mention the 'resurrection from the dead' explicitly each time:
19,1 : 'whom Jesus raised from the dead';
19,9 : 'whom he had raised from the dead';
19,17: 'the crowd which was with him when he called Lazarus forth from the tomb and raised him from the dead.'

It is interesting to note that the references are copied within the stories: within the story of the man born blind we find mention of the cure of the paralytic (during the Feast of the Tabernacles in preparation of the discussion on the last day and next to it the cure of the blind man), within the story of Lazarus we find mention of the cure of the blind man. Narratively it is a structure of 'hooking on' which has its special literary effect.

Different from the women's stories there is clearly no attempt to make the people anonymous as if the narrative character is of no importance once the story is told. In fact, the characters are brought back as individuals in the narrative itself. While they are fairly anonymous —a paralytic, a blind man—, they stay in the personal attention of Jesus, of the Judeans and of the narrator of the story.

- The stories refer mutually to one another. That is true also for their narrative structure. There are differences but there is also a great deal of parallelism. The variations are linked to the various positions in the main story.
Schematically:

the story of the paralytic	the story of the blind man	the story of the dead man
1. 5,1-9 the healing of the paralytic	1. 9,1-7 the healing of the blind man	1. 11,1-44 the raising from the dead
2.	2. 9,8-12 inquiry by friends and neighbours	2.
3. 5,10-13 inquiry by Judeans about the desecration of the sabbath	3. 9,13-17 inquiry by Pharisees about the desecration of the sabbath	3.

4.	4. 9,18-23 inquiry by the Judeans of the parents about the identity of the man	4.
5.	5. 9,24-34 judgment of the Judeans on Jesus and on the healed man	5. 11,45-53 procedure in the Sanhedrin and the judgment on Jesus
6.	6.	6. 11,54-57 the order to find Jesus
7. 5,14 Jesus is made known	7. 9,35-39 Jesus is made known	7. 12,1-8 Jesus is made known
8. 5,15-18 the healed man, Jesus and the Judeans	8. 9,40-10,6 the healed man, Jesus and the Pharisees	8. 12,9-11 Lazarus, Jesus and the High Priests
9.	9.	9. 12,12-18 revelation of Jesus and Lazarus
10. 5,19-47 Jesus' address	10. 10,7-18 Jesus' address	10.
11.	11. 10,19-21 the reaction of the Judeans	11. 12,19 the reaction of the Pharisees

In all three stories we find a basic structure: the 'healing' story; the story of an inquiry which leads to an ever widening judgment; the scene in which Jesus returns to the beneficiary and explains his position; the scene in which the three partners come together: Jesus, the beneficiaries, the opponents.

2. THE TEXTS

In this study we read the stories from a specific perspective. The determining point of reference are the women stories: how to describe the similarities and the differences? The texts themselves need to be studied for that more closely.

2.a. the cure of the paralytic (5,1-47)

The strong sense of unity is caused especially by the rather unique concentration of place and time, both rather special.

The *place* Jerusalem is the general reference. There are specifics in some sub-scenes: the pool in the opening scene and the Temple where Jesus finds the man again in the middle part of the story, but the general term of reference is Jerusalem. With the pool it is explicitly mentioned that it is located *in Jerusalem*, strengthened even by the use of the Hebrew name (5,2); the same naturally for the Temple, but even in the setting of the locale of the other subscenes: —the man who walks with his bed on his head (5,9-13) and the discussion between Jesus and the Judeans in relation to the man's identification (5, 15ff)—, Jerusalem is the public place where all activities happen and which guarantees the link between the various events.

The *time* creates a special problem. The story opens with the mentioning of 'a feast of the Jews' and in some manuscripts one finds written '*the* feast of the Jews'. Because this feast must be between Easter of 2,13 and the feast of 6,4, it could be the feast of the weeks (to be celebrated 6 weeks after Easter), the feast of the Tabernacles in the fall or the feast of the Temple in the winter. The text does not give a clear indication and thus it remains somewhat undetermined. It is not very important as long as we keep in mind the time determination which we find a bit further on: it all happens on the sabbath (5,9). It is a feast which brings Jesus to Jerusalem and which coincides with the sabbath or in which a sabbath occurs. It is the sabbath which leads to discussions and argument and which carries the dramatic element of the story.

2.a.1. the healing (5,1-9)

Stylistically this is one of the few narratives in John which resembles the Synoptic miracle stories. This opens the way to a possible double interpretation. One can read the story from the viewpoint of the Synoptics —exegetically this has been done mostly in a historising way (see e.g. Brown 1966, 298ff; Smith 1987, 197ff; Schnelle 1987, 108ff). One can also try to see where the story participates in its own way in what is proper to John's language (see esp. Witkamp 1985). It is a simple story but there are, in some places, hidden Johannine characteristics which, once seen, are very clear. In this study, through the connection with the subsequent stories about the blind man and the dead man, is the Johannine interpretation reinforced.

Jesus visits the sick near the pool in Betzata. In the story as told till now this is the first time that Jesus actively goes out to people. The disciples took the initiative to go with him. Jesus encouraged this but did not do much to make it happen. His mother pointed out to him the need of the couple in Cana and Jesus did what she asked him to do. Nicodemus went to Jesus as did the king's man. Jesus responded to them but it was not his initiative. Even with the Samaritan woman Jesus was not really active. He asked for water and is not originally open to the woman. We discussed this extensively before. It is clear that Jesus shows a new pattern in this story. In Betzata Jesus sees the man lying there and he knows that he has been a paralytic for 38 years and he asks him: do you want to be healed? Jesus is moved from within by the need of this man.

It is interesting to note in this concrete story that the man becomes gradually the focal point of the story. The story begins with a description of the place and the building (5,2). Then come the people, the mass of the sick: the blind, the lame and the people with withered limbs (5,3). In the longer text then follows the description of the chances for healing: the angel who stirs the water so that the first person will then be healed (5,4). It ends with the description of the man himself (5,5). The story allows the reader and Jesus to encounter the other actor in the story: a man who because of his physical handicap does not stand a chance ever to reach the water first.

Jesus puts his question to this man and he answers Jesus in a remarkable way: 'Lord, I have no one to throw me into the pool, when the water has been stirred. While I go, someone else enters before me'. It is a description of what happens around the pool. In the short text this explanation is needed, because the reader still does not know anything of the miraculous things which surely must have led to inhuman situations. The man's words sound rather aggressive: 'to have someone', 'throw someone into the pool'; 'I' over against 'the other who is first'. It shows how there was a struggle and how disappointed people were each time they suffered defeat.

On the level of relating the communication between Jesus and the paralytic, we see that there is a misunderstanding, a Johannine misunderstanding (cf. Witkamp 1985, 24ff). Jesus knows what he will do and from that perspective he asks the paralytic whether he wants to be healed. It is more or less a parallel with 6,5 where it is stated explicitly that Jesus asks Philip 'to test him'(6,6). It is not stated here but that is what happens. The answer of the paralytic makes clear that this man's imagination does not go beyond what he knows. The misunderstanding is that he is incapable of seeing the question as an offer; he can not see his possible healing as an reality coming from Jesus.

In the story the healing takes place immediately after the man has answered Jesus, in two sentences which run parallel as command and execution of the command: get up, take your bed and walk (6,8-9). It is the style of the miracle stories. There is no delay between the word of power and its effect.

The subsequent sentence, about the sabbath, which kind of limps in at the end is of great importance for the rest of the story. It will determine the discussion between the man and the Judeans, but it also determines the transition in the man from not knowing to knowing who Jesus is.

2.a.2.   the inquiry by the Judeans about the desecration of the sabbath (5,10-13)

Two narrative interrelated realities determine the importance of this short scene. It is the first time in the story that someone is questioned because of something Jesus has done; and in the questioning the attention shifts from the event (the act of healing) to the one who performed the action, to Jesus.

Communicatively-narratively the most important element is the fact of the interrogation. The election of the man by Jesus causes conflict. There is an essential difference with the women stories. There people come together or are brought together, while here we find a 'judicial inquiry'. In the story of the paralytic it is still a rather simple interrogation which does not carry very far-reaching consequences, but the trial has started. The act of healing by Jesus becomes for the Judeans a cause for discussing the sabbath: what is important is not the wellbeing of the man, but the law.

The content of the trial is originally about this possible transgression of the law. The narrator uses two ploys to transform this theme: that not the act but the person of Jesus is most important.

Firstly, Jesus' word —take up your bed and walk—, is repeated three times:

- 'it is not allowed to carry your bed', spoken by the Judeans (5,10);
- 'pick up your bed and walk', said by the man who is healed (5,11);
- 'who is the man who said to you "pick up your bed and walk"', spoken by the Judeans (5,12).

It is like a drone which stays with us while we are reading and which points back time and again to the miraculous word of Jesus.

Secondly, it happens because of the lucky find to let the discussion between the Judeans and the man take place in the absence of Jesus: 'because there were so many people there, Jesus had retired' (5,13). As the one who is absent, Jesus becomes the one whom they look for and becomes the centre of attention with each word spoken. It leads to the typically Johannine word that the man must say that 'he does not know who Jesus is' (5,13).

2.a.3. *the revelation of Jesus (5,14)*

I make this single sentence into a separate sub-scene, mainly because of the parallel-scene in 9,35-39 where the revelation of Jesus is developed more broadly (cf. Martyn 1968, 69). The essential elements can be found here too: Jesus finds the man a short time later (but still on the sabbath?); he speaks to him and the man understands that his healer is called Jesus. This is not expressly stated in this scene, but is implied in the continuation of the story (5,15).

The sentence which Jesus addresses to the man is often seen as non-Johannine, as the original conclusion of the pre-Johannine story (see esp. Haenchen 1965, 107ff). The sentence connects sin and sickness, a connection which in other places (Jn 9,3) is rejected by Jesus. I suppose, then, that the connection is not made here either. One can think of all manner of sin, but in the story the only one mentioned is the desecration of the sabbath, because he carries his bed. Can we not suppose that Jesus says to the man that he should not continue to sin (μήκετι), because otherwise something worse might happen to him; that the man should not carry his bed any longer, because otherwise he might be condemned to death as punishment for this offence against the law? In such an interpretation Jesus protects the man against his attackers. It is a protection which fits in with the need Jesus has to find the man after he has been interrogated by the Judeans. What Jesus says is not about a general link between sin and sickness, but it is an expression of his concern. Jesus has included this man in his love.

2.a.4. the healed person, Jesus and the Judeans (5,15-18)

The interpretation of the man's action (5,15) depends on the meaning one gives to the verb ἀναγγέλλω. It could be a neutral 'notify': the man notifies the Judeans that Jesus is the healer, but this is close to 'informing the authorities about Jesus'. This interpretation has a number of adherents among exegetes. It is sometimes linked to the practice to inform on someone judicially, as if the verb μηνύω has been used: the healed paralytic as a first Judas.

The paralytic has a bad press anyway, if compared to the blind man. He is an *Anzeiger* (Bultmann 1941, 182); a *betrayer* (Smith 1987, 202). Martyn thinks that 'the lame man represents the Jew, who though presumably thankful to be healed, nevertheless remains wholly loyal to the synagogue' (1979, 71) and Martyn thinks that this is really beyond redemption. The 'grumbling crotchety' which Brown mentions (1966, 209) is repeated in Carson (1991, 243) as 'the crotchety grumblings of an old and not very perceptive man who thinks he is answering a stupid question'.

The vision changes completely, when one understands ἀναγγελία in the same way as in other places in John's Gospel:

4,25: 'when the Messiah comes, he will *announce* all things';
16,13: 'when he comes, the spirit of truth, he will *announce* you the things to come';
16,14: 'because he will receive from me and *tell* it to you';
16,15: 'he will take what I give him and *tell* it to you';
16,25 (in some mss): 'I will *speak* to you openly about the father';

All these words come from a revelation context. De la Potterie (1977, 445ff), therefore, translates the verb always as *révéler*. In any case, there is something of 'making known what was hitherto unknown'; 'proclaim something which was as yet not known'.

If we may attribute this positive meaning to the paralytic who was healed, his is not a cowardly act, or an act of deceit and/or betrayal. It is rather an act of courage and freedom: he, the one who is being interrogated, makes it known to his interrogators that Jesus is the healer. From his point of view this is a proclamation, a confession of faith, because he now knows who Jesus is.

His statement makes it possible for the Judeans to concentrate all their attention on Jesus. The healed man is not longer the one who broke the sabbath rule, but Jesus. That is for them a good reason to prosecute him (διωκω 5,16). They do not even exclude murder ('they even wanted to kill him' 5,17). The specific action of Jesus creates narratively a conflict situation which plays all through the story. Because Jesus is good towards this man, other people are evil towards him. Love evokes hatred.

Jesus puts his action in an even larger perspective. He connects his work on the sabbath with the work of God on the sabbath. As God does not stop to do justice on the sabbath, so will Jesus not stop. The healing of the paralytic is an act of life and death. Jesus gave him life as God does (cf. the reference of Mek Ex 31,17, ch. 1 p.28-29). When Jesus refers back (in 7,22-24) to his healing act, he uses a similar argument. If it is allowed to circumcise someone on the sabbath, it must be allowable to heal someone completely. The sabbath as sign of the covenant of God with Israel signifies the fullness of life. In the discourse of Jesus right after the accusation by the Judeans he does not refer to the interests of the man. He places himself in the centre, the effect of his relation with the father-God, and the proof of his being right via oral and written witnesses.

In this interpretation —which is surprisingly rather unique—, the paralytic is a typically Johannine character. He comes into a situation of misunderstanding; via the interrogation by the Judeans he realises that he does not know who Jesus is; when Jesus frees him in his second encounter from the obligation to provoke the Judeans —there is no longer any need to carry his bed—, he makes a public confession before the Judeans. The paralytic is the first man to be selected by Jesus himself. And so he opens a way which will become progressively more clear.

2.b. the healing of the blind man (9,1-10,21)

There are few stories in the Gospel where the reading divisions are
so universally accepted. Jn 9 is a story which is narratively clearly
constructed in sequential scenes. The changes in persons, time
and/or place are seen by all exegetes —as far as I can see—, as
reader indications for the narrative progression of the story. Jesus
heals the blind man (9,1-7); neighbours and acquaintances identify
him (9,8-12); the Pharisees investigate the desecration of the
sabbath (9,13-17); the Judeans determine, via the parents, the
identity of the man (9,24-34); Jesus makes himself known to the
healed man who professes his faith (9,35-39). Jesus gives his
judgment in the presence of the healed man and some Pharisees
(9,40-41) (cf. a.o. Bligh 1966, 131; Brown 1966, 203; Painter
1986, 37; Panackel 1988, 150).

Such widespread agreement among the exegetes hides the fact
that the beginning and the end of the story are not so clear. The
opening sentence in 9,1 —'in passing he saw a man who was blind
from birth'—, makes it clear that there is a close connection
between the preceding chapters and this new story. It is the last day
of the Feast of the Tabernacles. Jesus has made this feast his own
by identifying himself with the water (7,37ff), with the light (8,12)
and with the name of God (8,58). This causes a lot of conflict. The
Judeans picked up some stones to throw at him, a first attempt at
stoning which remains unsuccessful, because Jesus hides himself
and leaves the Temple (8,59). Narratively-chronologically the story
then continues. It is, therefore, reasonable to think that the story of
the healing of the blind man took place during the Feast of the
Tabernacles. But how far does it extend? The question is important
because of possible allusions to the Feast of the Tabernacles. The
story opens with an explanation by Jesus about the difference
between night and day, and with a statement about himself, that, as
long as he remains in the cosmos, he will be the light of the world
(9,4.5). Furthermore, he sends the blind man to Siloam (9,7): all
realities which are linked directly to the Feast of the Tabernacles
—the light, the difference between night and day, Siloam as the
place where water is drawn, cf. Succah 4,9: 'The water-libation.
How so? A golden flagon holding three logs was filled from the
pool of Shiluach (and brought to the altar)'; Succah 5,1: 'They said
that anyone who had not witnessed the rejoicing at the Libation
Water-Well had never seen rejoicing in his life'; Succah 5,3: 'From

the worn-out drawers and girdles of the priests they made wicks and with them they set alight (the Temple court); and there was no courtyard in Jerusalem that was not lit up with the light at the Libation Water-Well ceremony'. The text takes on special meaning through these references.

If one accepts this, there are two additional observations to be made. First: the allusions to the Feast of the Tabernacles are limited to the opening phase of the story. The healing from the blindness and the difference between seeing and not seeing play a role all through the story; but after verse 9,13 there are no more references to the Feast of the Tabernacles: see especially the 'disappearance' of Siloam in 9,15. Second: the formulation of 9,14 is typical, more so in comparison with the parallel in 5,9. Vs 9,14 says: 'It was a sabbath day when Jesus made mud and opened his eyes' —implying some kind of past tense—, while 5,9 says: 'it was sabbath *on that day*' —so remaining within the narrative present. Does not this mean that, according to the narrator, the events of 9,1-12 (or at least 9,1-7) happen on the last and most important day of the Feast, a day which now, afterwards, is described as a sabbath; and that in 9,13 a further period in time begins looking back on a recent past?

This interpretation solves a number of narrative problems. The easy transition from the closing of chapter 8 and the opening of chapter 9 is respected. There is no need that the whole story plays in one day which is filled with events anyway. From the point of view of the reader there is room to look at the vague timing less strictly or even to assign different times or even different days to the various events.

That as far as the opening phase of the story is concerned. There are questions also about the end of the story. The general agreement among exegetes that the story ends with 9,41 (but see recently Beutler-Fortna 1991), hides the fact that communicatively-narratively the story continues way into chapter 10. Jesus addresses the Pharisees. Immediately till 10,5 which is followed by a short remark from the writer: 'Jesus was thinking of them in this parable but they did not understand what he wanted to say to them' (10,6). Jesus then explains the parable in various ways and his explanation evokes two kinds of reactions (9,19-21), a schism in which some reject Jesus as someone possessed by the demon and others accept him because his words are intelligible and because he performs miracles. Narratively-structurally one can compare this end-scene

with the end-scene of chapter 5. After a kind of basic sentence
(5,16-18 and 9,40-41) follows a discourse by Jesus in which he, in
the first part, speaks about himself in the third person singular
(5,19-29 and 10,1-5, apart from the use of λέγω ὑμῖν in 5,19.24.25
and 10,1 and the use of μου, με in 5,24), while in the second part
he speaks about himself in the first person singular (5,30-47 and
10,7-18). Just as his discourse in chapter 5 belongs to the healing
story, so also belongs the discourse of chapter 10 to the healing
story of chapter 9.

2.b.1. the healing of the blind man (9,1-7)

The theological impact of the problem about the relationship
between sickness and sin, brought up by the disciples (9,2) and the
answer which Jesus gives (9,3-5), made the exegetes forget to look
at the communicative-narrative meaning of this passage. This can
happen easily in Johannine texts. The content of the text is more
important than the communication aspect. In this text this is true in
a particular way. It is a kind of discourse and action in which the
central figure, the man born blind, remains the one about whom
they speak. Where in the story of the healing of the paralytic, the
man is at least asked for a reaction —whether he wants to be healed
(5,6)—, in this story even this question is lacking. Everything
happens without him. Jesus 'sees that the man has been blind from
birth' (9,1) a pre-knowledge which is also the point of departure for
the disciples in their questioning Jesus. The blind man is for them
only a theological problem. To some extent he is that also for
Jesus, but at the same time Jesus makes clear that the blind man
and he himself have a role to play in the larger plan of God. It is
communicatively remarkable that the man is not addressed at all. It
is not beyond the text to imagine that the man is seated (see 9,18:
'is not this man the one who sits and begs?'), over whose head
Jesus and the disciples talk. People talk about him without his being
involved and it is far from clear what profit he will gain from it all.
He is pulled in through 'in him God's work will become manifest'
(9,3), but when will this happen? The 'necessity for Jesus to work
as long as the day lasts' (9,4) —referring to 5,17 and showing that
Jesus is focused on giving life always—, shows that this moment is
not excluded from that. The closing sentence in which Jesus says
that he is the light of the cosmos (9,5) —as he did in 8,12 in the
Temple at the high moment of the Feast of the Tabernacles—,

refers here to the blindness of the man and the possibility for Jesus to change it. But will that happen? The words spoken give a perspective, but they do not determine the moment. When the blind man tells the story to other people (in 9,11 and 9,15), this discourse and Jesus' announcement are not mentioned.

He only talks about the mud which Jesus prepared and put on his eyes and how he gave him the command to wash in the water of Siloam. This action of Jesus is the most remarkable event. Again here is an active Jesus who, so to speak, bluntly enters into the life of this man. Jesus made his choice and without asking the man or saying anything to him, he makes it possible for the man to be healed. There is a difference with the story of the paralytic. The blind man must actively answer Jesus' invitation. He must go to Siloam and wash himself in the pool of Siloam which plays such an important role in the Feast of the Tabernacles —when its water is carried to the altar in a solemn procession. Jesus makes it his own again 'go to the pool of Siloam which means "sent"' (9,7; for the messianic meaning of Siloam see Müller 1969; Reim 1978; Grigsby 1985). Jesus sends the man to himself via a verbal detour. Obviously, this is theological language, but it has also a great affective content. From a undeserved special love of Jesus he asks the man to go to him. The man does what Jesus asks him to do and he is saved but, as we will see, he is also damned.

2.b.2. the inquiry by neighbours and acquaintances (9,8-12)

The healing brings the man in situations which progressively take the form of a judicial inquiry. It starts rather innocently. The healed blind man is confronted with people from his own social circle: neighbours and acquaintances. They ask him three questions: his identity, the way he was healed, who Jesus is. These questions will return again and again in variations and an ever clearer answer will be given. In this scene the questions serve the purpose to prove the reality, extent, and nature of the miracle (cf. Gourgues 1982, 387; Painter 1986, 34). The quarrel among these people whether this man is the same man as the beggar they have always known, a quarrel which the man definitively stops by stating that he is; ánd the similarity between what the man tells the people and what the readers have heard the narrator tell them before, make the reality of the story more obvious. It happened precisely as it is told.

There is only one small informative difference. The healed man calls Jesus by name: 'the man who is called Jesus' did it (9,11). This knowledge of Jesus becomes greater as the story unfolds. When the people ask him 'where Jesus is', he can only say for the moment 'I do not know'. The typical words "where?" and "I do not know" are important codes for Johannine readers. The story will further fill in these empty places.

2.b.3. the inquiry by the Pharisees (9,13-17)

The people 'bring' the man to the Pharisees. This is the first juridical word. These people, and from what went before we must think they are the neighbours and acquaintances, are not too far from the Pharisees: they too have problems that someone makes mud on a sabbath and heals on a sabbath. It is remarkable that the man is still an object of concern. Because he has been brought before the Pharisees, a judicial procedure is beginning.

The accusation is formulated indirectly in the determination of time about the sabbath and the precise statements about what is not supposed to happen on a sabbath: making mud and healing. The inquiry begins with the question about the way the healing took place. The man answers in a somewhat ambiguous way: he reformulates his story in such a way that it is not clear that Jesus has done anything illegal. The making of mud is no longer mentioned nor the anointing: 'he (Jesus' name is not mentioned) put mud on my eyes, I washed myself and I can see' (9,15). It looks as if the man protects Jesus. In any case the story, compared to the one he told neighbours and acquaintances, becomes shorter. Literally that means that he begins to waver.

The Pharisees are becoming divided by the events: a good deal of attention is given to that. It is remarkable that the manner of the healing is no longer the central point but the question 'who is Jesus', in the third person as if he is absent: is he from God or is he a sinner. Such a shift happened also in the story of the healing of the paralytic but here it is even stronger. That is because of the double option and the conflict this causes for the Pharisees. The negative solution is accentuated.

From the viewpoint of this dilemma they ask the man what he thinks: what do you say about him? (9,17). His answer is clear and shows the progression in insight which began in 9,11. The man Jesus has become a prophet. The healed man becomes a witness and his witness is a profession of faith: the opening of his eyes made Jesus a prophet for him.

2.b.4. The inquiry by the Judeans of the parents (9,18-23)

The further we enter into the story, the stronger the impression that it is a judicial inquiry. In this scene the juridical allusions are more prominent. The Pharisees are now called Judeans which exacerbates the situation. About these Judeans it is said that they will not believe the man unless they have cited his parents. Believing (πιστεύω), calling (φωνέω) and the questioning (ἐρωτάω) are words used in a judicial inquiry. The Judeans have become investigating judges who will determine the man's identity, the manner in which the event happened and who is ultimately responsible.

Because his parents are now called, the man himself is again sidelined. Other people speak about him and judge him. At least that is what the Judeans have in mind. The story tells us how this misfired. When it comes to the crunch, the parents refuse to cooperate. They are quite subtle about it. The Judeans ask them to identify their son and whether they are willing to testify how the healing took place: 'is this man your son?' and 'how is it that he sees again?' (9,19) The parents answer the first question in the affirmative. But the second question receives a two-pronged answer: 'How he sees now we do not know' and 'who opened his eyes we do not know' (9,21).

Such an answer is theoretically possible. The parents do not know what happened to their son. The closing sentence of the author in 9,22.23 shows that such a reader's interpretation is not correct. Not because they do not know but because they are afraid, the parents refer the Judeans to their son. They are not willing to stand with him, because they are afraid they might be thrown out of the synagogue.

Vs 9,22.23 is a sentence which has had enormous influence in the historical research on the Johannine Gospel. Everyone knows the sentence is an anachronism. The precise dating (whether the words are connected with the *birkat ha-minim* or not) evoked a long discussion in which all historical possibilities have been defended (see esp. Martyn 1968, 37-62; Wengst 1983, 48-61; and, critically, Schnelle 1987, 135). These studies are less relevant for a narrative analysis. In fact, almost the whole Johannine Gospel is anachronistic and says more about the way people at the end of the

first century saw things than about the 'historical' Jesus.
Narratively relevant is that at the end of the first century people
believe that 9,22 is historically possible. The story of Peter's denial
of Jesus —the fear of Peter, rightly or wrongly felt, that he might
be involved in what is happening to Jesus—, has possibly helped in
this.

Whatever, even if one is willing to read the sentence from the
point of view of the narrativity of the text, it is not a simple
sentence. The parents are not willing to tell them what happened to
their son and that Jesus healed him, 'because whoever professes
that Jesus is the Messiah will be thrown out of the synagogue.' i.e.
the story of the healing and naming Jesus is identified with the
profession of Jesus as the Messiah. That is clearly not so. But the
text just posits this without any objection: and so that is what it says
and that is what it is. After this scene one can no longer discuss the
manner of the healing without being forced to make a statement
about who Jesus is. The question 'how did it happen' is necessarily
linked to the question 'who is Jesus'.

The author manipulates his readers in a different way too. He
presupposes that the fear of the parents is realistic. They are
prepared to say what is necessary —it is our son and he was
blind—, but, fearful of the consequences, they stop right there. That
means that whoever goes beyond that point, will be given the
approval of the author as a hero and a witness. The blind man will
do exactly that.

2.b.5. judgment by the Judeans of the man and of Jesus (9,24-34)

The trial reaches its climax. The man has become the accused who
is threatened with a severe punishment. He is alone now:
neighbours and acquaintances brought him to the Pharisees; his
parents refuse to testify for him. While the fact that he is chosen by
Jesus has brought about this situation, Jesus himself is nowhere to
be seen as yet. As far as the Judeans are concerned, the man is
tried instead of Jesus. The man is 'cited' again: ἐφώνησαν, as were
his parents (9,24). But it all sounds much fiercer. The inquiry
begins to sound like a cross-examination in which the positions are
established and the conclusions drawn: the healed man only needs
to confess.

The story relates how it all works out differently. The narrator
assigns the positions to the two parties so that the reader is given a

choice. While the sub-scene of the inquiry by the Pharisees tells about divisions among the Pharisees (9,13-17), the different positions are now assigned to the Judeans on the one hand and the man on the other. He represents the side of Jesus or, better still, he represents Jesus himself.

The author prepares the parameters from the outset: 'give glory to God' (9,24). This is a secular expression to invite someone to tell the truth, but —John can never be taken simply—, in this context it is given a literal meaning. The inquiry is about the question whether God is being given 'glory'. The question about Jesus is a question about God. When one speaks about Jesus, one forms oneself an image of God.

Four short discussions, each with its own theme, determine the narrative form of the cross-examination:

9,24-25: knowing whether Jesus is a sinner.
The Judeans see the healing on the sabbath as a violation of the law. They judge unhesitatingly and it becomes a condemnation. The healed man does not agree and points to what happened. The implication will be developed by him further on. Narratively this means that there is a change in role playing: the accused becomes the one who judges.

9,26-27: the question about the 'how' and the ironic answer.
The Judeans put the question about 'how' once more, but the healed man refuses to tell the story one more time. He accuses them of not having listened. He becomes ironic, when he asks whether they maybe want to become disciples of Jesus.

9,28-33: turning away from Jesus and turning towards him.
The two sides are now definitively opposed: the Judeans understand that the man has become a follower of Jesus. About themselves they say that they do not know where Jesus comes from. Jesus had told them this already in the foregoing discussion (8,14). Now they themselves reach this conclusion. Furthermore, they create an opposition between being a disciple of Jesus and being a follower of Moses. From their point of view these can not be combined. It is the ideological basis for the divisions between the synagogue and the followers of Jesus.

The man opposes with his own reasoning. He can not deny what happened but neither can he see God would not be somehow part of it. If that is so, Jesus must be linked to God. He arrives at a new confession of Jesus: Jesus comes from God (9,33).

9,34: the final conclusion of the Judeans.
The inquiry concludes with a condemnation referring as to content
to the opening phrases of the story about the relation between sin
and sickness (9,2). What Jesus had rejected is simply taken up
again by the Judeans. There is a second reference: the
condemnation refers also to the judgment on Jesus at the start of the
inquiry. As Jesus is said to be a sinner (9,24), the man, healed by
Jesus, is now also called a sinner. In the judgment by the Judeans
the man and Jesus belong together.

The story of the judicial inquiry forms one whole and has it own
structure which, for Johannine ideas, is fairly logical and simple.
The gradual transition from oral to physical violence is narratively
important. The Judeans switch from the original 'speaking'
(9,24.26) to 'cursing' (9,28) to 'throwing the man out' (9,34).
What the parents feared, happens to the man: if one professes
Jesus, one is thrown out.

2.b.6. the revelation of Jesus (9,35-39)

The story ends with one of the most remarkable scenes of the
Johannine Gospel: Jesus asks faith in himself. After all the things
which the man had to go through, Jesus finally becomes active. The
repetition of 'throwing out' in 9,35, in conjunction with hearing,
seeking and finding Jesus, makes Jesus a partner in the events.
From the beginning he was the discussed, judged and condemned
subject and now he enters anew in relation with the man who was
given his preferential love. When Jesus hears what happened, he
'finds' him and asks whether he believes in the Son of man. After
the violent expositions full of unwillingness and lack of
understanding, this scene is filled with reverence, understanding,
and true communication.

To understand the meaning of the discussion, the narrative
situation of Jesus is important. In chapter 6 he saw almost all his
disciples disappear. Only the twelve in Peter's name remained
faithful and among them is Judas who betrayed him. In chapter 7
the conflict with his brothers and sisters ended with the dissolution
of the familial communion: Jesus entered Jerusalem alone without
his relatives. At the Feast of the Tabernacles Jesus got into a real
conflict with the Pharisees and the Judeans. That ended with the
threat of physical violence. When Jesus finds the man whom he
healed, he knows that this man experienced this violence. It is for

Jesus the first time that he finds a possible follower after all the conflicts and difficult divisions.

The scene itself is about believing, a word that is repeated three times: as a question, as future, and as judgment. Jesus' question is for the man a command as it was in the opening of the story. This is the first and only time that Jesus asks for faith in himself and it happens in a typical way, in the third person: 'do you believe in the Son of Man?' (9,35), 'you have seen him and who speaks to you is he' (9,37).

The last expression ὁ λαλῶν μετὰ σοῦ ἐκεῖνός ἐστιν reminds one of what Jesus said to the Samaritan woman: ἐγώ εἰμι, ὁ λαλῶν σοι (4,26). Is this meant as a reference and, above all, is the difference in attitude intended? For the Samaritan woman Jesus' identity is not yet completely clear at the end of the conversation. Talking to the inhabitants of Sichar she asks herself 'whether Jesus could be the Christ?' (4,29). The healed man entrusts himself unconditionally to Jesus: 'who is that, Lord? (9,36); 'I believe, Lord' (9,38); 'and he adored him' (9,38). Jesus has found a new follower. His adoration of Jesus changes the tone of the story: the accused Jesus speaks as judge. Jesus, the Son of Man, has come into the cosmos to distinguish between those who see and those who do not see. Everything is turned upside down. Jesus has become the leader of Israel.

In the following conversation between Jesus and the Pharisees (9,40-10,18), this leadership of and in Israel is discussed. It is an exciting text where, however, the relation between Jesus and the healed man no longer plays a role. That comes back only at the end of the story in the description of the reactions of the Judeans to the discourse of Jesus (10,19-21). While many reject Jesus, because they are convinced he is possessed by a demon and speaks dangerous gibberish, some develop a way of reasoning which resembles what the blind man uses: 'these are not the words of a man possessed. Can a demon open the eyes of a man born blind?' (10,21). It is an argument from the negative which indicates something of the hesitation but also of resistance against too easy condemnations.

The story of the healing of the man born blind indicates much more explicitly than the story of the healing of the paralytic what happens, when people are touched by Jesus' preferential love. The

story of Jesus and the man born blind is in the real sense a story of
a judicial inquiry. One could call it 'the story of *the* case against
Jesus'. The occasion is similar to the story of the paralytic and the
story runs parallel in structure. But there is more content and form.
Jesus is the active one who enters into the discussion of the
disciples about the question of guilt; unasked and unexpected he
determines the narrative development of the story. Although absent
he is the only accused in the inquiry. The desecration of the sabbath
is again the immediate cause of the judicial inquiry and the question
is again about the how and who.

The real difference with the preceding story is in the narrative
development of the events. The inquiry about the healed man has
been developed according to various juridical modalities: the man's
identity is determined several times; the interrogators divide
themselves in groups of defenders and accusers; in a later phase
there is a hardening of the positions; the position of the healed man
becomes gradually clearer and he himself changes in the course of
the inquiry: from the interrogated he becomes the interrogator;
from a passive subject he becomes an active participant. He makes
professions of faith in Jesus which become ever more explicit till,
at the end, he is found again by Jesus and can tell him personally
what he has understood through all the events which happened:
Jesus is the Son of Man who may judge about light and darkness,
about guilt and innocence, about sin and forgiveness.

2.c. the resurrection of Lazarus (11,1-12,19)

One can read the story of Lazarus from different points of view: as
an 'independent' story covering 11,1 till 11,44; as a story which is
embedded in the main story about Jesus and then 11, 45-53 is an
essential part of it. From the perspective of this chapter the
appearances of Lazarus in ch. 12 are part of it: his attendance at the
festive meal in 12, 1-8; his condemnation in 12, 9-11; the people's
memories of the events when Jesus enters Jerusalem (12, 12-19).

It has been said several times that the Lazarus story serves as a
climax. If we compare this story with the healing stories of the
paralytic and the blind man, this is true on different levels than
those we indicated in chapter 4. Not only the miraculous event in
the story (the raising from the dead), but also other events and
aspects of the story are at the top of the narrative crescendo.

- While Jesus confers his benefaction on the paralytic and the blind man without a previous positive relationship, Lazarus' resurrection is based on an explicit loving relationship. Jesus' love for Lazarus is mentioned several times (11,3.5.11.36).

- Jesus' foreknowledge grows constantly. In the case of the paralytic Jesus knows he has been sick for a along time but probably not precisely how long (5,6). In the case of the blind man Jesus knows that he has been born blind (9,1). In the case of Lazarus he knows that Lazarus will die (11,4) and when he died (11,11).

- The characters as discussed subjects. In the analysis of the story about the blind man I pointed out that he was, for a good part of the text, a discussed subject: discussed by neighbours, acquaintances, parents, Pharisees, and Judeans. In the case of the paralytic this is hardly the situation. He is addressed by Jesus and by the Judeans explicitly on their own initiative (5,6 and 5, 10.12). The Lazarus story represents the other side. Lazarus is exclusively a discussed subject. Not only when he is inside the tomb —not so surprising—, but also after he has been brought back to life, he does not speak a word, while many people react to him and to his situation.

- The persecution because of being elected by Jesus is told in the form of a climax too. The paralytic is subjected to questioning and when Jesus liberates him from his adversaries he is free. The blind man gets involved in a real judicial inquiry and is physically threatened because of his growing relationship to Jesus. Lazarus is condemned to death, albeit without any judicial procedure. They make plans to kill him (12,10), something substantially more serious than what happened to the paralytic or the blind man.

2.c.1. the resurrection of Lazarus (11,1-44)

The way the story of Jesus' miraculous action is related, is different from the case of the paralytic or the blind man: it is very broadly spun out. It is an elaborate story which gives the reader insight and knowledge in the various circumstances within which the sign takes place. There is no need to discuss all the aspects of the story here. Some —the relationship between Jesus and Martha and Mary—, have been discussed in the women stories. Here the relation between Jesus and Lazarus must be the topic: Jesus preferential

love for this man, leading again to rejection and violence by the
leaders of the people.

The narrative reality is special. Lazarus belongs to the small
group of people —the beloved disciple, Peter, Martha, and Mary—,
where the affective relationship of Jesus is discussed in various
ways. It brings Lazarus in a way very close to the beloved disciple
where the loving relationship is the core of the literary existence as
we explained. Some exegetes think, therefore, that the beloved
disciple can be identified with Lazarus (see Kügler 1988, 446-448
for a description of some historical data in relation to this
identification). This will probably remain a mystery and I think that
it is a way of reading the text, which narratively has serious
consequences, but which is textually not indicated. It does indicate
that Lazarus is a special case. I would like to summarise this from
the focal point of this chapter:

- the terminology:

The lexemes /$\phi\iota\lambda\acute{\epsilon}\omega$/ and /$\dot{\alpha}\gamma\alpha\pi\acute{\alpha}\omega$/ are used several times: in
11,3.5.11.36. It is remarkable that the love always comes from
Jesus. There is no mention of how Lazarus reacted to it.
Narratively even more important is the fact that all who speak in
the story, talk about this love. In 11,3 Lazarus' sisters use Jesus'
love for Lazarus as an argument to make Jesus act. In 11,15 it is
the narrator of the story. In 11,11 Jesus himself speaks about
Lazarus as 'our friend', implying that the disciples are part of this
relationship. In 11,36 a group of the Judeans see Jesus crying and
feeling miserable and they conclude correctly that Jesus must love
Lazarus a lot. It is a public love, a love which can not be
misunderstood and which has serious consequences.

- Jesus is made active

The Lazarus story is a special story for more than one reason.
Special is the way in which Jesus takes over the initiative from the
sisters and makes it his own. Martha and Mary send a message
which implies a question about the way Jesus acts. He responds to
the question in his own way. Having received the message he
remains for two days where he is and only then he convinces his
disciples to come with him and visit Lazarus. He acts this way from
his foreknowledge of Lazarus' death and from the fact that he
knows that he will call Lazarus forth from the tomb. He announces
this twice: in 11,4 more indirectly and in 11,11.14 more directly.
For the disciples it is still a secret language, but it is sufficient to

make them come. Arrived in Bethany Jesus acts in much the same way towards Martha. He gets involved in a discussion to convince her and it is successful. Mary then exercises an active influence on Jesus. Her emotional behaviour brings Jesus to come from speaking and announcing to acting. This constant seesawing of Jesus makes it clear that Jesus follows God's plan for him, but also how closely Jesus is involved with Lazarus and his family.

- Jesus' commitment

That this taking over the initiative by Jesus is connected with his special love for Lazarus is clear from what Jesus commits in his coming there and in his action. When he tries to convince his disciples (11,7-16), this plays a role. After two days the rest in the land where John baptised is over. He wants to go forth with his disciples whom he sees originally as his adversaries. While Jesus says: 'let *us* go back to Judea' (11,7), his disciples confront him, from what happened before (cf. 10,31.39), with the threat of death which awaits him and they ask him: 'are *you* going there? (11,6). They oppose Jesus' inclusive 'we' with their own exclusive 'you': they see Judea as a place of death. Jesus objects to that. He thinks it is too early to say that: the day has twelve hours and as long as there is light one can go; danger comes only when it gets dark. There is still time. Darkness has not yet won victory over light. He also connects to the previous story: his hour has not yet come and he has light in himself (8,12.20; 9,4).

Initially the discussion between Jesus and his disciples seems to get stuck. The narrator begins anew so to speak: 'he said this and then he told them: our friend Lazarus sleeps, but *I* will go to wake him up' (11,11). Jesus himself brings in death, as yet in secret language, but later directly: 'Lazarus has died ... let *us* go to him' (11,15). The transition of the 'I' sentence: '*I* will go to him' to the 'we' sentence: 'let *us* go' (11,15), shows the difference in tone. Jesus knows he has convinced his disciples. The mysterious phrase of Thomas to his co-disciples at the end makes it explicit: 'let us go too' —parallel to the opening and closing sentence of Jesus: let us go (to him)—, 'to die with him': is that Lazarus or Jesus? Jesus has convinced his disciples, at least Thomas, to be part of his own commitment, his readiness to put his life in the balance out of love for Lazarus and in favour of the life of Lazarus.

2.c.2. the judicial inquiry in the Sanhedrin and the judgment about Jesus (11,45-53)

In the story of the blind man and the paralytic, the healed one is addressed first of all. The breaking of the law serves as the occasion to indict Jesus. In the Lazarus story this sequence is inverted. First we get the official reaction of the Sanhedrin on the way Jesus acts. Only later in the story Lazarus gets involved. There has been no breaking of the law but, narratively, that has not been the motive for some time. Jesus as a person is under suspicion.

The opening sentence of the scene points forward to the motive which will be used in the Sanhedrin as a counter-argument. Many of the Judeans 'believe in him' (11,45), over against 'if we let him go on, *all* will believe in him (11,48). Again Jesus has found a following because of his action. The Sanhedrin is afraid that this might lead to serious political implications (cf. Grimm 1974; Grundmann 1984; Bittner 1987, 171). The personal act of friendship has become a political issue which stimulates the main story. We are back in Judea as the place of death. The scene itself connects directly with the story about the first gathering of the High Priests and Pharisees during the Feast of the Tabernacles (7,32.45-52). Jesus must be made to disappear.

An action by the Judeans leads into the story of the session itself. Again two groups are opposed to each other, as a model of possible attitudes towards Jesus: one can believe in him or one can go to the Pharisees. Within the Sanhedrin there is also a division: the High Priests and the Pharisees who do not know what to do, and the High Priest Caiaphas who wants an active role to make sure that the power over the people will be maintained. In that sense there is some sort of climax which from very positive (the Judeans who believe in Jesus) runs to hesitation (the Judeans who accuse Jesus) to uncertainty (what shall we do?) to the plan to murder him (Caiaphas). In the closing sentence the author turns the climax around again.

The Pharisees and the High Priests are presented as people who are at a loss. They foresee a future in which they, because of the people's faith in Jesus, will be driven from power by the Romans. That causes their irresoluteness: what shall we do? Caiaphas alone defends the opposition. He knows a solution for the problem: it is better that one man dies for the people than that the whole people perishes. He agrees with the political analysis of the other party:

there is a danger that everyone will believe in Jesus and that then the Romans will come and that they will take the place and the people away. Jesus death will end all that: they will not believe; the Romans will not come; the people will not perish.

Every listener to this story will understand that there are misunderstandings here. The closing sentence of the author underlines that clearly. The future is completely different: there will be many people who will believe in Jesus; the Romans did come and took away the power over the city and the people from them. The Sanhedrin was, therefore, right after all, but that is only because they gave in to Caiaphas who put the Sanhedrin in the wrong. For the readers of the story the Sanhedrin as well as Caiaphas sink into the morass of Johannine truth.

2.c.3. the order to find Jesus (11,54-57)

The reaction of the Sanhedrin gave Jesus' loving act a political meaning far exceeding the parties involved. For the time being Jesus retires with his (male) disciples to a lonely place near the desert. There is no mention of the length of time involved. It is the time between the Feast of the Dedication of the Temple in winter (10,22) and Easter (11,55; 12,1): about three or four months, divided between their stay in Bethany on the other side of the Jordan (10,41-42), the day in Bethany near Jerusalem (11,18ff), and the time near Ephraim, the city near the desert (11,54).

When the preparations for Easter begin, no one has yet forgotten the events around Lazarus. The readers are informed indirectly about the danger which threatens Jesus. From the discussions among the pilgrims we, as readers, hear that the Sanhedrin has taken measures: 'the High Priests and the Pharisees —the same group which in 11,47 called a meeting—, gave the order that whoever knows where Jesus is must report it' (11,57). The use of the words ἐντολή and μηνύω indicate the judicial character of the procedure. That shows also the difference with the parallel sentence in 7,11-13. Then, the possible arrival of Jesus evokes a discussion among the people. Some are positive, some negative. Out of fear for the Judeans they are forced to discuss this in secret, apparently because the Judeans have tried to limit the damage caused by Jesus' public stature by forbidding the people to discuss him (contra Brown 1966, 445-6 who undervalues the narrative function as well as the relation to 7,11-13).

At the end of chapter 11 this ban on discussion is over. The authorities are actively looking for Jesus. An order has been given to denounce him. Such a duty to denounce Jesus to the authorities can only be understood against the background of a society in which there is a tyrannical rule. In the Attic law the μήνυσις gives a possibility to the citizen to protect the state against the danger of high treason, stealing state money or —what is important in our case— *religious subversion* (cf. Pauly-Wissowa s.v.). In 11,57 the highest organ of state is active. One can compare it to the system of informants during the time of the Roman Emperors, most strongly present during the time of the tyrants Nero and Domitian (cf. Suet. Nero 32,2; Domitian 12,2; 31). In the eyes of the authorities Jesus has become an enemy of the State.

2.c.4. the revelation of Jesus and the judgment to kill Lazarus (12,1-11)

Jesus does not leave his people alone. He searches for the paralytic to reveal himself to the man and to protect him against his enemies. He looks for the blind man, when he hears that the man has been thrown out and he accepts him as a disciple. In the case of Lazarus the second meeting is even more important. Jesus is given a festive meal by the family to thank him. The existing friendship continues, but all personages play a special role. We have said enough about Martha and Mary but Lazarus' position is peculiar too. One would expect him to be the host. It seems to follow from the phrase: 'they prepared there a meal for him' (12,2), but immediately after it is said about Lazarus: 'Lazarus was one of the people who was at the table *with him*', as if he is a guest at his own table —as are, then, also Martha and Mary in a certain sense. In the eyes of the narrator Jesus is the most important personage.

This, however, is not true for all the people, as is clear from the closing phrases of this passage. A great crowd of Judeans comes to the house 'not only because of Jesus but also to see Lazarus whom Jesus had raised from the dead' (12,9). This has serious consequences for Lazarus. The High Priests decide to murder him. The motive is again (cf. 11,48) 'faith in Jesus', now connected with the verb ὑπάγω: the departure of many Judeans (from where?) to come to Jesus. One begins to see what the High Priests were afraid of. The sign which Jesus gave them, creates a division in the people, a division between people and leaders.

The decision to kill Lazarus shows most clearly the distance between the women stories and the men stories. While the women gather people without a conflict —the Samaritan woman a whole city; Martha and Mary the Judeans who are present (see esp. 12,17); Mary Magdalene the disciples—, the men come into ever more serious problems because of their contact with Jesus. This is true in a special way for the Lazarus story where women play an important role too. Lazarus is threatened to be killed, while Martha and Mary, the real initiators of the event, go scot-free.

2.c.5. Jesus, Lazarus, and the Pharisees (12,12-19)

Five days before Easter Jesus goes to Jerusalem and is received by the people as King-Messiah of Israel. The question of the people about Jesus in 11,56 is positively answered. In hindsight it is the preparation for this triumphant entrance. Jesus is not kept in check by the search warrant issued by the High Priests and Pharisees. At the same time it has become impossible to evade public appearances: wherever he comes people come together. It is not clear, as we said already, whether the disciples are there too (12,16). For our topic it is important that the people themselves bring up the resurrection of Lazarus (12,17). The phrase is a reflection of the author about the mass of people present at the entrance of Jesus. This is caused by the testimony of 'the crowd which was with Jesus when he raised Lazarus from the dead. That is why the people ran towards Jesus, because they had heard that he had performed this sign' (12,17.18) That Jesus is brought into the city as King-Messiah is the result of the people's experience at Lazarus' resurrection. The power over death which Jesus demonstrated, made his kingship in God's name public.

As in the other stories we have here a reaction of the opponents, the Pharisees in this case, who see their plans founder. They give a rather downhearted commentary (12,19). One could ask why only the Pharisees are mentioned here and whether there is a relation with 12,10 where the plans to kill Lazarus seem to be the High Priests' only. The High Priests certainly play a very special role in the passion story (cf.18,3.10.13.15.16.19.22.24.26.35;19,6.15.21), distinct from the role of the Pharisees (only indirectly in 18,3). The High Priests are responsible for the judgment to kill. The Pharisees make sure that the people will be thrown out of the synagogue (cf.

ch. 9 and esp. 12,42) but, in the way the narrator tells the story, their influence does not go beyond that.

The Lazarus story is told in a phase of the main story in which the events lead to a climax. Narratively the story brings the climax closer, causes it and influences it permanently. Jesus' death is directly linked to his act of love for his friend Lazarus and his friends Martha and Mary. In the series of the men stories the Lazarus story is in many aspects narratively the last. It demonstrates also in the most explicit manner the decisive distinction between the men- and women stories. Whoever as man is touched by Jesus' love, comes into a crisis situation in which one's moral, spiritual and physical potential is tested.

It is not so easy to give the reasons to clarify this distinction. Is it related to the political value of men as opposed to women? Because women are not supposed to profile themselves in the public arena and do not run so much danger to be threatened publicly or to be accused? What seems important is that Jesus identifies himself with the men. In his own person he identifies with the men whom he loves. He attracts them and does not let them go. The narrator identifies himself with this: he allows the characters in the story to return to the events and most clearly again the Lazarus story where a crowd of people gives witness about what they have seen in Bethany. It is a narrative procedure which does not appear in any of the women stories. Jesus identifies himself with these men and they, therefore, suffer the same fate as he does: Lazarus in the most literal sense of the word, via death and resurrection and a threat of being killed. Against such a background it is not totally incomprehensible why the natural death of the beloved disciple creates a crisis among the brethren. When a man is touched by the love of Jesus, the expectation is that Jesus' life will replay itself in him.

SUMMARY

The majority of exegetes treat the Johannine Gospel as a text which can be read at random anywhere. In the same manner, so they believe, we can discontinue our reading at any moment, as if neither the preceding text nor the following would influence the meaning of that particular text in any way. This way of thinking presupposes that the Johannine text has been built up episodically; that it is an agglomeration of individual pericopes, which —according to the idea of many scholars—, have a univocal meaning. One episode is a repetition of what has been stated in another. A limited number of basic themes are being repeated in varying combinations. The Johannine Gospel knows a quite distinct mythology which is repeated with a certain number of variations, and consequently there is only little or no difference in content at all between the various chapters of the book. I have called this a 'discursive way of reading'. The text is perceived as a discourse, which can consequently be compared with other, similar forms of discourse: e.g. the Johannine Gospel as a discourse in christology (Ashton), as a discourse on the holy spirit (Burge); as a discourse on understanding and reality of truth (de la Potterie). These exegetes hardly pay attention to the narrative character; if they do so, they do it in an initial way only, like de la Potterie, when he deals with the individual Johannine stories.

A particular form of this discursive way of reading is the historical reading. One reads the text as a historical document. This can be done in different ways. One can read the text as a text which provides information about the life of Jesus in Palestine in the thirties (like in the studies of Bammel), or about the church situation in the nineties (this happens in a number of studies, as in those on John the Baptist, on the early gnosticism etc.). Most influential, however, is the way of reading which uses John's Gospel in order to reconstruct the history of the Johannine community. Of this way of reading Martyn and Brown are the most prominent promoters, but also Neyrey, Wengst and Ashton follow this way of reading. There are certain assumptions that play a role, like the assumption that christology has developed from so-called low-christological to high-christological confessions; or the assumption that the conflict with the Jews has developed from an ideological discussion on the meaning of Jesus to juridical procedures and physical violence; or that the history of the Jesus narrative serves as a mirror for the history of the Johannine community. It is a way of reading which follows the story of the Johannine Gospel from a distance, and yet it does not keep in focus the narrative itself. At the contrary, in spite of the narrative told, one wants to obtain information about a history, which is not being told from the perspective of the narrator who tells the story.

The narrative reading of the Johannine Gospel is in opposition with all these approaches. Point of departure is the assumption that John's Gospel is a narrative which tells the history of a part of Jesus' life in Palestine in the thirties. This does not define yet the precise nature of the narrative. The narrative reading, however, assumes that the Johannine text is a narrative and —even more than that—, it assumes that from the perspective of the author/narrator the text is meant to be understood as a narrative. This implies, to say the least, that there is a difference between the beginning and the end of the narrative; that there are narrative connections between the various episodes; that the place of a particular episode within the story as it is told contributes to the meaning of that episode; that the various and at times extensive speeches of Jesus should not be considered as independent doctrinary tracts from the Johannine school, but as interventions of the narrative's main character within the setting in which he is situated at that moment. For instance, in the dialogue with Nicodemus in John 3 at the beginning of the story on being born; in John 10 at the parable of the good shepherd in Jerusalem, right at the heart of the conflict between Jesus and the Pharisees about the leadership in Israel; and in John 13-17 at the intimacy of a meal where Jesus is at table with his friends for the last time on lasting love relationships. The narrative reading of the Johannine Gospel is but one possible choice. As contemporary exegesis of John clearly demonstrates, it is absolutely not the only one plausible, but an option made in favour of the narrative reading has far-reaching consequences for the interpretation of the text.

In the foregoing project I have used the narrative reading. The Johannine Gospel is a narration, in which —I found—, love becomes real in a narrative way. It is of course possible, as in fact has been done in many ways, to talk about love in the Johannine Gospel in a discursive way by defining the concept of love, by analysing and clarifying the religio-historical background of the texts where the word 'love' appears, by comparing the concept of love in the Synoptics, Paul and John, etc. All these I have omitted. It is obvious for every reader of John's Gospel that in John 'love' is important indeed. What I wanted to know was the answer to the question in what way love in the Johannine Gospel is given form in a narrative manner, whether or not it is being realised by the characters of the narrative, by Jesus in the first place, as well as in the variety of characters beside him: the father and mother of Jesus, his brothers and sisters, his disciples and individual men and women.

Now, the narrative analysis of a text does not necessarily coincide with what an author wants to represent imaginarily. There are many possible ways to make a narratological analysis of the Gospel. In reality, only a few are being practised and these experience a constant pressure due to the dominant discourse within the exegetical field (cf. Carson's critique on Culpepper in his new commentary). In theory, however, it is possible to make a link-up with all kinds of variations which, in the field of literary sciences, are being proposed as models of analysis. And these can be applied in a variety of ways. We may call an analysis 'narratively imaginative' when —of course within a certain narratological framework—, the narrative realisations within a concrete text are being viewed as an imaginatively realised figure, placed beside other imaginatively possible figures. The concrete love story is considered a selection from many other love stories, as a narrative-factual love story among the many love stories possible.

In order to obtain a clearer view of this imaginary possible which is being told in the actual Gospel of John, I have used the biographical code: the concrete family constellation of Jesus' family, John the Baptist's relationship with his disciple Jesus and the relationship of Jesus, the teacher, with his beloved disciple and with his other disciples; the relationship of the disciples among one another and the preferential relationships of Jesus with a number of men and women. In a certain sense I have confronted one narrative, the Johannine Gospel, with another narrative, the biographical code which unfolds as a narrative discourse: the family, (birth), learning,

the formation of a group or school of disciples and entering into
relationships with women and men. This study shows what happens
when we bring about a confrontation between these two models of
reading.

I started my study with a critical analysis of the narrative family
constellation of Jesus' family. Love originates in the family and the
actual family situation determines the physical, emotional and
intellectual possibilities of loving. The specific family constellation
in which Jesus is found, determines his sympathetic and benevolent
openness towards the world and its inhabitants.

In the imaginary world of the Johannine Gospel Jesus finds
himself in a particular family situation. He has a unique relationship
with his mother, a non-relation with his father, a conflictual
relationship with his brothers and sisters, and a extremely close and
extensively described relationship with his 'father who sent him',
and who narratively speaking, exists only in Jesus' imagination.

Jesus and his mother

In two scenes which are particularly relevant to the narrative, the
mother of Jesus plays an important role: at the beginning and at the
end of the story; in Cana at the wedding meal and in Jerusalem
near the cross, when Jesus as a king is elevated at the cross in
order to return to his father. At both instances the distant word
'woman' is used: 'woman, what do you want from me?', 'woman,
this is your son', which expresses reverence and distance as well.
The numerous excuses produced by scholars in order to explain
why Jesus addresses his mother this way, can not conceal that
something important is being said. It certainly does not express
intimacy.

I began with a reflection on the Cana story. It has been a
surprise to many persons that from the narrative point of view the
story follows its own course. They have no wine, which is noticed
by the mother of Jesus, and she tells her son. But he, at least so it
seems, turns her down: 'woman, what do you want from me? My
hour has not come yet.' Whatever the meaning of this statement
may be, the mother continues to make arrangements. She tells the
servants to do whatever her son will tell them to do. As I have
shown, this is an extremely important sentence from the point of
view of communication. With her sentence the mother of Jesus
makes her way into the centre of the story in such a way, that

nobody, and most of all Jesus himself, can withdraw from her influence. Whatever he does, he always acts in consonance with whatever his mother has organised for him.

In the scene at the cross something more complicated takes place. In my opinion, it is the following: Jesus is about to die. Not parents will bury their children, but children will bury their parents. The commandment of the law: 'honour your father and mother' is at stake. Jesus will fulfil this commandment till the end, even beyond his own death. By way of his last will Jesus entrusts his mother to his beloved disciple. Jesus continues to take care of his mother. Jesus accepts the responsibility to care for his mother beyond death, and so he proves to be an obedient son. As far as relationship is concerned, the story is a continuation of the Cana story, however, with an inverted effect: the concerns of the mother have turned into concerns of the son.

Jesus and his brothers and sisters

Also Jesus' brothers and sisters play a role in the Johannine Gospel. No matter how modest their role, it is not unimportant. After Jesus' mission in Galilee has completely failed and all people have walked out on him for reason that his words are hard to believe, and after in spite of Simon Peter's impressive confession in the small group of the twelve disciples, the evil one has taken possession of Judas, the ἀδελφοί of Jesus think that he should leave for Judea: 'so that also your disciples can see the works you perform!' Their motivation is not friendly. Consequently the author of the narrative explains that also they have no faith in Jesus. And for him this is a complete dismissal.

The mutual relationship between Jesus and his brothers (and sisters) is extremely bad. Jesus' ἀδελφοί want to get rid of him, or at least under false pretext they refer him to the feast in Jerusalem, where he can show himself in public. Doing so, they pretend not to know that Jesus out of fear for his life decides not to go up to Jerusalem. Jesus blames them for not understanding him: 'my time has not yet come; the world hates me, because I accuse the world, but the world can not hate you'. Jesus and his ἀδελφοί do not match well. Within the circle of his family Jesus has become an alien whom they do not understand. He is forced to abandon his own family to realise himself and this calls forth conflict.

Jesus and his father

Also Jesus' relationship with his father is quite peculiar. An —as I called him—, 'earthly' father is totally absent, while his 'heavenly' father is supposed to be present from the very beginning of the book unto the end. It is with this heavenly father that Jesus entertains the most cordial and loving relationship. The main character of the narrative has no relationship at all with his father of flesh and blood. His own father is a father who dwells in heaven, which means that the main character of the narrative identifies himself with a imaginary father, a father who is alive in his imagination and his longings.

In a sense it is the only theme repeatedly mentioned by Jesus, and in which, although in various ways, the same is said time and again. There is a perfect, reciprocally positive relationship between Jesus as the son of God and God as his father. Both father and son realise the highest one can think of in this culture: the best father and the best son in the best relationship possible.

With a number of basic metaphors this point of departure receives a special colour.

- God is the father-*kyrios* who provides his son with a house in which this son may feel at home and to which he can invite his friends. It is a house with many rooms which is available to Jesus and which he can prepare for his friends (14,2). Materially speaking this refers to the Temple of Jerusalem as the house of God, his father. Being the son, Jesus is responsible that this house will be used in accordance with the will of the father. When people abuse this, Jesus will take action, because the zeal for the house of his father consumes him.

- God is the father-king, who sends his son to a far and strange country in order to reveal himself as the envoy of God the father. To be an envoy is a basic metaphor of which many aspects are elaborated, and which repeatedly occurs in Jesus' words. As the son of God he is the unique caretaker. Israel has never experienced this and should rejoice in this caretakership. The fact that this does not happen is a source of frustration and polemics.

- God is the father-educator, who personally has instructed his son for the task which he has to carry out. The father of Jesus has taught him everything he needed to know and Jesus has been his best disciple. In particular he has learned how he should act as king-judge in questions about life and death: the resurrection and the eternal death as the extreme experiences for those who are related to Jesus' performance.

Between Jesus and his imaginary father everything is grandiose. His father is the greatest, the strongest, the most loving; the son is the chosen one, he is unique. The oneness between father and son can not be broken even by the ruler of this world. The father will not abandon the son nor the son the father. The oneness exists in possessions, in knowledge and in love which is completely incomparable. Therefore, the son has access to the father and nothing will be denied him. He can ask anything. He can also intervene for others who want to ask something. All this is still re-enforced because it exists on 'the highest levels', on the level of a king-judge who has the power of life and death; of God himself who guarantees life for eternity from before the foundation of the cosmos.

This qualitative and quantitative expansion of the importance of the male code does not mean that there is no criticism on the culturally determined male dominance in John's Gospel. Jn 1,13 and 3,5-6 put it to the readers that the surplus value of the male in the fertile sexuality between man and woman is of no importance in comparison to the birth from God. Not the male dominance in fertile sexuality but the sperm of God determines men's destiny. Against this background the absence of Jesus' 'earthly' father and the active presence of his 'heavenly' father gets a special meaning. With this Jesus reveals in person origin and destiny of all the children of God. The text of John presupposes that the family story of Jesus is of importance for everybody 'born from water and spirit'.

John has pictured a very typical family constellation: a mother who is intensively present, an absent father, a conflict with brothers and sisters and the image of an imaginary father who assumes heavenly proportions. As far as I could see this is a unique presentation of affairs in antiquity.

My problem is —if at least it is a problem—, the fact that in the 20th century discourse on family constellations this is not unique at all. In fact, according to Freud's description of family constellations, it is the typical model of a family which tends to produce and develop a homosexual son. Of course, this hypothesis has been the subject of many discussions, but it looks as if at this moment psycho-analysis presumes the proposition mentioned above (Marmor, Green, Friedman, Isay). Even though such a family situation is not predeterminant —it is not bound to lead up to homosexuality—, it is conducive to a homosexual inclination among the male children.

the teacher's love for his favourite

The main contribution of this study to Johannine research is the proposal to understand the character of the beloved disciple against the background of the Hellenistic 'institute' of a teacher who loves in a special way one favourite among his disciples. It is a narrative reality which comes closest to what moderns would call male homosexual behaviour: the love of an older man for a younger one. From chapter 13 on we find the anonymous character: —'the disciple whom Jesus loved'—, who from that moment on will play an very important role in the narrative. The beloved disciple is a character who is unique for the Johannine Gospel among the gospel stories. Obviously, this evoked a mountain of literature, but the characteristic of 'to love' and 'to be loved' is conspicuously absent. In the scientific exegetical discourse it is not mentioned at all.

This vacuum should not be taken for granted. In fact I assume that via the lexeme of the 'beloved disciple' a reality is being called into existence which in classical and Hellenistic antiquity has its own structure: the teacher who has a particular, affective relationship with one of his disciples, and who attributes to this disciple a special role with regard to his succession in the future. This is more or less an institutional reality. Consequently one can speak of a repetition in the Johannine Gospel: like Jesus in a special way has been promoted by John (the Baptist), in the same way the beloved disciple of Jesus is granted a special place by Jesus. The Johannine Gospel tells that John, Jesus, and the beloved disciple realise the classical ideal of the $\pi\alpha\iota\delta\epsilon\rho\alpha\sigma\tau\iota\alpha$: the *paidagogic* love which is the source of divine knowledge and love of God.

This has different meanings in the relationship of John (the Baptist) towards Jesus and of Jesus towards his beloved disciple. In both it is the teacher who is active. In the case of John (the Baptist) this means that he is the active one in the presentation of Jesus to Israel. In his own imaginary presentation of affairs (especially in the mashal of 3,29) he has acted as the best man for Jesus, who as the son of God married the bride Israel. In the story as told this marriage does not play a role of much importance as far as I can see. In the fantasy of John (the Baptist) it is essential, because it justifies his lower position. He is the friend of Jesus which makes him use, unknowingly, the same words and sentences as Jesus, or he is prepared to let himself be influenced and/or corrected by his friend.

In the relation between Jesus and the beloved disciple Jesus is, in a way, also the active one. He is the lover. He has expressed his preference. He has elected this disciple over the others. Jesus realises the classical philosophical ideal of the teacher-disciple model. In practice each scene, in which the beloved disciple plays a role, refers to this model. Jesus takes the beloved disciple into the intimacy of himself. When Jesus dies, he appoints him as *kyrios* over his mother; as his successor and as his (quasi-) adopted son. He has taken him into his love to such an extent that he will not allow anyone to interfere in letting him 'remain till he comes'.

The beloved disciple becomes a participant gradually. While Jesus lives, he is the passive subject of Jesus' love and after Jesus' death he is the active witness of this love. His activity culminates in the writing of the book. According to 21,24, he is the explicit author of the book about Jesus' deeds and words, for always hidden behind the words of the real author, but in a truthful way as the we-group in 21,24 tells us. In short, while Jesus lives, he is the passive subject of Jesus' love and after Jesus' death he is the active witness of this love.

For Jesus' social role this means that the author, imaginarily, ascribes to Jesus a marriage as well as a special friendship. The difference is that the marriage is imaginary 'in the second degree' (i.e. in the presentation by a character of the narrative = John, the Baptist), while the friendship is narrative reality. In our culture such a social role could exist only at the expense of the masculine sense of identity, while in the classical culture it reinforces the masculine code.

As I wrote in the concluding words of chapter 2, if we combine this with contemporary discourse about the family constellations and the consequences in relation to the behaviour for a son in this setting, we have to come to a curious conclusion. The Johannine Gospel tells a story, according to the code of modern discourse, about a family constellation which is positively attuned to the development of possibly homosexual behaviour. It is a possibility which we see also realised in the story of the relation between Jesus and his beloved disciple. But in the code, contemporary to the story as told, such imaginary homosexual behaviour is not an expression of homosexuality. It is an expression of παιδεραστία, the love for a παῖς as the perfect entrance into the knowledge of God's love for his son and consequently of God's love for the cosmos. The love relation between Jesus and his beloved disciple shows the aim of Jesus' love: the propagation of his love relationship with his father-God.

Jesus' disciples as his friends

This exclusive friendship of Jesus is embedded in the positive relationship which Jesus entertains with the larger group of his male disciples. The beloved disciple is the favourite, because he is the elected one from among a larger group. More can be said about the disciples of Jesus in the Johannine Gospel than until now has been attempted in exegesis. In the context of love relationships it is of special importance that Jesus considers this group of disciples as a group of friends: the greatest love a person can have for his friends is to give his life for them; you are my friends; I do not call you slaves any longer, because I have told you everything I have heard from my father (15,11-17). Jesus has surrounded himself with a group of persons who are his disciple-friends.

This is indicated in a most impressive way by the scene of Jesus' last meal with his disciples. It is the longest scene of the Johannine narrative —which in exegesis hardly has been considered a narrative unit! Jesus is willing to do everything: he washes the feet of his disciples; he shows the way to the person who will betray him; he keeps Peter in check; he shows his intimate feelings for his beloved disciple in a visible way; he maintains the dialogue with his disciples, even when they do not understand and even though their words are not trustworthy. Jesus is willing to intervene for his disciples with his father, in words which speak only of good things and forget what is evil (especially in 17,6-8), because Jesus is the *agagogue* between God and his people. It is his task to unite the scattered children of God. This he carries out by taking care that his disciples are at home with the family and in the house of God.

This friendship of Jesus for his disciples is indicated even more by Jesus' preparedness to give his life for his friends. It is a preparedness which in the story told is carried out and which is significant for the evaluation of the cultural meaning of this special narrativisation of friendship. In philosophical ethics it is a topic which is ascribed to various persons as the highest ideal, but actually these persons are all mythological and early-historical persons: Achilles, Alcestis, Damon and Phintias. In John's narrative, however, Jesus does not merely speak about this, but he realises it. In the relationship between Jesus and his disciples something similar happens as in the relationship between Jesus and his beloved disciple. What was upheld in philosophical ethics as the highest norm, is completely carried out by Jesus. Jesus' love for his disciples is an extension of his love for his beloved disciple.

It shows more clearly that love contains a 'fantastic' quality, the preparedness to overlook actual behaviour which is not in line with the supposed love relationship. Jesus' love uses this imaginary knowledge which is so important and, in fact, necessary for the continuity of love itself, as is made clear in 17,6-8 and yet more in his death in favour of the world. In his own story, Peter appeals to this attitude of Jesus (21,15-19). It is connected with the overflowing love of God for his people: 'God is greater than our heart and knows all things' (1 Jn 3,20). Without this benevolent fantasy love is not possible at all.

Jesus urges his friends also to love one another. This is not to be taken for granted and in fact the disciples —except for some kind of mutual kindness—, make a poor show. The opening scene of the last supper, Jesus washing the feet of his disciples and their reaction to this, expresses this quite well. It is in a way the basic story of the *oikos* of Jesus and his friends: the washing of the feet as sign of the high stake of Jesus' love, but also as an act of hospitality; the disciples who need to behave themselves as mutual friends: ultimately ready to lay down their lives for the brethren, but in the meantime ready to be guest-friends of each other; Peter as the spokesman of the people who claim to be ready for this but who have their shortcomings; Judas as the representative of the worst that can happen among friends: doing evil, notwithstanding the fact that friendship has been offered; the presence of the beloved disciple shows that all of this does not necessarily harm the perfection of love.

The mutual love which Jesus impresses on his disciples is a principle of democracy within a society which is strongly hierarchically organised. The outcome of Jesus' life (and Peter's cf.

21,18.19; and the blind man's cf. 9,34.35; and Lazarus's cf. 12,10) shows that the actual world can not allow this. The alternative of love evokes the hatred of the world. It is part of the most fundamental message of the Johannine Gospel that love ultimately wins victory.

loving women

Jesus' love is not restricted to these disciples. He moves around and meets men and women. With some of them he starts a specific relationship. As shown, his relationship with women is quite special, but it is also somewhat ambiguous. The beginning and the end of the stories show quite a difference. In the beginning of the various stories Jesus is inviting and open; he opens the conversation and listens to them; he helps the conversation to progress. He also receives a lot: personally, because the women make it possible for him to express himself in a way which in other situations is not given to him or not yet given; and beyond the personal, because time and again the women win people for the Jesus movement and in this way make the covenant between God and Israel visible and open for new possibilities.

But each time there is a phase in the story where this openness is closed off: the active Samaritan woman is made anonymous (in 4,35-38); the theological Martha is accused of not having faith (in 11,40); the affective Mary hears an interpretation which is surprising (in 12,7); the radiant Mary Magdalene with her message that she has seen the Lord is rated lower than the beloved disciple who does not see him and yet believes (in 20,29). The implied author developed imaginarily a vision of Jesus which rather closely fits what has been said so far. At decisive moments Jesus retreats from his relation to women: he finds refuge in his relation with the male disciples (in the case of the Samaritan woman); he retires into himself (in the case of Mary and Martha) and, in the closing stories, he goes back to his relation with the beloved disciple (in the case of his mother and Mary Magdalene). One can surmise that the women are left empty-handed even though the story does not say so. The return to the male partner(s) is in the story something self-evident and demonstrates once again that the social role of Jesus in the Johannine Gospel is clearly circumscribed.

beloved men

The study ends with an analysis of the stories in which Jesus engages in a special relationship with three men, which presumably like the women belong to the circle of disciples, yet in a way different from the disciples who follow Jesus on his journeys and who are present during the last supper. These are stories in which Jesus expresses his preference for these men, a selection by Jesus which is immediately connected with their situation of deficiency: a man who is paralysed for 38 years, a man who is blind from birth, the beloved Lazarus who after a period of sickness dies and is buried. Jesus' love extends itself to persons who are marked by life.

Various narrative devices result in a typical difference between these stories on men and the stories on women.

Jesus is active in a manner which does not occur elsewhere in the narrative. He himself takes the initiative to action, or —like in the story on Lazarus—, he claims the initiative to action. Particularly distinctive is the fact that Jesus returns to the people. Once more he looks for them: the paralytic in order to liberate him from his assailants, the blind in order to bind him to himself, Lazarus out of benevolence. This is an activity of Jesus which is completely conform to his social role. In his love Jesus is positively directed towards men. He does not abandon them when difficulties occur.

This characteristic of Jesus is evaluated positively by the narrator, as it is shown most clearly by the number and the nature of the retrospective references. Different from the women's stories there is clearly no attempt to make the people anonymous as if the narrative character is of no importance, once the story is told. In fact, the characters are brought back as individuals in the narrative itself. Jesus refers to the cure of the paralytic (in 7,21-24); the people who see Jesus cry because of Lazarus, refer to the cure of the blind man (in 11,37); the narrator of the story refers to Lazarus several times in his narrative (in 12,1.9.17). While the men are fairly anonymous —a paralytic, a blind man—, they stay in the personal attention of Jesus, of the Judeans and of the narrator of the story.

The most remarkable difference with the stories on women is, as it has been shown earlier, the situation of 'persecution' in which various men end up due to Jesus' action. One may notice a certain crescendo: the lame man is submitted to a simple inquiry, the blind man is faced with a quasi-juridical process and he is physically expelled from the community, Lazarus is officially sentenced to death. The stories mirror concretely the social position of Jesus at a particular instance of the narrative: an inquiry, a physical expulsion, a death threat. The concrete stories on men indicate that those who as a man have experienced the benevolent love of Jesus, must opt for his way. The fact that this has not been the situation of the beloved disciple clarifies the confusion among the brothers (21,23) as well as his special election.

I should come to a concise and final conclusion. The Johannine Gospel is a very particular narrative. It pictures a value, which is of certain importance in the modern discussion on love and love relationships. That Jesus loves people is not an abstract sentence. His love is embedded in a pattern of relationships of different kinds. His love for the one, anonymous beloved disciple is the centre of his affective life. It is a preferential love, which colours all other relationships: the relationship with his mother, his father, his disciples, with women and men as well. In the opinion of the writer this beloved disciple is even the author of the book as the guarantee for the narrative told. I suppose that there is no greater authority for the value, appreciated by God and Jesus, of this and similar love stories.

SELECTED LIST OF LITERATURE

Archer L.J., 1990, *Her Price is Beyond Rubies. The Jewish Woman in Graeco-Roman Palestine*, Sheffield, JSOT Press

Arnim H. von, 1905-1924, *Stoicorum veterum fragmenta*, Leipzig, Teubner

Ashton J., 1991, *Understanding the Fourth Gospel*, Oxford, Clarendon Press

Babut D., 1969, *Plutarque et le stoïcisme*, Paris, Presses Universitaires de France

Barrett C.K., 1967 (1955), *The Gospel according to St. John*, London, SPCK

Barrett C.K., 1982, *Essays on John*, London, SPCK

Bartholomew G.L., 1987, Feed my Lambs: John 21:15-19 as Oral Gospel, in, *Semeia* 39, 1987, 69-96

Becker J., 1969, Aufbau, Schichtung und theologiegeschichtliche Stellung des Gebetes in Johannes 17, in, *ZeitschrNTlicheWissenschaft* 60, 1969, 56-83

Bernard J.H., 1972 (1928), *Gospel according to St. John* ed. by A.H. McNeile, Edinburgh, Clark

Beutler J., 1984, *Habt keine Angst. Die erste johanneische Abschiedsrede (Joh 14)*, Stuttgart, Kath. Bibelwerk

Beutler J. — Fortna R.T., 1991, *The Shepherd Discourse of John 10 and its Context. Studies by Members of the Johannine Writings Seminar*, Cambridge, Cambridge University Press

Bieber I. et al., 1962, *Homosexuality: A Psychoanalytic Study of Male Homosexuals*, New York, Basic Books

Bieber I., 1965 (1962), Clinical Aspects of Male Homosexuality, in, J. Marmor (ed.), *Sexual Inversion. The Multiple Roots of Homosexuality*, 248-267, New York, Basic Books

Bittner W.J., 1987, *Jesu Zeichen im Johannesevangelium. Die Messias-Erkenntnis im Johannesevangelium vor ihrem jüdischen Hintergrund*, Tübingen, Mohr

Blidstein G., 1975, *Honor Thy Father and Mother. Filial responsibility in Jewish Law and Ethics*, New York, KTAV

Bligh J., 1966, Four Studies in St John, I: The Man Born Blind, in, *HeythropJourn* 7, 1966, 125-144

Blok J., 1987, Sexual Asymmetry. A Historiographical Essay, in, J. Blok — P. Mason, *Sexual Asymmetry. Studies in Ancient Society*, 1-51, Amsterdam, Gieben Publ.

Boer W. den, 1979, *Private Morality in Greece and Rome. Some Historical Aspects*, Leiden, Brill

Boismard M.-E., 1953, *Le prologue de saint Jean*, Paris, Du Cerf

Bolotin D., 1979, *Plato's Dialogue on Friendship. An Interpretation of the Lysis, with a New Translation*, Ithaca-London, Cornell University Press

Boring M.-E., 1979, The Influence of Christian Prophecy on the Johannine Portrayal of the Paraclete and Jesus, in, *NewTestStudies* 25, 1979, 113-123

Boswell J., 1980, *Christianity, Social Tolerance, and Homosexuality. Gay People in Western Europe from the Beginning of the Christian Era to the Fourteenth Century*, Chicago-London, Chicago Press

Bouwman G., 1990, *De zonde van Sodom. Ontstaan en verstaan van een bijbelverhaal*, Hilversum, Gooi en Sticht

Bremen R. van, 1983, Women and Wealth, in, A. Cameron — A. Kuhrt (ed.), *Images of Women in Antiqutiy*, 207-241, London-Canberra, Croom Helm

Brooten B.J., 1982, *Women Leaders in the Ancient Synagogue. Inscriptional Evidence and Background Issues*, Chico, California, Scholars Press

Brooten B.J., 1985, Early Christian Women and their Cultural Context: Issues of Method in Historical Reconstruction, in, A. Yarbo Collins (ed.), *Feminist Perspectives on Biblical Scholarship*, 65-91, Chico, California, Scholars Press

Brown P., 1988, *The Body and Society: Men, Women and Sexual Renunciation in Early Christianity*, New York, Columbia University Press

Brown R.E., 1966-1970, *The Gospel according to John*, Garden City, New York, Doubleday

Brown R.E., 1979, *The Community of the Beloved Disciple. The Life, Loves, and Hates of an Individual Church in New Testament Times*, New York, Chapman

Brown R.E., 1983, *The Epistles of John*, Garden City, New York, Doubleday

Bühner J.-A., 1977, *Der Gesandte und sein Weg im 4. Evangelium. Die kultur- und religionsgeschichtliche Grundlagen der johanneischen Sendungschristologie sowie ihre traditionsgeschichtliche Entwicklung*, Tübingen, Mohr

Buffière F., 1980, *Eros Adolescent. La pédérastie dans la Grèce antique*, Paris, Les belles Lettres

Bultmann R., 1968 (1941), *Das Evangelium des Johannes*, Göttingen, Vandenhoeck und Ruprecht

Calloud J. — Genuyt F., 1985, *Le Discours d'Adieu. Jean 13-17. Analyse sémiotique*, Lyon, L'Arbresle

Carson D.A., 1991, *The Gospel According to John*, Grand Rapids, Eerdmans

Ceroke C.P., 1959, The Problem of Ambiguity in John 2,4, in, *CathBiblQuaterly* 21, 1959, 316-340

Coakley J.F., 1988, The Anointing at Bethany and the Priority of John, in, *JournBiblLit* 107/2, 1988, 241-256

CPJ = Tcherikover V.T. — Fuks A., 1957-1960, *Corpus Papyrorum Judaicarum, I-II*, Cambridge, Harvard University Press

Culpepper R.A., 1981, The Pivot of John's Prologue, in, *NewTestStudies* 27, 1981, 1-31

Culpepper R.A., 1983, *Anatomy of the Fourth Gospel. A Study in Literary Design*, Philadelphia, Fortress Press

Dagonet P., 1979, *Selon saint Jean. Une femme de Samarie*, Paris, Du Cerf

Dannecker M., 1981 (1978), *Theories of Homosexuality*, tr. of 'Der Homosexuelle und die Homosexualität', Frankfurt, 1978, London, Gay Men's Press

Dauer A., 1972, *Die Passionsgeschichte im Johannesevangelium. Eine traditionsgeschichtliche und theologische Untersuchung zu Joh 18,1-19,30*, München, Kösel

Davies W.D., 1965 (1948), *Paul and Rabbinic Judaism. Some Rabbinic Elements in Pauline Theology*, New York-Evanston, Harper & Row

Dibelius M., 1953 (1927), Joh 15,13. Eine Studie zum Traditionsproblem des Johannes-Evangeliums, in, *Botschaft und Geschichte*, 204-222, Tübingen, Mohr

Diels H., 1922 (1903), *Die Fragmente der Vorsokratiker, Griechisch und Deutsch*, Berlin, Weidmannsche Buchhandlung

Dodd C.H., 1968 (1953), *The Interpretation of the Fourth Gospel*, Cambridge, Cambridge University Press

Dodd C.H., 1968b, *More New Testament Studies*, Manchester University Press

Dörrie H., 1976, *Von Platon zum Platonismus. Ein Bruch in der Überlieferung und seine Überwindung*, Opladen, Westdeutscher Verlag

Dover K.J., 1978, *Greek Homosexuality*, London, Duckworth

Downing F.G., 1988, *Christ and the Cynics. Jesus and other Radical Preachers in First-Century Tradition*, Sheffield, Sheffield Academic Press

Dozeman T.B., 1980, Sperma Abraam in John 8 and Related Literature. Cosmology and Judgment, in, *CathBiblQuaterly* 42, 1980, 342-358

Ernst J., 1989, *Johannes der Täufer. Interpretation-Geschichte-Wirkungsgeschichte*, Berlin-New York, W. de Gruyter

Falk W.W., 1978, *Introduction to Jewish Law of the Second Commonwealth*, Leiden, Brill

Fander M., 1990, *Die Stellung der Frau im Markusevangelium unter besonderer Berücksichtigung kultur- und religionsgeschichtliche Hintergründe*, Altenberge, Telos

Festugière A.-J., 1954, *Corpus Hermeticum*, t. 1-4, Paris, Les belles Lettres

Feuillet A., 1963, La recherche du Christ dans la Nouvelle Alliance d'après la christophanie de Jn. 20,11-18. Comparaison avec Cant. 3,1-4 et l'épisode des Pèlerins d'Emmaüs, in, *L'Homme devant Dieu, Mélange H. de Lubac*, I, 1963, 93-112, Aubier, Montaigne

Fiebig P., 1933, *Rabbinische Wundergeschichten des neutestamentlichen Zeitalters*, Berlin, de Gruyter

Flacelière R., 1960, *L'amour en Grèce*, Paris, Librairie Hachette

Friedman R.C., 1988, *Male Homosexuality. A Contemporary Psychoanalitic Perspective*, New Haven-London, Yale University Press

Gaechter P., 1963, Zum Form von Joh 5,19-30, in, *Neutestamentliche Aufsätze*, Fs f. J. Schmid, 65-68, Regensburg, Pustet

Genuyt F., 1986, La résurrection de Lazare. Évangile de Jean. Analyse sémiotique du chapitre 11, in, *Sémiotique et bible* 44, 1986, 18-37

Gerhardsson B., 1961, *Memory and Manuscript. Oral Tradition and Written Transmission in Rabbinic Judaism and Early Christianity*, Lund-Copenhagen, Gleerup-Munksgaard

Gerlach W., 1938, Das Problem des 'weiblichen Samens' in der antiken und mittelalterlichen Medizin, in, *Suddhoffs Archiv für Geschichte der Medizin*, 30, 1938, 177-193

Geytenbeek A.V. van, 1962, *Musonius Rufus and Greek Diatribe*, Assen, Van Gorcum

Gnilka J., 1983, *Johannesevangelium*, Echt, Echter Verlag

Goedt M. de, 1961/62, Un schème de révélation dans le quatrième évangile, in, *NewTestStudies* 8, 1961/62, 142-150

Goessler L., 1962, *Plutarchs Gedanken über die Ehe*, Zürich, Buchdrückerei Berichthaus

Gourgues M., 1982, L'aveugle-né (Jn 9). Du miracle au signe: typologie des réactions à l'égard du Fils de l'homme, in, *NouvRevThéol* 114, 1982, 381-395

Green R., 1980, Patterns of Sexual Identity in Childhood: Relationship to Subsequent Sexual Partner Preference, in, J. Marmor (ed.), *Homosexual Behavior. A Modern Reappraisal*, 255-266, New York, Basic Books

Grigsby B., 1985, Washing in the Pool of Siloam — A Thematic Anticipation of the Johannine Cross, in, *NovTest* 27, 1985, 227-235

Grimm W., 1974, Die Preisgabe eines Menschen zur Rettung des Volkes. Priesterliche Tradition bei Johannes und Josephus, in, O. Betz — K. Haacker (Hrsg), *Josephus-Studien. Untersuchungen zu Josephus, dem antiken Judentum und dem Neuen Testament*, Fs O. Michel, 133-146, Göttingen, Vandenhoeck und Ruprecht

Griswold C.L., 1986, *Self-Knowledge in Plato's Phaedrus*, New Haven-London, Yale University Press

Grundmann W., 1959, Das Wort von Jesu Freunden (Joh XV,13-16) und das Herrenmahl, in, *NovTest* 3, 1959, 62-69

Grundmann W., 1988 (1984), The decision of the Supreme Court to put Jesus to death (John 11:47-57) in its context: tradition and redaction in the Gospel of John, in, E. Bammel — C.F.D. Moule (ed.), *Jesus and the Politics of His Day*, 295-318, Cambridge, Press Syndicate of Cambridge

Haenchen E., 1965, *Gott und Mensch. Gesammelte Aufsätze*, Tübingen, Vandenhoeck und Ruprecht

Hahn F., 1974, Die Jüngerberufung Joh 1,35-51, in, *Neues Testament und Kirche*, Fs R. Schnackenburg, 172-190, Freiburg, Herder

Hanson A., 1976/77, John I.14-18 and Exodus XXXIV, in, *NewTestStudies* 23, 1976/77, 90-101

Hanson A., 1991, *The Prophetic Gospel. A Study of John and the Old Testament*, Edinburgh, Clark

Heinemann I., 1962 (1929-1932), *Philons griechische und jüdische Bildung. Kulturvergleichende Untersuchungen zu Philons Darstellung der jüdischen Gesetze*, Hildesheim, Olms

Hengel M., 1963, Maria Magdalena und die Frauen als Zeugen, in, O. Betz — M. Hengel (Hrsg), *Abraham Unser Vater*, Fs f. O. Michel, 243-256, Leiden, Brill

Hofrichter P., 1978, *Nicht aus Blut sondern monogen aus Gott geboren. Textkritische, dogmengeschichtliche und exegetische Untersuchung zu Joh 1,13-14*, Echt, Echter Verlag

Hofrichter P., 1986, *Im Anfang war der 'Johannesprolog'. Das urchristliche Logosbekenntnis - die Basis neutestamentlicher und gnostischer Theologie*, Regensburg, Pustet

Holladay C.R., 1977, *THEIOS ANER in Hellenistic-Judaism: A Critique of the Use of This Category in New Testament Christology*, Missoula, Scholars Press

Hollenbach P., 1979, Social Aspects of John the Baptizer's Preaching Mission in the Context of Palestinian Judaism, in, *Aufstieg und Niedergang der römischen Welt*, 19,1, II, 850-875

Hudry-Clergeon C., 1981, De Judée en Galilée. Étude de Jean 4,1-45, in, *NouvRevThéol* 103, 1981, 817-830

Isay R.A., 1989, *Being Homosexual. Gay Men and Their Development*, New York, Farrar-Straus-Giroux

Jagu A., 1979, *Musonius Rufus. Entretiens et fragments: Introduction, traduction et commentaire*, Hildesheim-New York, Olms

Jaubert A., 1976, *Approches de l'Évangile de Jean*, Paris, Ed. du Seuil

Jewett R., 1971, *Paul's Anthropological Terms. A Study of Their Use in Conflict Settings*, Leiden, Brill

Kaser M., 1955, *Das Römische Privatrecht, I-II*, München, Beck'sche Verlagsbuchhandlung

Keuls E.C., 1985, *The Reign of the Phallus. Sexual Politics in Ancient Athens*, New York, Harper & Row

Klein M.L., 1980, *The Fragment-Targums of the Pentateuch according to the Extant Sources*, Vol I-II, Rome, Biblical Institute Press

Kleinknecht H.M. — Bieder W. — Sjöberg E. — Schweizer E., 1959, *TWNT* s.v. πνεῦμα

Koester C., 1989, Hearing, Seeing, and Believing in the Gospel of John, in, *Bibl* 70, 1989, 327-348

Kragerud A., 1959, *Der Lieblingsjünger im Johannesevangelium*, Oslo, Osloer Universitätsverlag

Krauss S., 1910-12, *Talmudische Archäologie*, Leipzig, Fock

Kügler J., 1988, *Der Jünger, den Jesus liebte. Literarische, theologische und historische Untersuchungen zu einer Schlüsselgestalt johanneischer Theologie und Geschichte. Mit einem Exkurs über die Brotrede in Joh 6.*, Stuttgart, Kath. Bibelwerk

Kuhn H.-J., 1988, *Christologie und Wunder. Untersuchungen zu Joh 1,35-51*, Regensburg, Fr. Pustet

Kurfess A., 1952/53, Zu Joh 2,4, in, *ZeitschrNTestlicheWissenschaft* 44, 1952/53, 257

Lacey W.K., 1983 (1968), *Die Familie im antiken Griechenland*, Übers. von U. Winter, tr. of 'The Family in Classical Greece', 1968, Mainz, von Zabern

Lazure N., 1969, La convoitise de la chair en 1 Jean, II,16, in, *RevueBibl* 76, 1969, 161-205

Lefkowitz M.R. — Fant M.B., 1982, *Women's Life in Greece and Rome*, London, Duckworth

Lenglet A., 1985, Jésus de passage parmi les Samaritains. Jn 4,4-42, in, *Bibl* 66, 1985, 493-503

Leo F., 1965 (1901), *Die Griechisch-Römische Biographie nach ihrer literarischen Form*, Hildesheim, Olms Verlagsbuchhandlung

Lesky E., 1951, *Die Zeugungs- und Vererbungslehre der Antike und ihr Nachwirken*, Mainz, Verlag der Akademie der Wissenschaften in Mainz

Lichtenberger H., 1987, Täufergemeinden und früh-christliche Täuferpolemik im letzten Drittel des 1. Jahrhunderts, in, *ZeitschrTheolKirche* 84, 1987, 36-57

Lindijer C.H., 1952, *Het begrip sarx bij Paulus*, Assen, Van Gorcum

Long A.A. — Sedley D.N., 1987, *The Hellenistic Philosophers*, Vol 1-2, Cambridge, Cambridge University Press

Lorenzen T., 1971, *Der Lieblingsjünger im Johannesevangelium. Eine redaktionsgeschichtliche Studie*, Stuttgart, Kath. Bibelwerk

Mahoney R., 1974, *Two Disciples at the Tomb. The Background and Message of John 20.1-20*, Bern-Frankfurt, Lang

Marmor J., 1980, Overview: The Multiple Roots of Homosexual Behavior, in, J. Marmor (ed.), *Homosexual Behavior. A Modern Reappraisal*, 3-22, New York, Basic Books

Marmor J., 1980/b, Clinical Aspects of Male Homosexuality, in, J. Marmor (ed.), *Homosexual Behavior. A Modern Reappraisal*, 267-279, New York, Basic Books

Marrou H.-I., 1965 (1948), *Histoire de l'éducation dans l'Antiquité*, Paris, Ed. du Seuil

Martyn J.L., 1979 (1968), *History and Theology in the Fourth Gospel. Revised and Enlarged*, Nashville, Abingdon

Mayer G., 1987, *Die jüdische Frau in der hellenistisch-römischen Antike*, Stuttgart, Kohlhammer

Maynard A.H., 1984, The Role of Peter in the Fourth Gospel, in, *NewTestStudies* 30, 1984, 531-548

Meier M.H.E., 1837, Päderastie, in, *Encyclopädie der Wissenschaften und Künsten*, Leipzig, IX

Merode M. de, 1982, L'accueil triomphal de Jésus selon Jean 11-12, in, *RevThéolLouv* 13, 1982, 49-62

Meyer R., 1938, *TWNT*, s.v. κόλπος

Michl J., 1955, Bemerkungen zu Joh. 2,4, in, *Bibl* 36, 1955, 492-509

Minear P.S., 1977, The Beloved Disciple in the Gospel of John. Some Clues and Conjectures, in, *NovTest* 19, 1977, 105-123

Müller K., 1969, Joh 9,7 und das jüdische Verständnis des Siloh-Spruches, in, *BiblZeitschr* 13, 1969, 251-256

Murphy-O'Connor J., 1990, John the Baptist and Jesus: History and Hypothese, in, *NewTestStudies* 36, 1990, 359-374

Neirynck F., 1975, The 'Other Disciple' in Jn 18,15-16, in, *EphTheolLov* 51, 1975, 112-141

Neirynck F., 1978, ΑΠΗΛΘΟΝ ΠΡΟΣ ΕΑΥΤΟΝ, Lc 24,12 et Jn 20,10, in, *EphTheolLov* 54, 1978, 104-125

Neirynck F., 1979, ΕΙΣ ΤΑ ΙΔΙΑ Jn 19,27 (et 16,32), in, *EphTheolLov* 55, 1979, 357-365

Neirynck F., a.o., 1979b, *Jean et les Synoptiques. Examen critique de l'exégèse de M.-E. Boismard*, Leuven, University Press Leuven

Neirynck F., 1981, La traduction d'un verset johannique. Jn 19,27b, in, *EphTheolLov* 57, 1981, 83-106

Neirynck F., 1990, John 21, in, *NewTestStudies* 36, 1990, 321-336

Neirynck F., 1990b, The Anonymous Disciple in John 1, in, *EphTheolLov* 66, 1990, 5-37

Neyrey J.H., 1979, Jacob Traditions and the Interpretation of John 4:10-26, in, *CathBiblQuaterly* 41, 1979, 419-437

Neyrey J.H., 1987, Jesus the Judge: Forensic Process in John 8,21-59, in, *Bibl* 68, 1987, 509-541

Neyrey J.H., 1988, *An Ideology of Revolt. John's Christology in Social-Science Perspective*, Philadelphia, Fortress Press

Odeberg H., 1968 (1929), *The Fourth Gospel, Interpreted in Its Relation to Contemporaneous Religious Currents in Palestine and the Hellenistic-Oriental World*, Amsterdam, Grüner

Okure T., 1988, *The Johannine Approach to Mission. A Contextual Study of John 4:1-42*, Tübingen, Mohr

Olsson B., 1974, *Structure and Meaning in the Fourth Gospel. A Text-Linguistic Analysis of John 2:1-11 and 4:1-42*, Lund, Gleerup

Onuki T., 1984, *Gemeinde und Welt im Johannesevangelium. Ein Beitrag zur Frage nach der theologischen und pragmatischen Funktion des johanneischen 'Dualismus'*, Neukirchen, Neukirchener Verlag

Painter J., 1986, John 9 and the Interpretation of the Fourth Gospel, in, *JournStudyNT* 28, 1986, 31-61

Panackel C., 1988, ΙΔΟΥ Ο ΑΝΘΡΩΠΟΣ (Jn 19,5b). *An Exegetico-Theological Study of the Text in the Light of the Use of the Term ΑΝΘΡΩΠΟΣ Designating Jesus in the Fourth Gospel*, Roma, Pontificia Università Gregoriana

Petzl G., 1982, *Die Inschriften von Smyrna*, Bonn, R. Habelt

Philips G.A., 1983, 'This is a hard saying. Who can be listener to it?': Creating a Reader in John 6, in, *Semeia* 26, 1983, 23-56

Pogey-Castries L.R. de, 1930, *Histoire de l'Amour Grec dans l'Antiquité*, Paris, Stendahl & Compagnie

Pohlenz M., 1948-49, *Die Stoa. Geschichte einer geistigen Bewegung*, Vol 1-2, Göttingen, Vandenhoeck und Ruprecht

Pomeroy S.B., 1975, *Goddesses, Whores, Wives and Slaves. Women in Classical Antiquity*, New York, Schocken Books

Potterie I. de la, 1962, Jésus et les Samaritains. Jn 4,5-42, in, *Assemblées du Seigneur*, Biblica, Bruges, 16, 34-49

Potterie I. de la, 1974, Das Wort Jesu 'Siehe deine Mutter' und die Aufnahme der Mutter durch den Jünger (Joh 19,27b), in, *Neues Testament und Kirche*, Fs. Schnackenburg, Freiburg, Herder, 1974, 191-219

Potterie I. de la, 1977, *La Vérité dans Saint Jean. I. Le Christ et la vérité; L'Esprit et la vérité; II. Le croyant et la vérité*, Rome, Biblical Institue Press

Potterie I. de la, 1984, Structure du prologue de saint Jean, in, *NewTestStudies* 30, 1984, 354-381

Potterie I. de la, 1986, Le témoin qui demeure: le disciple que Jésus aimait, in, *Bibl* 67, 1986, 343-359

Preuss J., 1969 (1911), *Biblisch-talmudische Medizin. Beiträge zur Geschichte der Heilkunde und der Kultur überhaupt*, Berlin, Karger

Price A.W., 1989/90, *Love and Friendship in Plato and Aristotle*, Oxford, Clarendon Press

Rebell W., 1987, *Gemeinde als Gegenwelt. Zur Soziologischen und didaktischen Funktion des Johannesevangelium*, Frankfurt, P. Lang

Reim G., 1978, Joh 9 — Tradition und zeitgenössische messianische Diskussion, in, *BiblZeitschr* 22, 1978, 245-253

Rengstorf K.H., 1942, *TWNT*, s.v. μαθητής

Richter G., 1965, Die Fusswaschung Joh 13,1-20, in, *MünchTheolZeitschr* 16, 1965, 13-26

Ritt H., 1979, *Das Gebet zum Vater. Zur Interpretation von Joh 17*, Echt, Echter Verlag

Ritt H., 1983, Die Frauen und die Osterbotschaft. Synopse der Grabesgeschichten (Mk 16,1-8; Mt 27,62-28,15; Lk 24,1-12; Joh 20,1-18), in, G. Dautzenberg — H. Merklein (Hrsg), *Die Frau im Urchristentum*, 117-133, Freiburg, Herder

Ritt H., 1988, Die Frau als Glaubensbotin. Zum Verständnis der Samaritanerin von Joh 4,1-42, in, H. Frankemölle — K. Kertelge, *Vom Urchristentum zu Jesus*, Fs f. J. Gnilka, 287-306, Freiburg, Herder

Rosen S., 1968, *Plato's Symposium*, New Haven-London, Yale University Press

Ruckstuhl E., 1988, *Jesus im Horizont der Evangelien*, Stuttgart, Kath. Bibelwerk

Samter E., 1901, *Familienfeste der Griechen und Römer*, Berlin, G. Reimer

Schaberg J., 1987, *The Illegitimacy of Jesus. A Feminist Theological Interpretation of the Infancy Narratives*, San Francisco, Harper & Row

Schenke L., 1989, Die literarische Entstehungsgeschichte von Joh 1,19-51, in, *BiblNotizen* 46, 1989, 24-56

Schnackenburg R., 1967-1984, *Das Johannesevangelium*, Vol 1-4, Freiburg, Herder

Schnelle U., 1987, *Antidoketische Christologie im Johannesevangelium. Eine Untersuchung zur Stellung des vierten Evangeliums in der johanneischen Schule*, Göttingen, Vandenhoeck und Ruprecht

Schottroff L., 1982, Maria Magdalena und die Frauen am Grabe, in, *EvangTheol* 42, 1982, 3-25

Schürmann H., 1969, Jesu letzte Weisung. Jo 19,26-27a, in, *EvangTheol* 24, 1969, 105-123

Schütz R., 1967, *Johannes der Täufer*, Zürich-Stuttgart, Zwingli Verlag

Schumann von, 1975, *Sexualkunde und Sexualmedizin in der klassischen Antike. Auswertung der griechischen und lateinischen Originalquellen und der Sekundärliteratur*, München, UNI

Schweizer E. - Meyer R., 1964, *TWNT* s.v. σάρξ and σῶμα

Seckel E. - Kvelber B., 1969 (1935), *Gai Institutiones*, Stuttgart, Teubner

Segovia F.F., 1982, John 13,1-20, the Footwashing in the Johannine Tradition, in, *ZeitschrNTlicheWissenschaft* 73, 1982, 31-51

Segovia F.F., 1985, The Structure, Tendenz, and Sitz im Leben of John 13:31-14:31, in, *JournBiblLit* 104, 1985, 471-493

Seim T.K., 1987, Roles of Women in the Gospel of John, in, L. Hartman — B. Olsson (ed.), *Aspects on the Johannine Literature*, 56-73, Uppsala, Uppsala University Press

Sinaiko H.L., 1965, *Love, Knowledge, and Discourse in Plato: Dialogue and Dialectic in Phaedrus, Republic, Parmenides*, Chicago-London, University of Chicago Press

Smith D. Moody, 1987 (1984), *Johannine Christianity. Essays on Its Setting, Sources, and Theology*, Edinburgh, Clark

Socarides C.W., 1974, Homosexuality, in, *American Handbook of Psychiatry*, 291-315, New York, Basic Books

Sproston W.E., 1985, 'Is This Not Jesus, the Son of Joseph..?' (John 6.42). Johannine Christology as a Challenge to Faith, in, *JournStudyNT* 24, 1985, 77-97

Staley J.L., 1988, *The Print's First Kiss: A Rhetorical Investigation of the Implied Reader in the Fourth Gospel*, Atlanta, Georgia, Scholars Press

Stählin G., 1973, *TWNT*, s.v. φίλος

Stemberger G., 1979, *Das klassische Judentum. Kultur und Geschichte der rabbinischen Zeit*, München, Beck

Strack H.L. — Billerbeck P., 1955 (1926), *Kommentar zum neuen Testament aus Talmud und Midrasch*, München, Beck'sche Verlagsbuchhandlung

Taubenschlag R., 1955/2, *The Law of Greco-Roman Egypt in the Light of the Papyri. 332 B.C. - 640 A.D.*, Warszawa, Naukowe

Theobald M., 1988, *Die Fleischwerdung des Logos. Studien zum Verhältnis des Johannesprologs zum Corpus des Evangeliums und zu 1 Joh*, Münster, Aschendorff

Thyen H., 1976, Entwicklungen innerhalb der johanneischen Theologie und Kirche im Spiegel von Joh. 21 und der Lieblingsjüngertexte des Evangeliums, in, M. de Jonge (ed.), *L'Évangile de Jean. Sources, rédaction, théologie*, 259-299, Leuven, Duculot

Thyen H., 1979, 'Niemand hat grössere Liebe als die, dass er sein Leben für seine Freunde hingibt' (Joh 15,13), in, C. Andresen — G. Klein (Hrsg), *Theologia Crucis-Signum Crucis*, Fs E. Dinkler, 467-481, Tübingen, Mohr

Tiede D.L., 1972, *The Charismatic Figure as Miracle Worker*, Harvard, Society of Biblical Literature

Tilborg S. van, 1989, The Gospel of John: communicative processes in a narrative text, in, *Neotest* 23, 1989, 19-31

Urbach E.E., 1975, *The Sages - Their Concepts and Beliefs*, translated from the Hebrew by I. Abrahams, Vol I-II, Jerusalem, Magnes Press Hebrew University

Vanhoye A., 1974, Interrogation johannique et exégèse de Cana (Jn 2,4), in, *Bibl* 55, 1974, 157-167

Verbeke G., 1945, *L'évolution de la doctrine du pneuma du stoicisme à S. Augustin*, Pas-Louvain, Desclée de Brouwer

Vermes G., 1973, *Jesus the Jew. A Historian's Reading of the Gospels*, London, Collins

Wengst K., 1983 (1981), *Bedrängte Gemeinde und verherrlichter Christus. Der historische Ort des Johannesevangeliums als Schlüssel zu seiner Interpretation*, Neukirchen, Neukirchener Verlag

Westcott B.F., 1975 (1881), *The Gospel according to St. John*, Ann Arbor, Michigan, Cushing

Wicker K. O'Brien, 1975, First Century Marriage Ethics: A Comparative Study of the Household Codes and Plutarch's Conjugal Precepts, in, *No Famine in the Land*, Fs. for J.L. McKenzie, 141-153, Missoula, Scholars Press

Wilhelm F., 1915, Die Oeconomica der Neupythagoreer Bryson, Kallikratidas, Periktione, Phintys, in, *Rheinisches Museum f. Philologie* 70, 1915, 161-223

Wilkins M.J., 1988, *The Concept of Disciple in Matthew's Gospel, as Reflected in the Use of the Term Μαθητής*, Leiden, Brill

Wink W., 1968, *John the Baptist in the Gospel Tradition*, Cambridge, Cambridge University Press

Winkler J.J., 1990, *The Constraints of Desire. The Anthropology of Sex and Gender in Ancient Greece*, New York-London, Routledge

Witherington III B., 1988, *Women in the Earliest Churches*, Cambridge, Cambridge University Press

Witkamp L.T., 1985, The Use of Traditions in John 5.1-18, in, *JournStudyNT* 25, 1985, 19-47

Wolff H.J., 1961, *Beiträge zur Rechtsgeschichte Altgriechenlands und des hellenistisch-römischen Ägypten*, Weimar, Böhlaus

Woll D.B., 1980, The Departure of "The Way": The First Farewell Discourse in the Gospel of John, in, *JournBiblStudies* 99, 1980, 225-239

Woll D.B., 1981, *Johannine Christianity in Conflict: Authority, Rank, and Succession in the First Farewell Discourse*, Chico, California, Scholars Press

Ziegler K., 1951, Plutarchos von Chaironeia, in, *Pauly-Wissowa* s.v.

BIBLIOGRAPHICAL INDEX

BIBLICAL INTERPRETATION SERIES

ISSN 0928-0731

1. VAN DIJK-HEMMES, F. & A. BRENNER. *On Gendering Texts.* Female and Male Voices in the Hebrew Bible. 1993.
ISBN 90 04 09642 6
2. VAN TILBORG, S. *Imaginative Love in John.* 1993.
ISBN 90 04 09716 3
3. DANOVE, P.L. *The End of Mark's Story.* A Methodological Study.
1993. ISBN 90 04 09717 1. *In the press*